Dear Susan.
and went for -
I am so proud of you!
Love
Helen

Her ~~His~~ Worship

MOMENTS IN HISTORY, MOMENTS IN TIME

The city of Winnipeg's first
(and so far only) woman mayor tells her story

Susan A. Thompson

with Terry Létienne

Special Thanks

We would like to acknowledge the wonderful SPONSORS for this book. Without their support, this book could not have been published.

Tannis Richardson
Women of Winnipeg (WOW group)
Debbie and Sandy Riley
Carol Bellringer and Greg Doyle
Tom Dooley
John Prystanski
Margie Isbister
Sharon Boyd
Elba Haid and Edward Ransby
Gayle and Jim Carson
Eleanor and Tim Samson
Fiona Webster-Mourant

Note to Reader:

By all traditional rules of publishing, when a statement or sentence is in BOLD, it is translated as loud or showy, and perceived as an unnecessary emphasis on an already clear sentence. To me, BOLD is an expression of awe and excitement. It is meant to draw your attention to what I consider a moment of serendipity. Please keep this in mind as you read through this book.

With grateful appreciation,

Susan

This book is dedicated to our parents,
Maurice and Eleanor Thompson
and
Claude and Bella Létienne,
whose stars are no doubt shining brightly
in the heavens above.

Suite 300 - 990 Fort St
Victoria, BC, V8V 3K2
Canada

www.friesenpress.com

First Edition — 2016

Co-authored by Terry Létienne

Front Cover Photo
Courtesy of Albert Cheung, Photographer

Back Cover Photo
David Lipnowski, Winnipeg Free Press/January 18, 2014 Reprinted with permission

City of Winnipeg logo reprinted with permission from the
City of Winnipeg Archives

ISBN
978-1-4602-9476-5 (Hardcover)
978-1-4602-9477-2 (Paperback)
978-1-4602-9478-9 (eBook)

1. BIOGRAPHY & AUTOBIOGRAPHY

Distributed to the trade by The Ingram Book Company

Table of Contents

PART 3— THE NEXT CHAPTER

Foreword

by childhood friend Gayle Carson (Sykes)

Susan's request for me to write the foreword for her book was a daunting and challenging task. I was in minor angst! However, it was also a privilege, and my opportunity to pay tribute to a woman who dared.

Upon reflection, this was not the first time Susan had pushed me out of my comfort zone. She is of the same mind as Apollinaire... "'Come to the edge,' he said. They said, 'We are afraid.' 'Come to the edge,' he said. They came. He pushed them... and they flew." Along her life's path, she constantly challenges herself and those around her to fly higher, think bigger, and rise to the utmost standard of excellence.

Family, a good value system, and respect are very important to Susan. We are friends from childhood and when I married my husband Jim, she became a good friend to him as well. She is godmother to our three children...Jane, Ryan, and Joan. They refer to her as their "fairy godmother" for her unique ability to mark special moments in time with joy, curiosity, and a touch of magic. There was usually a learning component mixed with the delightfully unexpected in her thoughtful cards and gifts.

Susan is a spiritual woman who has a great sense of public service. When called to be mayor, her intestinal fortitude was constantly challenged. She dared to have a vision for our city and the courage to stay the course. Giving credit to others was a great consensus builder and she freely gave praise both publicly and privately. Not the norm in the blood sport of politics, Susan always took the high road even when personal criticism and factual inaccuracies were printed, aired, and viewed.

In life and work situations she embodies Tennyson's words... "strong in will to strive, to seek, to find, and not to yield."

This book is about Susan A. Thompson's public and private life, her struggles and rewards, her passion and conviction. She has been a business owner, visionary, mayor, diplomat, women's rights advocate, CEO, fundraiser, mentor, and life coach, but to me she will always be a "good friend first."

Please join me in reading about her inspirational journey.

Part 1

MOMENTS IN TIME

"Sometimes you have to look back where you came from to see where you are going."

Author Unknown

Ice jams on the Assiniboine River circa 1950

Chapter 1
My Early Days

My Very First Memory

My earliest memory — believe it or not — is of the 1950 flood. I was three years old. I remember looking out the large picture window in our living room, which normally overlooked the Assiniboine River, and seeing only a massive wall of sandbags. My father lifted me up onto his shoulders for me to see over the dike, which ran along the front of our living room window. There was a huge amount of water, rapidly rushing past our house. Even at this early age, I felt the danger before me. As the river swelled, our family had to face the agonizing fact that we had to evacuate to higher ground. Unfortunately, that also meant that we would be temporarily separated. My parents and I, and my eldest sister Lenore, moved in with some wonderful neighbours — the Mathers — who were up the hill at the top of the street. My brother Norman was attending and living at St. John's Ravenscourt School at the time, and was evacuated to Saskatoon. My sister Barbara moved in with the Moffats, who were friends of the family. They lived in the west end of the city, on higher ground.

Being three years old, I only understood that our property was in crisis. I don't recall much of anything else about it, even though it was such a historic event. Of course, it ended up being one of the most devastating floods the city of Winnipeg had ever seen. The Red River rose to its highest level since 1861 and the entire Red River Valley was affected. Nearly 100,000 people were evacuated and extensive damage occurred to thousands of homes. Little did I know at the time that I would be intensely involved in the next major flood to hit the city forty-seven years later. **How uncanny that I was the mayor of Winnipeg in 1997 for the Flood of the Century.**

Luckily, our house did not suffer any damage and we moved back into our home after approximately six weeks. My parents had the arduous task of removing all those sandbags from our yard, and I clearly recall the erosion of our yard due to the flood. The river side of our property had been gouged away, which resulted in our front yard now being no more than ten feet to the riverbank. For years afterwards, my father fought the City of St. James to adjust our property taxes, as our assessment was based on land that was no longer there.

Years later, I learned that my grandfather and father's business, Birt Saddlery, had suffered water damage due to the flood. The store was located at Market and Main Street, just four blocks away from Portage and Main, which also got flooded in 1950. Father and Grandfather had to move over 200 saddles and other stock out of the basement to higher floors in the building.

When I went through the harrowing experience of the 1997 flood as mayor of Winnipeg, these early memories came back to me, and I felt my father and mother watching over me and understanding the challenges that stood before me. At a very early age, I clearly learned the power and the danger of the river.

Memories of my Neighbourhood

Norman, Lenore (behind me in the cradle) and Barbara

Winnipeg has been home for most of my life. I was born in this great city where east meets west in 1947 at the old Grace Hospital on Arlington Street. Mother said I was born talking. I've been told that I was advanced in many ways, and being the youngest in the family, I was the centre of attention. My siblings — Lenore, Norman, and Barbara — were quite a few years older than me. By the time I was nine, my sister Lenore was getting married.

We grew up on Douglas Park Road in St. James, which is just off Portage Avenue, one of the two main arteries in Winnipeg. This street was quite unique, much like a small village in its own right. Similar to the '*seigneuries*' of rural Québec, the lots were at least 300 feet in length and all houses backed onto parks — Bruce Park to the west, Bourkevale Park to the east, and Assiniboine Park to the south. Yards were large, with plenty of room for children to play and adults to grow gardens and raise animals. Mr. Knight raised pigeons and Mr. Hillier golden pheasants. Mrs. Gifford grew gladiolas, Mrs. Boyd had the most beautiful, prize-winning flower gardens, the Sinclairs had the best crab-apple tree, and the Cookes had the best vegetable garden. The Cookes also grew unbelievable creeping bent in their front yard that looked like a carpet of green velvet. Mr. Cooke had learned how to properly grow this plant, growing up in England.

The family home

Our house was a very modest bungalow, originally a summer house, with white siding and brown trim, situated on a half-acre lot at the end of the street. The front of our house overlooked the winding Assiniboine River. The landmark Assiniboine City Park was located directly across the river from our house. Just imagine...I was able to look out our living room window and see this magnificent park! After the 1950 flood, the riverbank in our front yard eroded to the point that an island emerged near the edge of the river. The street-side part of our yard had a sandbox, a teeter-totter, and a double glider swing. At one time, there was a trapeze, a bow-and-arrow target made of bales of hay, and a shallow pool made with a canvas tarp bordered by sandbags. My appreciation for flowers came from being surrounded in our own yard with wood violets, lily of the valley, honeysuckle, dogwood shrubs, iris beds, and wild roses along the riverbank. The entrance to the upper yard was framed with two cedar trees and lilac hedges, and the north wall of the house was dressed with gorgeous ferns. Mother loved geraniums, and each spring she would create a great display. We all enjoyed bird watching, so we placed a bird feeder just outside our sunroom window. One year, I can remember my father feeding about 200 geese down on the island.

Douglas Park Road was a very eclectic street. Many famous Winnipeggers hailed from it, including A.W. Hanks, mayor of St.

James from 1960-1969 and former publisher of the *St. James Herald*. Gordon Sinclair Senior, night editor of the *Winnipeg Free Press*, also lived on the street, and his sons, David and Gordon Sinclair Junior, would grow up to become journalists at the *Winnipeg Free Press* too. Gordon is an award-winning feature columnist. Another notable resident was Bob Pollack, a well-known artist who painted landscapes of rural and urban Manitoba. He was especially famous for his paintings of City Park. He even depicted the Douglas Park Road Bonfire, a painting I have in my home. This was no ordinary neighbourhood!

The design of this cul-de-sac lent itself to neighbourhood interaction. I do believe that everyone knew each other. Douglas Park Road was also a street full of activity, in no small part due to my parents. In early years, Mother organized an annual New Year's Eve gathering and many families from the neighbourhood would partake in this special evening. Mother made her famous Christmas punch served in a beautiful, ornate Chinese bowl, which I still have today. Everyone contributed to the food for the evening. Mrs. Gifford brought her famous ham and Mrs. Boyd could always be counted on to bring delicious, homemade buns and baking. At an appointed hour, all the families — adults and children — formed a big circle around the dining room table and joined hands to sing "Auld Lang Syne," led by the exquisite voices of the Cooke family. Each year, this was the tradition.

Soon after Christmas, families in the neighbourhood were asked to bring their Christmas trees (most everyone had "real" trees back then) to our back yard, where they stayed all winter. This was the basis for an event my parents had created and organized each year — The Douglas Park Road Queen Victoria Day Bonfire and Fireworks Display. This was held in our back yard, usually just after the May long weekend. The tradition lasted fifty years.

The evening always began with a volleyball game in the upper part of the yard. One of my fondest memories is eighty-year-old Mr. Allen returning a serve with his head. He had played soccer in England when he was younger, and he used to delight all of us with his expert moves.

The annual neighbourhood volleyball game in the Thompson family yard

Neighbours were asked to bring their own lawn chairs, soft drinks, and fireworks. My father supplied marshmallows for roasting and some of the sparklers. The bonfire was a highlight event. Once darkness set in, a fire was started, and one by one, the Christmas trees brought to our yard earlier in the year were placed in the fire pit. They were extremely dry by then and I can remember a big whooshing sound every time a tree was added to the fire. Sparks would fly as the flames shot skyward. Sometimes the flames would reach great heights, all to the awe of children and adults alike.

The neighbourhood children were assigned to cut some of the willows for sticks on which to roast the marshmallows. My brother Norman, along with Mother and Father, supervised us as we searched along the riverbank looking for the perfect willows. Some neighbours were assigned the task of setting up sand pails and water pails for the fireworks display. Others ensured a first aid kit was nearby, just in case something went awry.

While the children roasted marshmallows, sipped pop, and played games, the adults sat around the fire pit in a circle and took part in great chats. The final event of the evening was the fireworks display. Of course, the most popular one was the "burning school house." Squeals of delight could be heard when that one burned up. The evening ended with the distribution of sparklers and all the children ran around the yard, lit sparklers in hand, capping off the magic of the evening.

When I look back now on what it took to organize this great neighbourhood tradition, I am in awe at how my parents made it all look so simple. To this day, I have the fondest memories of this significant yearly event. It instilled in me the importance of creating community and nurturing our neighbours.

My First Adventure

In the spring of 1951, I went for an extended visit to my Aunt Betty and Uncle Gordon McKay in Edmonton. At the time, my mother was confined to bed due to debilitating arthritis.

My parents obtained special permission to send me off on a plane to Edmonton, by myself, at the age of four less a day...with supervision by the airline stewardesses of course. (They weren't called flight attendants back then.) My father had painstakingly tried to prepare me for this grand adventure. He sat me on our kitchen chair, wrapped a tea towel around my hips to simulate a seatbelt, and stood behind me making propeller noises. He showed me where the button would be located to call for the stewardesses, who were actually trained nurses at the time. He assured me that the pilot was a nice man that I could trust. Despite all the preparations, I was still afraid.

My solo flight to Edmonton at age three

Mother and Lenore had made sure that I was well-dressed for this extraordinary adventure. I wore a beautiful, blue, soft wool coat with dark-blue velvet trim. I had a matching beret and brand new socks and shoes, and my hair was braided with white satin ribbons. My father had a small suitcase made especially for me from Birt Saddlery. I vividly remember stepping on that TransCanada Airlines plane.

I had been told that I would be on the plane for a long time — seven hours in fact — first to Saskatoon, and then to Edmonton. Once the plane left the ground, the airline pilot and stewardesses became my caregivers and took wonderful care of me. When we arrived in Edmonton, I stayed on the plane until the pilot was able to come and escort me down the stairs to meet my aunt and uncle. He held my hand and led me to the plane's doorway. I stood alongside him at the top of the stairs, looking down at a couple of strangers, one of whom snapped a photograph of me and the pilot. I was quite content to stay with my newfound guardian — after all, the people at the bottom of the staircase were unknown to me, and I had been taught never to go with strangers. Though I don't necessarily recall every detail of this experience, leaving my new airline friends was traumatic, and huge drama occurred as my aunt and uncle tried to take me to their home. I remember crying and screaming all the way to their house, only to be consoled minutes later when they presented me with a brand new tricycle. Then, I felt better...I had my own set of wheels!

The very next day just happened to be my birthday. My aunt had made me a cake with white icing and silver decorations; little silver balls that I had never seen before on a cake. I was so impressed with this lovely cake and remember feeling very special indeed.

My aunt and uncle had one child, a son named Leonard who was a year older than me. I remember thinking he was the greatest and we got along wonderfully during my six-week stay. I immediately got used to my new environment. Aunt Betty had an uncanny resemblance to my mother and she doted on me all the time I was there. In later years, I found out that she had always wanted a daughter, so while she had me there, she spoiled me like I was her own.

On May 30, 1951, I returned by plane — again on my own — to Winnipeg. The result of being "sent away" at such a young age was evident. When I first returned home, I had become "detached" from the rest of my family. I knew that they were my mother, my father, my sisters, and my brother, but I kept asking when I would be going away again. How soon independence had set in.

When I was ten years old, our family travelled to Victoria, BC where I was reunited with Aunt Betty, Uncle Gordon, and cousin Leonard. I was thrilled to see them again. Their house was right on the ocean, complete with a dock, a motorboat and a sail boat. All of this was quite a thrill for a prairie girl. Another consequence of my little adventure to Edmonton is that it instilled in me a confidence and desire to travel...a desire that is with me to this day.

Fun at Victoria Beach

The Thompson family's summer cottage was at Victoria Beach. Nestled on the north-eastern tip of a peninsula on Lake Winnipeg, this private haven, named after the British monarch Queen Victoria, is where I spent time every summer for over fifty years. In the early days, we took a train to get there, as there was no road access to the area. As I think back now, I can only imagine what my poor mother went through, travelling by train with four children in tow and enough luggage and supplies to last the summer. Father stayed behind to run the business on weekdays, but joined us on weekends. He always managed to take a few weeks' vacation each summer as well.

The log cabin on Sunset Blvd. at Victoria Beach, Manitoba

Ours was a log cabin built in 1921, with a double woodstove, coal-oil lamps, and an icebox refrigerator. For many years, we did not have electricity, running water, or a telephone. We had to get our water from a well and since we didn't have indoor plumbing, we had "the outhouse." In the 1950s, during my growing-up years, our amenities improved. A bathroom was eventually built inside our cottage, which was a wonderful addition, but we kept the outhouse "for emergencies."

My siblings and I had many chores to do while at the lake; from chopping wood for the fireplace and woodstove, to gathering twigs for kindling, to tending to the oil lamps by cleaning the chimneys and filling them with oil, to rubbing the blackened bottoms of our stove pots into the sand to clean them off. It was always a treat to take the wagon to the well to get water...when I was very young I could hitch a ride in the wagon, but as I got older it became more of a chore. The girls would help Mother with laundry; we all knew how to use a wash scrub-board very early on in age. Norman would help Father replace the oakum between the logs of the cabin.

Mother loved wild flowers and we would often head to the bush to pick wild roses, chokecherry blossoms, and forget-me-nots to decorate the cabin. When in season, we would also pick berries from the raspberry patch, as well as wild strawberries, saskatoons, and blueberries. Mother would then create some of the most wonderful pies and desserts in that famous woodstove.

Once our chores were done, it was off to the beach. We spent many days swimming and sandcastle-building on the beautiful white-sand beach and made many friends there. It is there that I met Margie Isbister. Though we both lived in Winnipeg, we were at different ends of the city, so we really became just "beach friends." We then attended the University of Winnipeg together and it was from then on that our friendship flourished.

At one point, my father bought an inflatable, double-seated, blue kayak, which was a hit, not only with our family, but with other kids at the beach. It was great fun and we all loved getting our chance to ride the kayak. Each evening, we would play family games — Chinese checkers, Monopoly, Scrabble, cribbage. These games also came in handy when we would hit a patch of rainy weather.

Elk Island was directly across from our cabin and when the lake was shallow enough, we could actually cross the 1.2 kilometres to the island on foot via a sandbar. Once we got on the island, there was lots of exploring to do. Many "adventures" took place at Elk Island, an uninhabited provincial park only nine square kilometres in size.

Victoria Beach was as unique to me as Douglas Park Road. There were only eight avenues in the entire community, yet it had its own community club where one could go to movies, dances, and swimming lessons. Victoria Beach was, and still is, its own municipality. It boasts its own newspaper and police force and has always been known to have a flurry of famous residents. In my growing up years, the beach also had tennis courts, a nine-hole golf course, a sailing club, and a government pier, where many took to fishing. The government pier was also where the summer regatta took place, a very special event. The club also hosted an annual dog show, where every dog won a prize. For as long as I can remember, Victoria Beach had a general store, Einfeld's bakery, and the Moonlight Inn. The two stores were convenient for the cottagers and even though it was a mile from our cottage, I thoroughly enjoyed walking to either of these great locations to pick up needed items and treats. The Moonlight

Inn was also a great place to pick up treats, and as a teenager, it was a great place to "meet boys."

Eventually, a road was built to Victoria Beach, though cars were not allowed into the cottage and beach areas. Residents had to park their cars in a large parking lot at the entrance of the beach, and would either have to walk over or take a "taxi" (usually an old beat-up station wagon) to their cottage. This was established for safety reasons, to protect children and adults from vehicle traffic. To this day, other than the taxi service, only bicycles and people are allowed on the road from June to September. As far as I know, this bylaw is unique to Victoria Beach.

Once the road was built...next came electricity...and running water and telephones! It was all so progressive. This made our cottage experience much more civilized, especially for my mother, although we still enjoyed bathing in the lake from time to time. The day the wood stove was replaced with an electric stove and the refrigerator replaced the icebox, our life had changed. We were no longer "pioneers."

This beautiful photo of a Victoria Beach sunset was taken by my sister Barbara.

Victoria Beach has the best sunsets in the world and our cottage was located on Sunset Boulevard...can you get any more serendipitous than that? Families gathered at the lakeshore every evening just before sunset, and as this beautiful spectacle took place before our eyes, children and adults alike clapped their hands and celebrated the end of yet another wonderful day at Victoria Beach.

Victoria Beach was my private haven. After my parents passed away, I inherited the cottage and continued to visit there each summer. I especially appreciated the private aspect of the beach when I became Winnipeg's mayor. Our cottage was on a cul-de-sac at the northern end of the beach area. It was quite secluded and when I could, I would try to "get away" for much needed down time. In the fall of 2005, the cottage was sold to a young couple whose family has been part of the Victoria Beach family for years. It was time to let that part of my life go. I will always have the most incredible memories of this very significant part of my family life.

My Father

Father and I on one of his visits to Calgary when I worked at Eaton's My father, William Maurice Thompson, was born in Edmonton, Alberta on October 23, 1910 to May and William Thompson. He went by the name Maurice. He was a highly intelligent man and had a very enquiring mind. He was raised in Edmonton, lived for a short while in Regina, and then he, my mother, and my sister Lenore moved to Winnipeg in 1935 where he joined his father in the family business — Birt Saddlery. Prior to that, Father had attended McMaster University and spent a few years as a small goods manager at Great West Saddlery in Regina.

Father read a great deal and was always exploring things and curious about new trends and technology. Birt Saddlery owned a computer very early on in the age of computers. It was really only a glorified bookkeeping machine, but it was the start of the computer age and my father was on board. He used a small pocket tape recorder extensively on business trips to ensure he captured important conversations, product information, and noted follow-ups. He would also take photos of the business people he met, along with the items they were meeting about. He was passionate about photography and was well known for his photo taking. He owned a "Polaroid" and had catalogues of photos. If he met you, he had your photo.

Father was fun. He loved to "do things" and "go places." Each year, he was the first in line for the helicopter ride at the Red River Ex. He took dance classes. He was thrilled to go to Expo '67 in Montreal. He had a very strong personality, although he sometimes showed signs of insecurity and shyness, especially in social situations. He was most generous and thoughtful to his friends and associates. On Christmas Eve, he would deliver turkeys to retired employees and others in need. Every time a girl on Douglas Park Road was getting married, he gave her a nice handbag from Birt Saddlery. As a parent, Father was strict. He always set the bar very high. It was never wise to talk back to him...it didn't work.

As a businessman, Father was shrewd and sensible. He was a hard worker and saw the family business as a 24/7 job. He was one of the founders of the Western Merchants Association, a small group of retailers in Western Canada. Within Birt Saddlery, he and my grandfather established a retail store, a wholesale business, a distributing company, and a catalogue business. He did business all over the world, importing saddles from England and Mexico, polo equipment from Pakistan, and horse equipment from Japan. He was one of the first few Canadians to open up that market. He worked largely with western clothing companies from the United States of America — including companies in Denver and Texas to name a few. He started buying in Denver shortly after World War II, just before the official Denver Western Buying Mart was established.

Father was totally committed to our community. He was a Rotarian, and a member of the Winnipeg Executives and the Winnipeg Chamber of Commerce. He served on the board of the St.

James YMCA, the St. James School Board, the Kiwanis, the Lions Club, the Bourkevale Community Club, and the Victoria Beach Club. Both our mother and father taught us to volunteer and give back to our community.

My Mother

Mother, Father and I in Sarnia for my sister Barbara's wedding

My mother was a woman of integrity and sheer determination. Had she been born in a different era, I have no doubt that she would have had a major career in a highly disciplined environment. She had a great sense of family and friendships, and hence, was the organizer of many social gatherings and events. She was a gracious hostess and a wonderful cook. Our table was always beautifully set and she had a great sense of style, be it her home or fashions for her and her children.

Mother had a great sense of duty. She was often called the "Mayor of Douglas Park Road," as she fought religiously to protect our street and our neighbourhood. When a developer once tried to convince the City of St. James that Assiniboine Avenue should be extended to connect to Deer Lodge Place via Bourkevale Park, Douglas Park Road, and Bruce Park, all hell broke loose. There was no way my mother was going to let that happen! These parks and our street were to be preserved and to this day, they still are.

Mother came from a very good Edmonton family — the Bellamys. Her father, Ralph Victor Bellamy, was one of the first eleven Rhodes Scholars from Canada. He was given that distinction in 1904 and the opportunity to study and graduate from Oxford University in England. His early career was that of a lawyer and he had previously studied at McMaster University and the University of Alberta. He and his father, Thomas Bellamy, both served as Aldermen for the City of Edmonton. Grandfather Ralph also ran unsuccessfully for mayor in 1935. My political blood ran deep. So did my desire for equality. My great-grandmother, Lorinda Jane Bellamy, was a suffragist and president of the Woman's Christian Temperance Union in Edmonton. In the early 1900s, she marched the streets of Edmonton against the sins of alcohol and for the rights of women. She was also a founding member of both the YWCA and the Baptist Church in Edmonton. So Mother came from a lineage that fought for what they believed in and were dedicated to public service. She fiercely believed in these values and instilled them in her children as well.

Like all people, Mother had many layers to her personality. At times, she was not to be tangled with, but at other times, she was a complete joy to be around. She had a tremendous spirit and a terrific gift of style and grace. I can definitely thank my mother for teaching me the important things in life.

My Siblings

There is a good reason why, at the mention of my eldest sister Lenore's name, most follow it up with "the one we adore." That is because Lenore is the dear heart of the family. She is a soul mate to people. She is a nurturer. When people meet her for the first time, they immediately sense her empathy towards others and her wisdom.

Lenore is one of those special people that seem to have it all. She is smart and well-informed. She is creative and a fabulous cook. People rave about her cooking and baking. She has a great sense of occasion...the "Martha Stewart" of her generation. Lenore is also the historian of the family. I believe it most important for each generation to have someone preserving the family history, and in our case, it is my sister Lenore.

My brother Norman is ten years older than me. He was the only boy and had three sisters...yikes! Somehow he made it work, however, and was never much bothered by us. He was mechanically inclined; a fixer. He built fantastic model planes. This was his passion, especially growing up. He was a mechanic by trade and loved cars and working on them. He was musically inclined and had a good singing voice. Now in his late seventies, Norman lives in British Columbia with his wife Carolyn. He is the father of two sons, and has two stepdaughters and eight grandchildren. He is retired and the maker of delicious wines and jams.

Sister Barbara, now in her mid-seventies, is the brains in the family. She has an English degree from the University of Manitoba. She is the organizer and the researcher of the family. Her career was with the YM/YWCA of Canada. Barbara lived most of her married life in Ontario — Sarnia, Peterborough, Cambridge, and Toronto. She has two children and four grandchildren. In 2004, at the age of 64, Barbara went back to school — Mohawk College in Brantford, Ontario — and became an instructor of the blind and visually-impaired; an orientation and mobility specialist. She received her certificate in October 2005. This was quite a feat, going back to post-secondary education forty-two years after her first degree, but she did it, and she did very well. She is now retired and resides in Saskatchewan.

Maya Angelou once said, "I do not believe that the accident of birth makes people sisters and brothers. It makes them siblings. It gives them mutuality of parentage. Sisterhood and brotherhood are conditions people have to work at. It's a serious matter. You compromise, you give, you take, you stand firm, and you're relentless... and it is an investment." How true!

Lenore, Norman, Barbara and I relaxing in my home on Elm Street in Winnipeg

Childhood Friends

The friendships I formed on Douglas Park Road have, to a great extent, remained to this day. My friendship with Gayle Sykes (now Carson) and her husband Jim has been a special one and has evolved over the years. I was honoured to be asked to be godmother to their three children and I cherish my three perfect godchildren as a result. Friendships have always been very important to me, partly due to the connections I made early on in life.

There is no doubt in my mind that my accomplishments as an adult are in part a direct result of what I learned as a child. I certainly came out of my childhood knowing that things were expected of me. I was expected to behave appropriately. I was expected to do well in school. I saw firsthand the importance of volunteering. I understood what it meant to participate in neighbourhood activities and give back to the community. I grew up knowing that responsibility was not something that should be taken lightly and that we were all put on this earth to help to make things better. As I became an adult, I tried to apply these principles every step of the way in my journey.

The neighbourhood kids from Douglas Park Road, playing in Bruce Park (Photo taken by R. Mathieson)

Left: Gayle Sykes and I conquering the blizzard of March 1966
Right: Gayle and I on our St. James Collegiate High School graduation day

University of Winnipeg graduation 1971

Chapter 2
My Education

My Adolescent Years

A good education is its own reward. I strongly believe in this statement today, however, I must admit there was a brief period during my adolescent years when I got sidetracked. Other things seemed much more important.

Growing up in the fifties had its rewards as well. Families were the nucleus of society. This was an era where most mothers stayed home to tend to their families. It was all very *Father Knows Best*[1]-like, so I benefitted from having a stay-at-home mother. I don't recall ever thinking there was any inequality in this...fathers going off to work, mothers staying home...at least not in my pre-teen years. I did all the cliché things the fifties are famous for...I wore a poodle skirt and bobby socks and saddle shoes. When the hula-hoop fad arrived, my friends and I spent hours and hours at Bruce Park learning how to use it.

1 Father Knows Best is an American television comedy that ran on CBS from 1954 to 1960. It portrayed a middle class family life in the Midwest. (Source: Wikipedia)

Learning the hula-hoop (Photo taken by R. Mathieson)

Though I didn't realize it at the time, economic times were good during these post-war years. This was also an exciting time in the world of technology. In the late fifties, the Thompson family purchased its first television set. Of course, the picture was in black and white (no colour television sets in those days!) and an antenna, which everyone called "rabbit ears," was used to improve the reception. I would rush home from school and watch *Rin-Tin-Tin* and *The Lone Ranger.* On Sunday nights, the family would gather to watch *The Ed Sullivan Show*. I recall seeing Elvis on that show and didn't quite get what the uproar was all about when he swayed his hips. I actually preferred his slower songs and his gospel music. In 1964, I watched the famous episode on *The Ed Sullivan Show,* where the Beatles performed on North American soil for the first time. I was also a big fan of Dick Clark's *American Bandstand.*

I was a typical teenager in the early sixties, swooning over teen idols like Bobby Vinton, Paul Anka, and Gene Pitney. My friends and I loved to dance to sounds of The Beach Boys and would even do a little "twist" now and again. I never liked the sixties fashion trends such as miniskirts and hot pants, preferring the glamorous styles of movie stars such as Grace Kelly and Audrey Hepburn. I followed the acting careers of Doris Day, Rock Hudson, the gorgeous Tab Hunter, and the ever so charming Cary Grant. I was a romantic...the schmaltzier the music or the movie, the better. Life in the very early part of the sixties seemed simple...and fun. This was prior to the unimaginable tragedies that were to come...the assassination of John F. Kennedy, his brother Bobby, and Martin Luther King.

The Cuban Missile Crisis, a thirteen-day confrontation in October 1962 between the Soviet Union and Cuba on one side and the United States on the other side, marked the first time in my life that I remember feeling the absolute impact of a global conflict on our daily lives. We were all very aware of the seriousness of the situation and fearful of what could happen. The school, along with many other schools across the continent, held drills whereby we all had to crouch under our desks in case of a nuclear attack. I remember thinking how silly it was that we could be protected by crouching under our desks. I had already made up my mind that if we were attacked, I would run home, which was only one block away, and head down to our basement.

I was very influenced by the Kennedy family. I thought John F. Kennedy was articulate, progressive, and ahead of his time. I admired Jacqueline Kennedy for her style and elegance. They created such an aura. They were so glamorous; they seemed so happy, so together. To a young girl growing up in St. James, they seemed to have it all. And then the unthinkable happened — November 22, 1963 - the assassination of JFK. I was in grade eleven. I remember going home at lunchtime and my mother had the TV on. It was awful. I was in disbelief. It was all so sad. When I returned to school, our teacher asked that we pray and have a moment of silence. I cried. There was a great sense of loss felt by all of us. It was one of those moments in history that will stay with me forever.

My Secondary Years

So suffice it to say that somewhere between moving from Linwood School to St. James Collegiate, sometime after I saw Elvis sway his hips on the Ed Sullivan Show but before the death of John F. Kennedy, school was not as important to me as it should have been. By the time I reached grade eleven, I was a social success and an academic disaster.

Heading out to high school graduation dinner and dance

My father did not take lightly to my new lifestyle and especially to my dating. He made it clear to each one of my boyfriends that they should not "mess with him." There was one boyfriend in particular that my father referred to as a "smoothie." He once drove me home after a date just before curfew, but our "good night" kissing extended to past midnight. My father, who had no doubt been looking out our window for me, started to flick the outdoor porch light as the clock struck twelve. At our peril, we ignored my father's warnings and continued to kiss. Suddenly, our passionate embrace was interrupted by the sound of air hissing out of the car's tires. My father had proceeded to release the air out of this poor guy's tires. I rolled down my window, only to see my father standing outside in his "shorty pyjamas" and I asked him "What are you doing?" to which he replied sternly, "It's past curfew!" and returned to the house. It's a wonder I had any dates at all!

I once had a boyfriend who lived in Fargo, North Dakota. I would visit him occasionally, flying North West Airlines, first to Grand Forks and then to Fargo. Many of the passengers getting on the plane were soldiers... boys my own age...on their way to Vietnam. It was at this point of my life that I got a more in-depth view of the Vietnam War. My boyfriend and his friends were exempt from military service as long as they attended university. As the war continued however, some of his friends signed up. Unfortunately, some were killed. It was all very sobering for me. It was a very different time for Canadian youth and American youth. As young Canadians, we all knew about Vietnam, but this was not our war. I do remember thinking though that it was such a useless war...so many lives lost.

In Canada in 1968, a new "star" was emerging on the political scene. Like so many others, I was intrigued with Pierre Elliot Trudeau and swept up in "Trudeau-mania." The Trudeau era once again represented glamour and glitz, but it also gave Canadians hope. I saw Pierre Trudeau as highly intelligent, eloquent, witty, and good-looking...what more could we want in a leader for our country? The Trudeau years gave me my first taste of the ups and downs of a political life, though I did not think for one moment during those years that I would ever enter the political arena, let alone break barriers doing so.

My teen years, like those of all teenagers, were about finding out who I was as a person. Life was about making good and bad decisions and basically "growing up."

Earlier in my life, I had solidified my religious beliefs. My parents were not churchgoers, but they did believe that we should have faith and include God in our lives. They were very clear in their belief that religion was culturally based, but also understood that religions were a vehicle to include faith in our daily lives. Therefore, at a very young age, I was allowed to decide which church to attend. I explored a number of religious affiliations over a period of time. I first attended the Presbyterian Church at the top of the street, and then went to the United Church for a while. I tried the Baptist Church, then the Catholic Church, and then settled in as an Anglican. My friend Gayle and I were active in the Anglican Young People's Association. I volunteered for a number of activities in the church and even taught Sunday school at one time. My sister Lenore and my brother Norman became Anglicans and my sister Barbara became a Baptist. I am very appreciative of the fact that my parents encouraged my siblings and me to choose our religion.

As a teenager and young adult, I began to question some of the decisions made by certain religions. I recognized that religions were man-made structures and noticed that some decisions were based on power and politics. It was offensive to me that women would not be considered as leaders or ministers of the church. I couldn't understand how the "powers that be" recognized certain skill sets and qualities in men but not in women. It made no sense to me. As I studied the hierarchy of various religions, I often found myself questioning their intent...certainly they were not serving the intent of God. In fact, in many instances, I think decisions have been made that would be contrary to what God would have wanted.

That being said, I still consider myself a person of strong faith. I base my devotion on what I think is the bigger picture of what God wants and how we should conduct our lives. I have complete faith that there is a greater power and that God will guide us in our darkest hour. I know it. I have experienced it. Some people have told me that they only believe in themselves. In response to that, I say those people are short-changing themselves. People of faith, I think, have something to draw upon during difficult times. I am a strong believer that faith is an important component in one's life.

Lessons Learned: Quitting School and Going Back

In the summer of 1965, I took a summer job at the University of Winnipeg library as a circulation clerk. I placed books on shelves, collected fees, filed, helped students find materials, and answered telephone enquiries. I am an extrovert, so it was fun to be in a job where I was in contact with many people. I am an organizer by nature and therefore loved the structure and orderliness of a library. I loved my job.

At the end of the summer, I was offered a full-time position. I made the decision to take the job and forego returning to grade twelve at St. James Collegiate. I so vividly remember the conversation I had with my father when I told him about my plans. I had actually told him over the telephone, and once I "dropped the bomb," there must have been a full minute of dead silence at the other end of the line. He then said, "Well then, starting tomorrow, you are paying rent." Ouch.

I worked full time in the library for one year. Though I loved the job, I decided that I couldn't afford "me" on $85 a week. A posting came up for a buyer's job at Eaton's, Canada's top department store at the time. Regardless of my lack of education and experience, I boldly applied and was actually called in for an interview. I thought I had it in the bag. After all, I was a born retailer...a natural. The interview went well until the interviewer began to review my application. She began asking questions about my schooling. I started into a long explanation about why I had missing grade twelve subjects, and one missing subject from grade eleven. The interviewer quickly interjected and said, "Oh, you mean all that you have is a complete grade ten?" I nearly died...it had never been put to me quite like that before. After telling the interviewer of my natural capabilities as a retailer, she retorted, "That may be, but at Eaton's, we only hire "born retailers" with university degrees. It is Eaton's policy." And that was that. I truly learned an important lesson that day, and decided to go back to school.

Over the course of my work in the library at the University of Winnipeg, I had met many great teachers from the University of Winnipeg Collegiate. I was so impressed by their dedication and commitment to their students that I decided that this would be the best place to finish my high school education. Mr. Wright, the librarian who hired me, gave me a flexible work schedule that allowed me time to study. I continued to work at the library on a part-time basis, and completed my grade twelve at The Collegiate. This was one of the best decisions I have ever made.

The teachers at The Collegiate were brilliant and caring. They took the time to help me along and ensured that my educational needs were met. One of the subjects I had failed at St. James Collegiate was math, and I had been told by a former teacher that I would likely NEVER pass grade twelve math. When my UW Collegiate math teacher, Miss Mills, got wind of this, she assured me that not only would I pass, but I would get a better than passing grade. She worked with me and a few other struggling students three times per week — after regular classes — to ensure that we passed. And we did! Miss Mills' dedication to her students is just one example of the teachers at the Collegiate...individuals who took a personal interest in their students...teachers who made you feel you could accomplish anything. We were cared for, but not babied. We certainly felt that we were in a university atmosphere and treated like adults. It was a beautiful balance.

University of Winnipeg Collegiate Gr. 12 photo

My year at The Collegiate was a unique and outstanding experience. To this day, I credit this school for teaching me to stand on my own two feet. I can honestly say that the teachers at the Collegiate, and particularly Miss Mills, were instrumental in putting me on the right path. They instilled in me a passion to learn, to work hard, and to persevere. Their lessons helped me to make the decision to continue my studies after high school and I enrolled in the Bachelor of Arts Program at the University of Winnipeg.

My Collegiate days were also the start of an ongoing admiration for the University of Winnipeg. To this day, I truly value and respect this institution. It was only fitting that I returned one day, many years later, as the President and CEO of its Foundation.

Life, Learning and Love

If there is one thing I learned more than anything else at the University of Winnipeg, it's that the relationships you form with the people on either side of you in a particular classroom, or at a table in a school canteen, can influence your life dramatically and stay with you throughout your life. You will discuss concepts and ideas with your peers with vigour and enthusiasm. With them, you will celebrate victories and share defeat. With them, you will envision the future.

Tony's Canteen at UW Collegiate (Photo courtesy of University of Winnipeg Archives)

In the late 1960s and early 1970s, the University of Winnipeg was a hub of political activism. Many people who attended there at that time later made their mark on our great city of Winnipeg. When I look back, it is quite extraordinary that I was at the university at the same time as Lloyd Axworthy, Tom Axworthy, Barry Shenkarow, and Nick Ternette, just to name a few. We all sat at our own tables with our own group of friends in Tony's Canteen. I remember a particular conversation, when Tom Axworthy and his cronies pondered when his brother Lloyd should become prime minister of Canada. I was amazed that this conversation was actually happening and was incredulous about the whole situation. **Thirty years later, I had a full-circle moment when these same people were involved in trying to save the Winnipeg Jets franchise. Barry was one of the owners of the Jets, Lloyd was a federal cabinet minister at the time and I was mayor. We were all trying to save the Jets and Nick was protesting that we shouldn't save them. It's all very uncanny.**

From a personal perspective, I met many great people and established some good friendships at the University of Winnipeg. This is also where I reunited with someone I'd had a crush on in my earlier years. This same man later proposed to me on the front lawn of the University and we got married in the University of Winnipeg chapel.

I had met Garry when I was thirteen. He was a lifeguard at the local Y. He was seventeen or eighteen and I thought he was appealing (didn't everyone have a crush on the local lifeguard??). He apparently had some feelings for me as well, as he wrote me a few, "I like you, you're swell" letters that summer, but our age difference prevented us from dating. After that summer, I returned to junior high and Garry went on to the University of Winnipeg Collegiate to take his grade twelve. The next time I would see him would be four years later, when I worked at the University of Winnipeg library and he was taking his master's degree. I was in a line-up at Tony's Canteen. I looked at the tall, good-looking man ahead of me and, low and behold, it was Garry, my "lifeguard crush." I immediately said, "Hello Garry," to which he replied, "Do I know you?"

Regardless, we reconnected that day at Tony's and saw each other occasionally as friends, but it was a while before our relationship began to flourish. We started off carpooling together and we dated other people for a time. At the age of twenty, when I was enrolled in my first year of university, we began to date. We broke up for a short time but then got back together a year later. Garry was quite persistent this time, and before long we were engaged. He proposed to me twice. The second time, he proposed to me on the front lawn of the university. It was a beautiful, sunny day in September 1968. He asked me to meet him out front after class and I was astounded when he popped the question. We'd had a conversation about marriage earlier on in our relationship, but that conversation felt like more of a suggestion than a proposal. Being a romantic, I wanted a full proposal. I didn't quite understand that's why he wanted to meet me out there on that particular day. Garry could be very eloquent and very sweet, so his words were quite extraordinary and the entire thing was terribly romantic. It was definitely one of the most touching moments of my life.

We were officially engaged in December 1968 when he gave me a beautiful ½ carat diamond ring. As Garry had just started his career, I wasn't expecting an expensive engagement ring and had told him that I would be just as happy with a plain gold band. He refused that idea and I gladly accepted the exquisite diamond.

We were married in September 1969. The university chapel was small, holding only fifty people, so the ceremony was quite intimate. We had a modest reception at the Hotel Fort Garry where guests were served hot and cold hors d'oeuvres and sparkling wine. Susan McMillan was my maid of honour, and my bridesmaids were friends Gayle (Sykes) Carson and Eileen (Roper) Stuebing.

The earlier years of our marriage were good. Garry had a successful career as a director with the Province of Manitoba. I completed my Bachelor of Arts degree at the University of Winnipeg, and then began to work at Eaton's. Had it not been for Garry's love and support, I don't know that I would have done as well in my post-secondary education. He helped me with my writing and he mentored me in study skills and subjects that gave me difficulty. In many ways, he was my coach. To this day, I am grateful that he was in my life during those years.

Garry and I on the steps of the University of Winnipeg chapel

Early in our marriage, we bought a beautiful home on Elm Street in the middle upper-scale River Heights area. It really was the home of my dreams...an older, large two-storey with an entrance foyer, a living room with a fireplace, a formal dining area, a kitchen with a pantry, a sunroom, a porch off of our master bedroom on the second level, and a study with another fireplace. I recall thinking that if this was our first home, what would our "next" home look like? Our plan was to pay off the house as quickly as we could, and then Garry planned to go back to school to become a lawyer. We spent our first few years working hard in our careers and renovating our home. We got along well and had many great friends, so we socialized quite a bit. What we failed to do was discuss issues that really mattered to us...faith, having children, finances, and our careers. At first, Garry was very supportive of my career, but later resented the fact that I was away so much. After four years of marriage, and due to a series of circumstances, it became evident that our marriage was not going to work and we parted ways. Our values were just too different.

Many years later, when I made the decision to run for mayor, I called Garry to let him know of my plans. At first, he did not even want to talk to me, but eventually agreed to meet me. We had a three-hour lunch at Dubrovnik's on Assiniboine Avenue, the top restaurant in Winnipeg at the time, and in addition to discussing how my entrance into politics could throw him into the public light, we addressed issues in our marriage that we should have dealt with years ago. From that point on, a respectful friendship evolved between us. In fact, Garry helped me to write many of my speeches when I was mayor. He helped me to eloquently put together my last "State of the City" address to the Winnipeg Chamber of Commerce, even though at that time, he was in the latter stages of lung cancer. Unfortunately, he was too sick to attend my last address, and instead listened to it on the radio — a CJOB broadcast — from his hospital bed. He called me later that day to tell me how great a job I had done and that he was very proud of me. Two days after that speech, Garry fell into a coma. He died the following day. It was tragic that he died at such a young age. He was only in his early fifties.

In good times, Garry was my best friend, my mentor, and a trusted confidante. He was a great communicator. You could talk to him about any subject. He was intelligent and intuitive. He could understand your very soul. I am grateful that we were able to reconnect after our marriage fell apart, and I think that I was helpful to him during his final days. I became his support person in many ways, and I know that he was appreciative. His family was also very important to me and remained a part of my life.

This photo was taken by my father-in-law Nelson Harvey in 1970.

Chapter 3
Working for a Living

After graduating from the University of Winnipeg, I recognized that though my school days had ended, my education was just beginning. As a result of my post-secondary education, I learned the value of good communications and was able to focus on tasks with more confidence. University reinforced in me that life was all about learning. Every day brought something new to absorb and retain.

I did have a "one-day working stint" earlier on in my life. In my teen years, my father made it quite clear that it was time for me to have the responsibility of a job and arranged for me to work at his store, Birt Saddlery on Main Street in downtown Winnipeg. I had been to the store many times and was quite excited for the opportunity to work there. My first duty upon arrival was to dust some merchandise in the Luggage and Fine Leather Goods department. I followed his orders and starting cleaning the handbags. As I went about my work, it occurred to me that the bags were placed somewhat unsystematically, so I took it upon myself to reorganize the entire section by colour and style. After a few hours, I stood back and proudly looked at the newly placed items, quite content with my work. A few moments later, my father entered the area and saw my handiwork. "What is this?" he exclaimed. Father took one look at the reorganized area and adamantly said, "Put everything back the way it was!" I tried to explain that this would be easier for the customer, but he rejected my reasoning and again told me to move things back to the way they were. I refused. Both of us stood there and looked at one another.

A moment later, he said, "You're fired!" and I said, "I quit!" When I returned to Winnipeg in 1980 and I walked through the doors of Birt Saddlery, I owned it.

Eaton's of Canada

Immediately after graduation from university, I explored full-time career opportunities. I was impressed with the fact that Eaton's of Canada offered university graduates management trainee positions, so I pursued and eventually accepted an offer from the company in 1971.

For as long as I can remember, the Eaton's downtown store has meant so much to me. As a child, I loved the sheer excitement of visiting the store and viewing the spectacular window displays at Christmastime. Our family would often take in the outstanding Eaton's Santa Claus Parade. We would then have lunch in the famous Grill Room on the fifth floor, where they had special orange children's menus in the shape of Punkinhead, Eaton's toy teddy bear. We then went up to see Santa Claus on the eighth floor. He was no doubt the "real" one because he looked and acted so authentic. As I reached my teens, Eaton's was not only THE place for Winnipeggers to go shopping — after all, they were known for their famous TransCanada Sale and $1.49 Days — it also became a centre of entertainment. At any given time, Eaton's would have an array of events happening — be it a fashion show, an "up and coming" local band playing, or spectacular displays and demonstrations. As a young adult, I loved to purchase my clothes at Eaton's and I enjoyed meeting friends and family at the great Grill Room. In my last year of university, as I pondered my job options, working at Eaton's seemed like the perfect fit. My first job at Eaton's was a part-time position at the men's shirts counter, alongside Lolly Roper, my good friend Eileen's mom. After I finished university, I moved to full time.

I always tell people that I started at the bottom and worked my way up at Eaton's. In fact, I literally did start at the bottom, working in Eaton's basement as a signature supervisor. In this position, I was responsible to authorize cheques, returns, and cash register transactions. I also learned how to become a cashier. This was an experience in itself. I quickly learned that I had to void a mistake instead of just throwing the receipt in the wastebasket. The first day that I did this, I had to retrieve every discarded receipt I had thrown out, so that we could void them and make sure the cash register balanced at the end of the day. I believe that this may be when I began to use the term "learning curve."

The main responsibility for all staff at Eaton's was selling merchandise. In order to do this effectively, many tasks needed to be done behind the scenes, such as pulling cage trucks full of merchandise from the receiving area to the appropriate departments, keeping the clothing racks properly organized, and working cash. It was important to be flexible and to pitch in where needed.

I found working in retail to be exciting and fast paced. You had to be creative and you had to know how to sell a product. If you were good at sales — and you knew soon enough if you were — it could be personally rewarding. I discovered that if I could convince someone to buy a few items, when they originally had planned to buy "just a lipstick," I was doing my job well. I think Eaton's developed the add-on sales technique long before fast food restaurants did. ("Do you want fries with that?") I loved working in retail and found that working for one of the city's top fashion centres influenced my style and lifestyle. I also became knowledgeable on determining the quality and value of a product.

The departments in Eaton's basement were constantly in sales-promotion mode. This made work incredibly busy all the time. It was like a mini world and it made for interesting encounters, as so many people from so many different nationalities shopped in Eaton's basement. I once had a customer who would regularly come in and buy many ladies' mouton winter coats. He bought these under the condition that I would take them over to the weigh scales in the meat department, so that he knew what his purchases weighed. I later learned that the reason for this was that he would send these coats to his relatives in the Ukraine, who could then sell them to get cash.

In those days, he was not allowed to send cash to his relatives. The communist government would not allow it.

Training was paramount at Eaton's. The company strongly believed that good training produced good employees. Generally, training involved more experienced staff teaching new employees "the ropes." I learned many lessons from the training I received at Eaton's. I developed organizational skills, became self-motivated, and learned to pay attention to detail. Most importantly, by handling customer complaints, I learned to rely upon my intuition when dealing with people. One of my best training experiences with Eaton's was called MIMIC (Make IT Meaningful In Cash). I was one of fourteen employees selected for this specialized training program. It was a unique experience for employees who were seen as future leaders within the company. It was an unbelievable course. All in all, Eaton's was the best place I could ever have had to start my career.

I soon became a management trainee and buyer for ladies coats, dresses, and pantsuits — still in Eaton's basement — and entered a whole new realm of the retail business. When you work in a department where the majority of your customers are low-income earners, or new immigrants, or people looking for a deal, maintaining low prices is critical. Mere pennies counted in the negotiations on the price of merchandise. We had to be very sensitive when pricing items, yet still do our best to maintain quality. "Junk" never sold.

My buying market was Montreal so I began to travel, which I absolutely loved. This position gave me a great opportunity to learn how to negotiate with the toughest of suppliers. It was hard work but I worked with a wonderful team that really pulled together. Many of the employees were women who had left school in grades eight, nine, or ten to go to work during World War II. They were required to do the jobs that the men had done at Eaton's before heading off to war. These women were amazing. Many of them wound up as single moms because they lost their husbands in the war. I believe that this generation of women were unsung heroes. They were never really recognized for their contributions and never properly paid for all the hard work they did. They were my teachers — no-nonsense people who praised you if you were doing a good job and told you plain and simple if you weren't. My very first supervisor, Anne Lonie, was one of the women who left school during the war and was a single mom. She and I became lifelong friends.

A major culture change was happening around the world in the early seventies and subsequently, within our company. Women were taking their place in the job market. The first wave of women baby boomers were graduating from university and most, if not all, found jobs. Women across the country were recognizing the need to work outside the home. More and more, women needed careers and incomes to maintain their family lifestyle. A shift had ensued and a woman's salary was no longer seen as a "supplement" to the family income, but instead a necessity.

I had personally always wanted to pursue a career and I don't know that the "feminist" movement necessarily influenced my decision. I never really saw myself as a feminist, however, over the course of my early days at Eaton's, I discovered an antiquated policy that made me recognize the need to fight for women's rights. I found out that I had been hired on a "woman's" pay scale. I was shocked. It had never occurred to me that there would be different salary grids for men and women, especially when they were doing the same job. When I asked for an explanation, I was told by one manager that most women were married and therefore "supported" by their husbands. He then went on to say, "Most of you eventually become pregnant and leave, and all that money spent training you is then lost." I was astounded by his remarks. I was not going to let this go. I know that I was extremely vocal about the unfairness of this ludicrous policy, and eventually the policy was changed.

Another incident while I was working at Eaton's made me a huge advocate of women's rights. A women's movement group was circulating posters to businesses around the city and one was pinned up in our staff room. The poster had a photo of a boardroom table with twelve men seated around it. The caption read, "Why are there no women at this table?" When I saw this, I took the poster in to my boss' office and asked him what he thought. His reaction still irks me to this day. He calmly said, “You want to be a board member? Can you grow a moustache?” Wow! I could not believe those words came out of his mouth. This is exactly the moment I became a feminist.

As much as I would have liked to have worked on one of the “upper” floors, Eaton’s basement taught me many things — how to obtain the best value for the customer...not to ever “waste” money... you were only as good as your sales and ROII (return on inventory investment)...how to identify great workers from pretenders...how to keep your receiver happy...the list can go on and on.

Working for Eaton’s was like being a part of a great big family. We all joked that we had the Eaton “E” branded into the middle of our foreheads. The loyalty of the employees to the company and the Eaton family was quite something. The company had a rich history and employees knew that. We were proud to be “Eatonians.”

My last promotion at the Eaton’s store in Winnipeg was to western regional buyer of women’s shoes for stores in Manitoba, Saskatchewan and Alberta. I travelled across the country to find suitable sport shoes, sandals, casual shoes, and women’s boots. This also involved flying to Montreal for national meetings. I absolutely loved that city and enjoyed going to meetings there. I also got some great exposure in every city in Western Canada. It was all a great experience.

Moving away from Winnipeg

After several years of working at Eaton’s in Winnipeg, I was promoted to group department manager in Calgary. This again was a wonderful opportunity, managing ten departments across Alberta, in Calgary, Red Deer, Lethbridge, and Medicine Hat. It also proved to be a challenge.

In the mid-seventies, Eaton’s was the number one department store retailer in Winnipeg. We were the best and we worked hard to be the best. The marketplace was changing as suburban malls began to expand and the downtown store was experiencing a decline, but we were still the most popular department store in the city. In Western Canada, things were different. The west was exploding as far as businesses and the economy were concerned. But Eaton's was not a predominant player out west. When I was promoted to the Calgary location, I was shocked to find out that Eaton's in Alberta was fifth behind Woodwards, The Bay, Sears, and K-Mart.

Subsequently, significant money was poured into existing stores in Alberta and expansions occurred as well. It was an exhilarating time. The economy was unreal. Calgary was booming. Oil workers in Fort McMurray would come in to Edmonton on their time off and then go down to Calgary. Jewellery departments in Edmonton and Calgary were selling exquisite one-carat and half-carat diamond rings by the dozen. This was definitely the sign of the buoyant economy. I believe a lot of "weekend" engagements took place.

Calgary was a young city, vibrant in so many ways, and Albertans had a very "can do" attitude. Housing was scarce and I had a difficult time finding an apartment. I eventually found a place close to downtown, on the other side of the tracks of 14th Avenue. It was smaller than my apartment in Winnipeg and double the rent, but only five minutes from work. It was a rather nondescript square box, but it did have two bedrooms so I was able to host friends and family who came to visit.

My staff at Eaton's store in Calgary

I had just been divorced and was glad to have a fresh start in another city. Other than a few family friends in Calgary, I did not know anybody. That soon changed and yet again, many of my coworkers became lifelong friends. Many employees were new to Calgary, transferred from all across Canada and all over the world. Bill McFarlane, who was our display person at Eaton's and then went on to a very successful twenty-five-year career with CTV/CFCN, is a good friend. Brian Peel and I met in Calgary, but then our careers took us to Vancouver and Montreal respectively. Years later, we reconnected in Winnipeg, where Brian became my communications person during my time as mayor of Winnipeg. To this day, he is still a guiding force in my life.

Part of the Calgary experience included what I call serendipity. On one particular day at Eaton's downtown Calgary location, yet another amazing opportunity presented itself to me. We were in the midst of a cosmetics fair and by all accounts, I must admit, it was sensational. We knew we were doing a great job and the event proved to be more successful than our main competitor — The Bay. It was noon, when all good managers should really be on the selling floor. I was in my cosmetics department when I noticed three men in dark-blue pinstripe suits walking towards my area. Retailers have a way about them, and I knew as soon as I saw them that these were not just regular customers shopping at our store. They were our competitors and they were "checking us out." Knowing that networking usually starts with a conversation, I approached them and asked them who they were, in as friendly and helpful a tone I could muster. I soon found out that two of them were managers from The Bay in Calgary and one was the senior national merchandise manager from The Bay in Montréal. I proceeded to introduce myself and give them a tour, knowing full well that this was opening the door to the possibility of networking with them in the future.

A few hours later, one of the gentlemen who had visited the store called and invited me over for coffee. The end result of this encounter was that I was asked to go to Montréal for an interview with Mr. Herber, the senior merchandise manager. Montréal...my favourite city outside of Winnipeg! I jumped at the chance. My interview went extremely well. In fact, I can honestly say that this was the best interview I have ever had. Mr. Herber knew how to engage conversation and the interview was interesting, informative, and respectful. We really hit it off and knew immediately we could work well together. At the end of the interview, as I was walking out the door, he said, "Oh by the way, you do have a university degree right?" to which I replied, "Yes of course." It was one of those full circle moments and all I could think about was, *Thank you, University of Winnipeg!* Soon thereafter, I was offered what I considered to be the job of a lifetime.

Onward and Upward to Montréal

So off I was to "La Belle Province." Finding an apartment in downtown Montréal was no small feat, not because there were none available, but because they were old, cramped, and expensive. The economy was not booming like it was in Calgary. In fact, people were starting to move out of Montréal in droves due to the political climate. This was at the height of the Québec separatist movement and many English-speaking residents were leaving the province.

I was assigned a realtor who was brash and unfriendly, and she barely made time for me. She took me to a number of apartments that were very small, smelling of mildew, and in unkempt condition. This was late winter and it was a typical slushy day in Montréal, so we got colder and wetter as the day progressed. By noon, the realtor abandoned me, leaving me only with a list of potential rentals. I continued to call and make arrangements on my own, but most landlords I called did not speak English. Every place I checked out was unacceptable and most of the landlords wanted to rent to bilingual tenants. This went on for two days. Finally, I came across a place in Westmount, the city's English suburb. It was in an eight-storey block near the corner of Sherbrooke and Landsdowne, and I saw that as a sign, since these were both street names that could be found in Winnipeg. The building appeared well-built and well-maintained, and the suite was much larger than any of the others I had seen. It had a great foyer, a dining room and a big master bedroom with a walk-in closet. I also liked the fact that there was a doorman, as security was important given the political climate. I must say however, that the poor man was quite shocked when I arrived to see the apartment. The woman who lived there previously had just died one day earlier. Such was the real estate market in downtown Montréal! The rent was higher than I anticipated and I had no idea how I was going to be able to afford this place, but I also knew it would be foolish to pass up on the opportunity. I snapped it up.

I worked about 20 minutes away from my apartment and drove my baby blue Mustang to work every day. The Bay's offices were on the top two floors of The Bay downtown, on Rue St. Catherine. There were approximately two hundred buyers, mostly women, all working in overcrowded conditions, and each with a small cubicle. Austerity at its finest! Central buyers were in cubicles but principal buyers had their own separate offices.

The Bay buying offices group in Montréal

Within a few months, I was promoted to principal buyer of jewellery for The Bay. This was without a doubt my dream job. I had three central buyers reporting to me and we were responsible for three major areas: (1) precious jewellery (diamonds and gold); (2) fashion jewellery; and (3) watches and clocks. We purchased these items for all of The Bay's retail stores across Canada. It involved travel all over the world and I was well paid. I swear I sometimes had to pinch myself. I couldn't believe that I was an international buyer at the age of thirty-two. Incredible is the best way to describe it. I made more great friends — Sharon Rundle and Jill Morton to name just a couple — and immersed myself in my newfound life. In fact, Sharon's son Christopher is my godson.

In spite of the tough political times, I loved Montreal. I loved the lifestyle and I quickly learned "the French way" of doing things. Québecers, especially Montréalers, had a sense of style about them that I admired. I was immediately impressed by my coworkers, who were incredibly beautiful women and always looked so "put together" throughout the day at work. I would often wonder how they kept looking so fresh when I appeared dishevelled by lunchtime. I learned a lot from them and developed my own sense of style as a result.

I also loved the Montréal way of life. They call it "joie de vivre" (translation: joy of living) and it truly is a refreshing way to live. Montréalers work hard but they also pause and enjoy things. They take the time to enjoy good food, good wine, good entertainment, and the company of friends. When I held my first dinner party, I originally asked people to arrive at 6:00 p.m. I was quickly told that the timing was wrong. I was advised that no dinner party in Montréal starts before 8:00 p.m. These parties went on quite late into the evening, however, as dinners included many courses and wines and liqueurs in between each course. Even lunches were to be savoured. We once went for a group business lunch and after more than an hour of sitting at a beautiful outdoor restaurant at Place Ville Marie, I turned to my boss and said, "Shouldn't we be heading back to work?" She replied, "Susan, we put in incredibly long hours, travel extensively, and have little time for home life. Enjoy this time, the beautiful weather, the wonderful food, and all of us being together." I eventually built this attitude in my own life, even though it was contrary to the way I had been brought up. When I could, I took the time to savour moments, no matter how busy life had become. Much later in my career, I also remembered this and took the opportunity with my staff, be it at the mayor's office or at the University of Winnipeg Foundation, to take a pause from our hectic days and relax and enjoy the good things in life over lunch.

Every so often, I did get the feeling that I was not welcomed in Montréal. At times, it felt like I was in another country. I was once stopped by a police officer because I was about to park in a no parking zone, and as he looked at my Alberta licence plates, he asked me, "What are you doing here if you are from Alberta?" He warned me that my car could be a target for break-ins and I quickly changed to Québec plates.

As time went on, I tried to understand the reasoning behind Québec separation and asked friends and co-workers many questions about the issue and discussed their views. I found out that the War Measures Act that had been enforced on the province in October 1970 had a major impact on its citizens. They were horrified that tanks were filling their streets and military were strong-holding their people, and many never forgot, or in some instances, forgave the Liberal government of the time for implementing such perceived brutal force. As an Anglophone, and a western Canadian, the separatist movement certainly became a significant reality, and quite frankly, it terrified me that our country might break apart.

In May 1980, I participated in the historic Québec referendum. I was proud to be part of history and I waited nearly two hours in line to vote. Later that evening, I watched television intently for the results. Many of us at The Bay were from other provinces, and not Francophone, and because of that, we always had an exit strategy, should Québec separate from the rest of Canada. The federalist side won that night, but I knew immediately that didn't mean the issue had gone away. I think people were afraid that if the "yes" side had won, the threat of having tanks driving down the streets of downtown Montréal could re-emerge, this time by René Levesque and his followers. As a Canadian, this experience had a huge impact on me. I became much more passionate about my country and about the importance of a unified country. I paid more attention to my responsibilities as a citizen of Canada and valued citizenship more than ever before.

Near the Arno River in Florence, Italy

A year passed, very quickly I might add, as I thoroughly enjoyed my life and my career with The Bay in Montreal. I was starting to envision future career opportunities within The Bay, and possibilities existed within the company for me to move outside of Canada, to either Florence or Hong Kong. I was ready for this next step and anticipated that when I was ready, I would apply for an international posting and start living abroad.

And then, one of those curves that life throws at you occurred, and in a second, my life was about to change more drastically than I had ever imagined.

Susan Thompson minding the store: "Anything to reinforce the positive."

Photo featured in a Winnipeg Free Press Article on Birt Saddlery in 1988 (Gerry Cairns/Winnipeg Free Press, April 9, 1988 Reprinted with permission)

Chapter 4
Becoming a Business Owner

Taking Care of Business

I had been living in Montreal for a little more than a year when my father came for a visit. It was early 1980 and he had come here on business, but also made sure that he could spend some time with me. I took him to our buying offices in downtown Montreal and gave him a glimpse of what I did for a living. As I described my responsibilities and showed him my office, he looked at me in awe and said, "Are they really paying you to do this job?" He was very proud of what I had accomplished. I told him of the opportunities around the corner, and more precisely, the possibility of landing a posting in Hong Kong or Florence. Again, he was in awe.

Following our visit to my workplace, we went to an expensive restaurant in downtown Montreal. I remember that it was expensive because Father nearly fell over when he saw the bill. During dinner that evening, he told me something that caught me completely off guard. Father had been diagnosed with cancer and the prognosis was not good. He was worried about his health, of course, but he was also concerned about the future of Birt Saddlery. I knew immediately what I needed to do. **Within seconds, my life changed.**

The family business had been a part of my father's life for almost fifty years. In the early thirties, father worked as a manager for Great West Saddlery in Regina. In 1935, he moved to Winnipeg to work for my grandfather, William Josiah Thompson, who had just purchased Birt Saddlery in Winnipeg. Father eventually became vice president and continued to run the company after my grandfather passed away. Father worked hard for the business to succeed. He had a true entrepreneurial spirit and knew the importance of networking. He was one of the people who established the Western Merchants Association and he belonged to a number of business organizations. He devoted many long hours...his life really...to ensure that the business was successful. Now, he was struggling with what was going to happen, due to his illness.

When my father told me about his cancer, I knew I had no option but to return to Winnipeg. I knew that he and my mother should have the opportunity to make the most of the time they had left together. I felt strongly that I had to put aside my personal ambitions. This was one of those moments when you step up to the plate and honour your family obligations. As difficult a decision as this was, I knew in my heart and soul that it was the right thing to do.

It took almost a year to work things out for me to come back. I had decided early on that I could not return and "run" the business. I needed to buy the company outright. The negotiations were very difficult and very sensitive. After all, this was my father's pride and joy... his legacy. Part of the negotiation was the fact that my father wanted to stay involved in the business as much as his health would allow. He once told me: "Your mother and I have been married for fifty years. She has saved up fifty years' worth of projects for me to work on at home. You will have to tell her that you need me at the store." I agreed to his request and, much to my mother's dismay, he remained involved for a few years, until his health deteriorated.

I returned to Winnipeg on October 1, 1980. I knew there was no looking back...what had to be done had to be done.

The Rich History of Birt Saddlery

The original Birt Saddlery building at Main and Market

Birt Saddlery had a rich history in the Winnipeg landscape. It was a descendent of Great West Saddlery, which was founded by the Hutchings family in the early 1900s. The Winnipeg operation of Great West Saddlery was in manufacturing and wholesale. Birt Saddlery was a retail store, established by John Birt, who was married to a Hutchings. My grandfather purchased the business from Mr. Birt in 1934. Its original location was on the corner of Main and Market, right across from the old City Hall. As a young child, I used to love going to my grandfather's store, just to see that beautiful "gingerbread castle" across the street, not knowing at the time that it was Winnipeg's old City Hall building. I later recognized that the store was in a prime location in downtown Winnipeg and that Birt Saddlery was part of Winnipeg's business community.

Birt Saddlery sold everything from saddles and harnesses, to whips and carriage equipment for the horse trade. As more automobiles made their way into the marketplace, a shift occurred in the business. Horse equipment continued to be popular, but after World War II, luggage and leather goods were added to the retail mix.

Steamer trunks were a popular item in those days. Soon, western clothing became a prominent seller.

Birt Saddlery Main and Bannatyne location

In 1965, Birt Saddlery moved to a different location, still on Main Street, but further south, at Bannatyne Avenue. The Duffin Block, a one-storey building originally built in the late 1800s by one of Winnipeg's pioneering photographers, Simon Duffin, has a rich history as a Winnipeg landmark building. The Baker Block, which was built in the early 1900s, is a three-storey building with a red brick facade. Both of these historical buildings housed Birt Saddlery and both are still intact today. The retail store took up the ground levels of both buildings. Either side of the front entrance was adorned by the profiles of two white horses with blue eyes (which coincidentally matched the colour of father's eyes). The remainder of the three-storey building housed the wholesale portion of the business and inventory storage.

My father was a brilliant, visionary businessman. In its heyday, Birt Saddlery was a retailer, a wholesaler, and a distributor, and it had a catalogue division for the saddle part of the business, all due to my father's business acumen. After World War II, Father bought directly from many countries including Japan, Finland, England,

Pakistan, and the U.S.A. In the early fifties, father talked Lee Jeans into giving him the Western Canadian distributor rights...a coup, you might say, for a small independent retailer in Winnipeg, Manitoba. Eventually, big department stores like Eaton's and The Bay ended up buying directly from Lee Jeans as well, but my father's ingenuity put him on the map as a shrewd businessman. He ran his company successfully for many years. When Father's health took a turn for the worse in the early 1980s, the state of his business was also deteriorating, though I do not know that he was aware of how bad things were. A combination of many circumstances — a declining downtown, the advent of suburban shopping malls, the barricading of Portage and Main (which literally cut off thirty percent of our customer trade) — made it very difficult for family businesses in the area to survive.

My father was a very proud man and I don't know that he understood the situation that the business was in when we were negotiating the buyout. Downtown Winnipeg was declining, particularly on Main Street. Many businesses that had been functioning for years were struggling, and unfortunately, many ran their course during these difficult years. Father thought that our building alone was worth over a million dollars. It was not. By the time I sold in 1995, the selling price was $150,000. In retrospect, my father likely knew that many businesses in downtown Winnipeg were facing some financial struggles, but it was difficult for him to accept that his own business was facing those same woes.

Taking Over the Reins

In order to purchase the business, I had to assume a huge debt. Unfortunately, this came about during difficult economic times. High inflation and ballooning interest rates dominated in the early 1980s and though I knew there was a risk in borrowing money, I also knew it was the only way to get this done.

There was no question that I was on a major learning curve when I first took over the business. Being trained in retail at two major department stores, I was taught that turnover of inventory and return on investment were critical. Father had a different approach.

He thought inventory was like gold. More than half of our 22,000 square feet of our buildings were filled with inventory. We had everything from blue jeans dating back to the 1960s to horseshoe nails. I believe we had over 10,000 nails...enough to supply horseshoes for every horse in Canada for years. Eventually, I formulated my own policy on how much inventory we should have.

Within six months of purchasing Birt Saddlery from my father in 1980, I almost lost the whole thing. By March 1981, interest rates skyrocketed to nineteen, twenty, and twenty-one percent, and I found myself paying $110,000 in interest during my first year. Winnipeg's downtown continued to be in trouble and Main Street was especially hard hit. The recession was setting in, the Canadian dollar was falling rapidly, and the cost of importing American cowboy boots and other goods was skyrocketing. City business taxes doubled and a city-wide reassessment of properties resulted in our property taxes increasing significantly. And then, to add to the stress, the city announced it was going to stop providing steam heat to its customers, which included ninety-plus historic buildings in the exchange district...ours included. We suddenly had to find the funds to purchase a furnace to heat 22,000 square feet of store space. What most people don't realize is that back in the forties when the steam heat was provided by the city, most of these buildings had removed their furnaces. They were no longer needed. When the city introduced this new policy, the building required a major retrofit — at a cost of $30,000 cash — just to install a furnace that would heat the basement and main floor. We couldn't afford to heat the other floors.

Encountering resistance took on a whole new meaning in those early years. Small businesses often faced challenges in dealing with banks, as did women business owners. Despite the obstacles, I worked hard to make the business successful. I retained the services of an extremely good financial advisor, Bob Stuebing, and together we developed an excellent business plan. I worked tirelessly to develop a good relationship with the bank. I hired good staff. I developed strong networks and became hugely involved in the community, such as the

Winnipeg Chamber of Commerce, the YM-YWCA, and the Winnipeg Symphony Orchestra.

For the most part, the original staff at Birt Saddlery was most welcoming. Many of them had wanted to retire but stayed on because of their loyalty to my father, and did eventually retire when I came along. Others remained and continued to treat our company with respect and dedication. A few unfortunately, were not as respectful to me or my father. Through a security process, I discovered that two long-standing staff members had been stealing from us, for years. This was devastating to my father, who, in addition to hiring them, had helped these people out with home loans at one point. Overall however, the employees at Birt Saddlery were amazing. Over the years, I was fortunate to find new people to join the company, who also became dedicated and wonderful staff. During difficult times, I was grateful for the people around me who supported me in so many ways.

The early days of owning Birt Saddlery were definitely difficult. In some ways, however, they were also completely gratifying. I loved being an owner. I loved making decisions without having to jump through hoops to have them approved. It also solidified my thinking that you better love what you are doing or you will not survive. Private business is 24/7. I developed a great respect for business owners — their ingenuity, their sense of responsibility. There is no process like figuring out how to meet payrolls, pay suppliers, and even pay yourself, etc. when you are faced with not enough cash flow. I learned that somehow you have to find a way to make things work.

Just when I wasn't sure I could continue to run the business, I was blessed with — of all things — a movie that made cowboy boots and western apparel fashionable once again. Birt Saddlery no doubt benefitted from the returning fashion trends due to the popularity of the movie *Urban Cowboy*, which was released in Canada by early 1981. I've always wanted to meet John Travolta, just to thank him for his part in making that movie so successful. It certainly was a godsend for Birt Saddlery at that time.

Being a Woman in Business in the 1980s

Financial stability was not the only challenge that presented itself during my Birt Saddlery days. I have always believed that networking is a vital factor to business success. As such, I felt it was important for me to join organizations. In the early months at Birt Saddlery, my father made many attempts to introduce me to his network. He would take me to meetings with him as a way of introducing me. Astonishingly enough — at least to my father — his network rejected me. These exclusive clubs — Winnipeg Executives, Carleton Club, Manitoba Club...and most other service clubs — rejected me because I was a woman. None of these clubs would allow women members. Yes, this was 1980, not 1880. Incredible! I could be a Rotary Anne, a Lionette, or a Kinette — usually reserved for spouses of Rotarians, Lion's Club members, or Kinsmen — but not a bona fide member of these organizations. The Winnipeg Chamber of Commerce was the only open door.

As a woman business owner, I could not believe the patronizing attitudes of the business community. There was a definite lack of acknowledgement that I was the owner, particularly when my father was still involved. Women were just not seen in the same light. This absolutely irked my father. We once went to a business meeting where the organization's membership threatened to quit if a woman was allowed to join. My father expressed to this organization quite clearly that the "rules of membership" did not include any wording that might suggest members were required to have a penis.

On the following page is another example of Father's attempt to have women recognized among local executive groups. Despite the resistance and the challenges for many years, I was eventually appointed to significant federal, provincial, and local boards. One of the proudest moments I can remember, not long before my father passed away, was a call by the Prime Minister's Office to sit on the Economic Council of Canada. It was so ironic that through the networks I had built, I was catapulted into a playing field that was well beyond my father's experience and he was in awe of these doors that were opening for me.

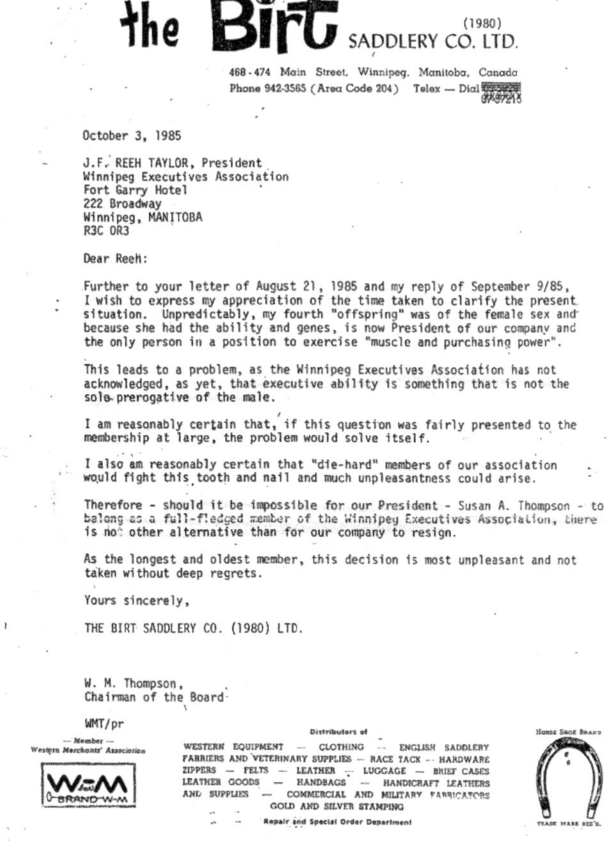

the Birt SADDLERY CO. LTD. (1980)

468 - 474 Main Street, Winnipeg, Manitoba, Canada
Phone 942-3565 (Area Code 204) Telex — Dial 07-57215

October 3, 1985

J.F. REEH TAYLOR, President
Winnipeg Executives Association
Fort Garry Hotel
222 Broadway
Winnipeg, MANITOBA
R3C 0R3

Dear Reeh:

Further to your letter of August 21, 1985 and my reply of September 9/85, I wish to express my appreciation of the time taken to clarify the present situation. Unpredictably, my fourth "offspring" was of the female sex and because she had the ability and genes, is now President of our company and the only person in a position to exercise "muscle and purchasing power".

This leads to a problem, as the Winnipeg Executives Association has not acknowledged, as yet, that executive ability is something that is not the sole prerogative of the male.

I am reasonably certain that, if this question was fairly presented to the membership at large, the problem would solve itself.

I also am reasonably certain that "die-hard" members of our association would fight this tooth and nail and much unpleasantness could arise.

Therefore - should it be impossible for our President - Susan A. Thompson - to belong as a full-fledged member of the Winnipeg Executives Association, there is no other alternative than for our company to resign.

As the longest and oldest member, this decision is most unpleasant and not taken without deep regrets.

Yours sincerely,

THE BIRT SADDLERY CO. (1980) LTD.

W. M. Thompson,
Chairman of the Board

WMT/pr

— Member —
Western Merchants' Association
W-M BRAND W-M

Distributors of
WESTERN EQUIPMENT — CLOTHING — ENGLISH SADDLERY
FARRIERS AND VETERINARY SUPPLIES — RACE TACK — HARDWARE
ZIPPERS — FELTS — LEATHER — LUGGAGE — BRIEF CASES
LEATHER GOODS — HANDBAGS — HANDICRAFT LEATHERS
AND SUPPLIES — COMMERCIAL AND MILITARY FABRICATORS
GOLD AND SILVER STAMPING
Repair and Special Order Department

Horse Shoe Brand
TRADE MARK REG'D.

My father had always taught me that success depended upon "fifty percent product and fifty percent network," so I knew that one of the most important things I could do was to establish my own network. He taught me that it didn't matter how small you were as a business, you should be connected. He never accepted that a job could not get done. He never accepted that discrimination would stop any woman from achieving anything. Certainly, the behaviour of his colleagues towards me shocked him, but that didn't change his conviction that I could find a way around, over, or through an obstacle. His belief in the power of perseverance is one of the most valuable legacies he gave me. My favourite definition of perseverance is: "When the world says 'give up,' hope whispers 'try one more time'. And so, that is what I did. I applied to the Rotary Club every year for at least eight years and was rejected every time. Finally, in 1989, I was accepted to become the first woman Rotarian in the city of Winnipeg. Perseverance pays off. It was most unfortunate that my father had passed away by then and did not live to see this day.

Setbacks and Struggles

I experienced other setbacks while I owned and operated Birt Saddlery. Often, these were due to policies and taxes imposed by our municipal government. These unfair policies may have had a hand in fuelling my desire to enter politics, to work for change from a business perspective within government.

It became inevitable that there would come a time when I would have to close Birt Saddlery's doors. My father died in 1987 and the years that followed were extremely difficult. I am thankful that my father did not have to see the worst of it. Owning your own business can really be one of life's tests. I tried in vain to make the business succeed, but in 1995, I made the decision that it was no longer possible keep the business afloat. I had survived for fifteen years in this business. When we finally closed our doors, we were one of the last of the Main Street stores to go...Big Four Sales was gone, MacDonald Shoes was gone...Silverman Jewellers was gone. After eighty-eight years, Birt Saddlery was no more. It was heartbreaking. The day the store was closed was truly one of the darkest days of my life. I felt that I had let down my customers, my employees, and my family. I had nothing left.

Through my entrepreneurial experience, I learned many things. I understood sheer terror in trying to meet a payroll and take care of employees and suppliers. I learned all about perseverance. I learned that I had guts and true grit. During my fifteen years with Birt Saddlery, there were times when I could only pay myself $25,000 a year — not your typical CEO salary. I drove a ten-year-old car, did not own a house, and had no savings.

I don't know that I realized how pivotal that decision was back in October 1980, when I gave up my career in Montreal to return to Winnipeg. Had I not understood family obligation, I would not likely have returned to Winnipeg, nor would I have necessarily gone through the struggles of being a business owner. I would not have encountered the prejudices against women, which really opened my eyes to some unfair practices, and I would not have had a hand in breaking down barriers for Winnipeg women. I may also not have realized my real passion for the city of Winnipeg. I learned very early on that passion in what you do is a key to success. You need to love what you are doing. **And so began a journey that would lead me on a path I would never have expected to take.**

Part 2

MOMENTS IN HISTORY

"I believe most women do not go into politics for power, but to make things better and to make a difference."

Susan A. Thompson

My official portrait, taken by local photographer Albert Cheung, hangs at Winnipeg City Hall

Chapter 5
The Road to Becoming Mayor

When Destiny Calls

I truly believe that we all have been given a destiny. Mine was to be the mayor of Winnipeg, and it came to me in my mid-thirties in the middle of the night. The details of how this unfolded are for another time and perhaps another book, but suffice it to say that I heard my destiny and I listened. I was going to be the mayor of Winnipeg. I did not know when, I did not know how, I did not even know why, but I did know that it was going to happen. I truly felt, and still believe, that I received a calling. There is no other way to describe it.

I really want to emphasize here that I had absolutely no political aspirations growing up. In my adolescent mind, my future consisted of getting married, being happy, and being rich. I did not ever see myself as a political enthusiast. I remember seeing Prime Minister John Diefenbaker at the old Winnipeg Auditorium when I was quite young. A family friend, Margie Dunwoody, had taken me there to see "democracy in action." I was horrified that those in attendance, including Margie, heckled the prime minister when he spoke. I thought that it was such bad manners to do such a thing and I remember thinking that I would not ever want it to happen to me. Of course years later, after I became mayor, I had to endure the same circumstances as Mr. Diefenbaker at a few public events.

I was managing Birt Saddlery when I heard my chosen path. It was 1982 and I was learning the ins and outs of being a business owner. I had just sold my soul to the Toronto Dominion bank, in order to finance my business. I was volunteering on the boards of a number of organizations and I had a very busy life. The last thing I needed was to enter a new career and one in politics, no less. For years, I continued to run my business, but I never denied the calling that I had experienced that I would one day run for mayor. It was always present.

I began to gather information. I set up some boxes in a section of the store vault. Prior to Birt Saddlery inhabiting the Baker Block, the building had once housed the Home Investment and Savings Association. As a result, interior renovations had been made to the building to include a large walk-in bank vault with a big, black, steel door. The vault itself was roughly the size of a small room and had rows of shelving. I sectioned off some of these shelves to accommodate this material. I labelled each box with a component of the campaign — policy, strategy, volunteers, fundraising, public relations — and filled these boxes with information and business cards of people who offered to help. I told everyone that I was going to be mayor one day. My friends tell me they were not surprised and never doubted that it would happen. I asked most people I knew or met if they would be interested in helping and most were. Whenever I sat beside a politician at a luncheon or business event, I would ask for advice. The late Peter Lougheed, former premier of Alberta, gave me some wonderful advice. He told me to "Stick to your priorities and don't get off track." I remembered his words many times during my tenure. "Once you are elected, you will be pulled in a million different directions. If you don't stick to your priorities — what you were elected to do — it won't happen." I once met Jim Durell, the mayor of the city of Ottawa and asked him how to win an election. His advice to me was, "Sew up the money" and he was right. We raised unprecedented amounts of money for my first campaign, as did the other leading mayoral candidates at the time. Collectively, we raised nearly a million dollars for the 1992 campaign, the highest amount raised in the city's history.

As for how to run a campaign, I had a strategy. I thought I would ask the provincial political parties for their campaign manuals to help me along. I boldly asked members of the Liberals, Conservatives, and the NDP if they would share this information with me. Not surprisingly, they declined. Perhaps I was a bit naïve in thinking any of these major parties would release this to me, but I also thought there was no harm in asking. It was then clear to me that we had to build our own campaign manual and we set about to do this. One of my student volunteers, Susan Mackie, found a Canadian publication entitled, *A Woman's Manual on Organizing an Election Campaign* prepared by a Women's Mentoring Program Advisory Committee in Newfoundland. This manual was developed by a number of prominent women in the Province of Newfoundland, including representatives from their Provincial Advisory Council on the Status of Women, the Newfoundland and Labrador Federation of Municipalities, local school board associations, and the Women's Policy Office. As fate would have it, the co-ordinator of this project was a Cathy Dunderdale, who later became the first woman premier of Newfoundland. She served from December 2010 to January 2014.

The manual was written on the belief that women needed to be more adequately represented in political decisions at all levels of government, and it served to assist them with key strategies to run a successful campaign. This manual proved to be a great resource for us and we often referred to it in the early planning stages. Susan also found a library book on how to run for the U.S. Senate. We used this book as background as well and eventually created our own campaign manual.

In 1990, long before the incumbent mayor announced his retirement, I started to pull together a small group of volunteers. Even though it was over two years before the next municipal election was to be held, I knew it was important to get a team together to start doing some background work. I also knew that in order to win, we needed people of extraordinary calibre and skill set. We knew only too well the challenge ahead of us. I had never run for political office before and generally, outsiders didn't do well against seasoned politicians.

I was completely inexperienced, had no political affiliations, had no personal money, and I was a woman. Historically, women had a difficult time raising funds for their political campaigns and I was painfully aware of this. As uphill as it all seemed, we were confident that with the right strategy and the right people, we could prevail.

Building the Dream Team

The Honourable Terry Stratton

I first met Terry Stratton at a United Way meeting in September 1991. We were on the same committee but did not know each other. Not long after that meeting, his name came up as someone who knew how to run successful political campaigns. Unbeknownst to me at the time, he was a key player for the federal Conservatives and served as campaign chair for the Province of Manitoba in Prime Minister Brian Mulroney's campaign in 1988. I was intrigued and thought he could be a great candidate to chair my campaign.

I called him up and asked if I could meet with him. I explained that as the business owner of a retail store, my days were quite busy and I would prefer to meet him after six p.m., once the store had closed. Mr. Stratton advised that he had a slot available a week from Tuesday from 5:15 p.m. to 5:30 p.m. Again I persisted in asking him to meet with me after store hours. There was a long pause at the other end of the line. He reiterated "I have a slot available a week from Tuesday from 5:15 p.m. to 5:30 p.m." I recognized by the tone of his voice that I had better accept this time slot. Our initial meeting began as tense and uncomfortable. I asked him precisely what type of political experience he had and how many campaigns he had won. He then asked me why I had decided to run for mayor. I quickly went into my explanation of what set me on this path...that it was my destiny...that it was my calling.

He stayed silent, looked at me as though I was crazy, and continued with a few pointed remarks. "So you have no political experience?"

"Right."

"...and no political backers?"

"Correct."

"You do realize that campaigns cost money. Do you have anyone in mind to fundraise?"

I told him that I had already had preliminary discussions with two people to co-chair the fundraising committee — Kathleen Richardson, a member of the prominent Richardson family of Winnipeg, and Bill Watchorn, a highly successful businessman who at the time was vice president of Federal Industries. To further emphasize my connection with these two well-known members of our community, I picked up the telephone right in the middle of our meeting, called Kathleen and had Terry talk to her directly. I'm not sure what Kathleen said to him at the other end of the line but when he hung up, he looked at me and said, "Impressive." Now he was intrigued.

I was extremely pleased and grateful that Kathleen Richardson and Bill Watchorn had indeed accepted my request to work on the campaign. During this pre-election phase, many of my colleagues and friends told me that they were impressed by the calibre of people I was attracting, and I must say, I was as impressed as they were. The fact that there were many talented and prominent community leaders involved contributed greatly to my win.

A few months after my initial meeting with Terry Stratton, I attended a Conservative fundraising dinner in Winnipeg. There were several people in attendance, including the "who's who" of the Conservative Party at both federal and provincial levels. Terry had asked me to sit at his table. For most of the evening, Terry was mingling amongst the guests. As the event progressed, guests began approaching me, telling me that they had heard I was running for mayor and that I had their support. It eventually dawned on me that Terry was "working the room," letting people know about my intentions, and asking for their support. By the end of the night, many in Terry's core influential base knew about me. As we walked to our cars in the parking lot, Terry turned to me and said, "You did good kid. You've got IT!" From that point on, Terry was on board. He became co-chair of the 1992 campaign and he is the one who suggested that we should also bring in a federal Liberal backer, which we did. David Unruh, secretary of the national Liberal Party and a prominent lawyer with one of Winnipeg's biggest law firms joined us and also became co-chair. We were off and running.

Robert Gabor, a Winnipeg lawyer, and Dennis McKnight, a local entrepreneur, were also critical players to the campaign team. They were the key operatives. Both had strong political experience and were extremely talented when it came to strategic thinking and execution. They worked diligently on formulating strategy, developing policy, and polling, all while working full-time at their day jobs.

When Terry Stratton agreed to help me with my mayoralty campaign, he set about "testing me." He had his tried and true political operatives and three of them were Robert Gabor, Lawrence Prout, and John Perrin. I guess Terry's process was to run possible candidates by these operatives to get feedback on potential political candidates.

An appointment was made for me to meet with Robert, Lawrence, and John. I didn't know any of them; I knew "of them." We met at Robbie's office. My impression was that this was going to be a meeting, but it turned out to be more of an interrogation. This did not sit particularly well with me. I guess I didn't understand the vetting process. At some point, I believe, I became quite "proactive" and basically asked what they could do to help me. To Robbie's credit, he "stepped up" and decided to help me out. Robbie had just finished being commissioner on the Royal Commission on Electoral Reform and Financing, so his involvement in my run for mayor was indeed a huge plus for me and my team.

Robbie Gabor

As things evolved, Robbie became my legal counsel and was the chair of the Strategy Committee in the 1992 Campaign and co-chair (with Dennis McKnight) in the 1995 campaign, but of course he was much more than that.

Robbie is brilliant and I soon came to appreciate his many skill sets and political talents. His dedication to me as a candidate and his all-encompassing commitment were remarkable. To this day, I still ask his wife, Miral, for forgiveness for all the time that our campaigns required Robbie to be away from his home and family.

As mayor, I asked Robbie to chair what was called TRANSPLAN 2010. This was an incredibly thorough and visionary plan for our city's future transportation needs. Robbie and his steering committee dedicated enormous volunteer time and effort to produce what would be an excellent plan forward for our city.

In politics, and indeed in life, you need to have people who will tell you the truth, no matter how difficult it is; who will be there with you and for you, no matter how rough things get; who are loyal and honest and to whom the word integrity is within the very fibre of their beings. Robbie Gabor is such a person and to this day a person that I admire, respect, and love.

Dennis McKnight or as I like to call him, Dino, is one of life's amazing people. He is a renaissance man, someone who never thinks inside the box, a person who is forever curious and an exceptional strategic thinker. He is in my opinion, one of the best political operatives and one of those special people that come into your life just once in a lifetime.

Dino

Dino is a born visionary, a futurist, and a person who can connect the dots of information, ideas, concepts, and trends better than anyone I know. He has an expertise in cities and the future of cities. One of the greatest joys in life is to be able to share a passion that you may have with someone. Dino and I share our passion for cities.

Dino worked on Jimmy Carter's presidential campaign in California in the 1976 election. He was a huge Tommy Douglas supporter in his home province of Saskatchewan. He understands the political "beast" and how the political machinations work. It is quite something to hear him speak... his depth and breadth on issues.

Dino came on to my first campaign as our pollster and a key strategist, and in the second campaign as co-chair. He knew the lay of the land and what the citizens were looking for in a mayor. When we began our campaign, I had less than two percent name recognition. Dino said, "That doesn't matter, Susan. We can deal with name recognition. What matters is that the people see the candidates who are already at City Hall as "the old boys" and part of the existing problem. People want someone new and being an outsider is an asset in this election...and being a woman is an asset. People trust women more than men, and the fact that you own your own small business is an asset. You are not big business or from the development community, and you do not belong to a political party. You are a-political. The fact that you are a political neophyte is seen as positive. You have no baggage. You are not beholden to anyone."

His polls were invaluable — accurate and highly advanced within the normal framework of pollsters. They provided us with critical information as to what Winnipeggers wanted in their new mayor, what the key issues were and whom they would support. My ideals and my vision for what I had hoped to do for our city if I became mayor meshed with what Dino was hearing and seeing in his polls.

From 1992 to this day, Dennis and I are both still very committed to the future of cities. Dino speaks on the subject around the world. In the very core of our beliefs is that the future of our world must be in healthy, sustainable, affordable, and liveable cities.

When we began the campaign, I asked Terry, Robbie, and Dennis to be with me for six years (two terms). It was later explained to me that most people worked six weeks on a political campaign and then were gone, but this was not true of Terry, Robbie, or Dennis. They were with me for a full year prior to the election and stayed with me for both my terms, all with unsurpassed dedication and commitment. Their devotion perpetuated to developing lasting friendships with each of them.

Next, I needed an official agent...someone with an impeccable financial background. A good friend of mine, Eleanor Samson, suggested that I contact Wally Hill, who at the time was a vice-president at Investors Group. Not only did Wally have an accounting designation, he also knew computers, an IT whiz you might say, plus he had worked on other political campaigns at the provincial level. Wally was invaluable. In addition to his regular duties as official agent, Wally devised a system on election night that had the city of Winnipeg envious. He set up a framework using four computers hooked up to a network, and with the help of an overhead projector, he was able to post results as they were being phoned in by our scrutineers. It was all very technologically-advanced for a civic election and even the media picked up on the fact that we were tabulating results faster than any other campaign. It looked like "Election Central" for a federal election at my headquarters on election night. Thank you, Wally! It must also be said that Vivian Hill, Wally's wife, was also an important campaign volunteer and contributor.

Left to right: Michelle Maskell, Mary Fox, Darlene Hildebrand, me, Glenda Hildebrand, Doris Mae Oulton, Gail Archibald, Judy Robertson, Elba Haid — the most amazing women's group a campaign team could ever have!

One of the biggest challenges for women is to NOT run a "man's campaign." To help me ensure that the woman's perspective was front and centre, a group of Winnipeg women also became a significant part of my campaign. Spearheaded by Doris Mae Oulton and Elba Haid, these professional women from all sectors of the community sought to mobilize the women's vote to get me elected. They had great connections with women in powerful roles and positions, including various levels of government, businesses, and non-profit associations. They established a series of meetings during the campaign and invited leaders of many local women's organizations and Winnipeg's ethnic communities. The attendees were invited for breakfast, lunch, or an afternoon or evening reception, and were from all facets of life — business owners, professionals, volunteers, stay-at-home moms. They were given the opportunity to meet with me and discuss my plans as mayor. As the campaign evolved, other women's groups hosted me at their meetings and events. This expanded to a wider network — wives of prominent Winnipeggers, and the general community. I was invited to many community centres and people's homes to let people know what I would do if I became their mayor.

More importantly, some of the key members of the women's group worked on my campaign team and helped me to establish my policy manual. The feedback from the weekly sessions became the basis for many of my policies. The regular meetings with this group became my safe haven during the election campaign. While other meetings were gruelling and often negative, the "women's group" get-togethers were less formal and uplifting. The women in attendance were clearly excited at the prospect of having a credible woman candidate running for mayor and I very much felt I was on safe ground when I attended these events. This group was never recognized or even mentioned by the media. They simply ignored the work of this group of women, who were so influential in raising my profile and so important to my campaign. Instead the media portrayed me as someone with "male handlers." As in so many situations, women are not recognized for their accomplishments. The influence of this group greatly contributed to my success in winning the 1992 civic election. This illustrious group of women worked steadfastly during my campaign and once I was elected, we continued to meet on a regular basis. This formidable consortium eventually evolved into a mentorship group called Women of Winnipeg, which is still active today.

Eileen Stuebing and I at my 1992 swearing in ceremony at Winnipeg City Hall

Many of my friends followed suit in their quest to help me become mayor. Eileen Stuebing, a close friend who had moved to Toronto, and her husband Bob, along with Blair Murdoch, actually organized a fundraising event there and it was a smashing success. It was heart-warming that people over a thousand miles away were interested in who was running for mayor in Winnipeg. Eileen and her husband Bob knew many former Winnipeggers living in Toronto and also knew that Winnipeggers were quite proud of their city. They put together a list and then asked for my input of potential supporters living in Toronto. The invitation said, "Portage & Main meets Yonge & Bloor" and referred to the event as "a Winnipeg 'Social' for the Politically Aware." The concept was brilliant. The event took place at the Imperial Room at the Royal York Hotel and was well-attended. The food theme was "Delight to the Tastes of Winnipeg" and we served Winnipeg specialty foods such as mini perogies and cabbage rolls, rainbow trout, wild rice croquettes, and partridge berry compote. Mike Lewis was a pianist who hailed from Winnipeg and he entertained guests as they mingled. We raised nearly $5,000.

I was completely shocked when a television crew from a major network's local affiliate showed up prior to the event, wanting to investigate what I was doing in Toronto. The impression they gave me from their negative and intimidating questioning led me to believe they were there to discredit me. I emphasized to them that this was a private event and proceeded to my hotel room. They followed me, accompanied me in the elevator, and came right up to my hotel room door. They expressed that if I did not explain why I was there, they would show me closing the door on them and refusing an interview. They completely missed the point (or NOT!) that many former Winnipeggers lived all across Canada and loved their city so much that they wanted to get involved in my quest for mayor even though they were not living in Winnipeg at this point in time. These former Winnipeggers were still in tune with civic politics and wanted to help to build a brighter future for the city they still called home. The appearance of the television media at this event emphasized for me the reality of how stories can be "spun" or how a bias can be invoked on a particular candidate in any election. Since then, I have always dealt with media, be it television, radio or newspapers, with great trepidation.

Many other events were organized by friends and colleagues. Margie Isbister and her mother Jean organized a coffee party at Victoria Beach on Lake Winnipeg in July 1992, before I actually announced my candidacy. The crowd was extremely supportive and it made for a lovely afternoon at the beach! Gayle Carson's mother and sisters put on an afternoon tea in St. James. Friends of friends invited me into their homes to "meet and greet" their friends. There was a real grassroots touch to the campaign and this allowed me to meet personally with many, many people. At each event, I spoke to them about my history, why I was running, and what I hoped to accomplish.

For the final six weeks of my campaign, Eileen, who co-hosted the Toronto event, came to Winnipeg to live with me and support me any way she could. She and Gayle Carson, along with many other good friends, were instrumental in getting me through the campaign. Elections can be ugly and this one was no different. I was criticized by my opponents and by the media. My friends comforted me when I was down and celebrated with me when I was up. They nurtured me, providing me with kind words and understanding as I faced some of the most negative and critical moments of my life. They also spent many hours at campaign headquarters, doing what they could to get the job done — answering phones, preparing for events, and anything else that needed to get done. I will be forever indebted to these special women for their dedication and compassion.

My family was also very supportive. My sister Barbara came to Winnipeg for both of my election campaigns, and my brother Norman helped where he could.

Overall, we sought out the best volunteers we knew for my first campaign and thankfully, they all agreed. We gathered a superb team of individuals who worked with diligence and determination to get me elected. Together, these people spearheaded a group of volunteers whom I can only describe as "unbelievably talented and dedicated." We shared a common vision and worked tirelessly to achieve it.

Preparing for a Win

Mayor Bill Norrie officially announced his retirement in early July 1992. Soon thereafter, a number of candidates threw their hats in the ring to take his place, including a mix of incumbent councillors and concerned citizens. My candidacy was one of the last announcements and this was a strategic move on our part. The plan was to announce in early September, along with the unveiling of our platform. In all, seventeen candidates ran for mayor in 1992. It was a ZOO!

Our campaign headquarters were located in the Birt Saddlery building, in a section of the smaller building off the main floor. The decision to set up in this location was two-fold. First of all, it allowed me to continue to run my business while I was campaigning, although inevitably, as the campaign unfolded, I devoted most of my time towards the campaign. Thankfully, Beth Grant, my office manager, took over the reins and continued to run the business efficiently in my absence. The second reason for choosing Birt Saddlery was that it was a cost-saving measure, as we did not have to pay rent for this space. Our headquarters were modest but efficient. We set up desks provided by Cunningham's, a local office furnishings store, and rows of tables equipped with telephones, and there was ample room for the many volunteers who came in as the campaign evolved. Once the election was in full swing, there were always people in the campaign office, making calls, recruiting volunteers, and arranging publicity events. In fact, when all was said and done, nearly 1,000 volunteers helped in various ways to get me elected.

We established very early on that it was important to get my name out. As such, a big part of my budget went to marketing initiatives. Years before I knew that I would be running in the 1992 election, I pre-booked some billboard spaces through Mediacom. This was a full three years ahead of the election call, but it proved to be a great strategy. Once the official campaign was announced that I was running for mayor, my billboards went up and we were the first out of the gate with public awareness.

We were also very efficient at preparing postcards, which we distributed door to door, and at public places and events. A number of "Eatonians," former Eaton's colleagues, were instrumental in hand delivering these cards. Ann Lonie, Jimmy Thomson, and John Maniella were retired at the time and organized a group of volunteers from Eaton's to blitz the city and deliver postcards to as many households as possible. They delivered thousands of postcards. I'm sure that the distribution of this information contributed to greater awareness of who I was.

We purposely avoided creating brochures, opting to spend more on other, more noticeable forms of publicity. We invested in television advertising and wisely chose some prime spots. We were able to obtain air-time during the 1992 World Series, which was a very good strategic move on our part. Who knew that a Canadian team (yeah Toronto Blue Jays!) would end up in the World Series that year...very fortuitous! Our television ads were very effective and we received accolades for our ingenuity. We also did the trendy self-promoting Burma Shave signs along Winnipeg's busiest streets. All in all, our publicity efforts proved to be very successful. In fact, very early on in the campaign, our research showed that only two percent of the Winnipeg population knew who I was. By the end of the campaign, I had almost ninety-eight percent name recognition.

The days of the campaign were long and arduous. I can remember leaving my home as early as 5:30 in the morning and returning home after 11:00 each night. Former CBC broadcaster Garth Dawley was one of our volunteers. He would pick me up before the sun came up and we would go to designated public places in the city to "meet and greet" the people of Winnipeg. My days were filled with team meetings, "meet the candidate" events, panel sessions, and debates. Often, these events were held in the evening, so working sixteen-hour days became the norm. It was gruelling, but all worth it in the end.

As the campaign unfolded, our polling indicated that we had a good shot at winning. I was confident in the expertise of our pollster Dennis McKnight, but I also didn't want to get ahead of myself or get overconfident. What helped reaffirm my belief that things were going well, however, was the "unofficial polling" that occurred.

In the days leading up to and during my time as mayor, I referred to my unofficial pollsters as my "touchstones in the community." They were my girlfriends who were business owners and those who were hockey moms. They were my grocer, my car mechanic, my hairstylist, my dentist, my florist, and my dry cleaner. They were the people I met when I campaigned in front of grocery food chains or department stores. If I wanted to get a read on things, reaching out to the community was the best way to do it. Many times as mayor, I would take a cab to get from one meeting to another, not because I didn't want to drive, but because it gave me the opportunity to talk to the taxi drivers. There again, by engaging in conversation with people who spoke to other people in Winnipeg on a daily basis, I was able to get a pulse on what my constituents were thinking. On a personal level, I must acknowledge one individual who was absolutely candid with me about everything I did or said during my tenure as mayor, and that was John Doole. A prominent business owner, an author, and an artist, John helped me many times to focus on what was important. We remained good friends until his passing in 2011.

Another unofficial pollster for the 1995 election was Sandy Cotie, someone I had met shortly after being elected. Sandy and her husband John run a business in south-eastern Manitoba, just off Highway #1. Geppetto's, which is still in place today, mainly sells wooden outdoor furniture but also has a take-out food kiosk where people heading east can stop by and get a bite to eat along the way. Many Winnipeggers have cottages or take vacations in this beautiful part of the country, either in Whiteshell Provincial Park in Manitoba, or at Lake of the Woods in Ontario. For many, Sandy's Snack Shack was the perfect half-way point to stop, stretch their legs, and order a hamburger or fries. Sandy's friendliness led her to chitchat with most of her customers, and she took it upon herself to discuss the municipal election with her customers in the summer of 1995. "So, who are you going to vote for?" she would ask. More often than not, she would get candid answers. She would ask people about what the real issues were and would give me feedback accordingly. It was great to get her input and I appreciated her assistance.

Public debates played a huge role in the 1992 campaign because there were so many candidates running for mayor. It was important that each of us had the opportunity to let the citizens of Winnipeg know what we stood for and to lay out our platforms. Opportunities abounded, as over thirty public debates were organized over the course of the campaign. The largest one was a mayoralty forum held at the historic Walker Theatre, a building where many political rallies had been held as far back as the early 1900s. The forum was sponsored by the Winnipeg Real Estate Board and was well publicized. The place was packed to the rafters — nearly 1,700 seats — and the atmosphere was electric. Sixteen of the seventeen candidates were in attendance and all were jockeying for attention. We were all seated alphabetically and once the event began, the moderator asked each of us to say a few words in this same order. This turned out to be an advantage for me, as I had a chance to hear what most others had to say and I adjusted my notes accordingly.

This forum turned out to be a real three-ring circus, as candidates performed attention-grabbing stunts. One candidate walked on stage sporting a gas mask (apparently there had been a lot of smoke in the air due to stubble fires the evening preceding the debate). Another held her middle finger up to the crowd proclaiming, "This is what I think of the establishment at City Hall." Yet another tried to prove his support for the disabled by telling the crowd that he had personally kissed a prominent disabled advocate prior to the start of the meeting. This compelled a number of other candidates to rise from their seats and proceed into the audience to plant a kiss on the activist as well. All these attention-grabbing stunts reinforced the craziness of political campaigns.

Once every candidate was given a chance to speak, a Q & A session took place. The moderator had some prepared questions but most of them came from the audience. It was obvious that the majority of the questions had been "planted" by campaign teams, so their candidates could respond by unveiling their own policies with intelligence and wit. Most of the questions ended up being directed at the four leading contenders — Dave Brown, Ernie Gilroy, Greg Selinger, and me. Every once in a while, others were given the floor, and I had a chance to sit quietly in the background. As I sat and listened to the litany of political jibber jabber, I glanced around at the magnificent building we were in — the Walker Theatre, an historic building in its own right. It was on this very stage that famed suffragist Nellie McClung had discussed women's rights issues in the early 1900s. As a member of the Winnipeg Political Equality League, Mrs. McClung once starred in a theatre production about a "mock government" made up of women who debated the merits of whether men should have the right to vote. This play, which was presented at the Walker Theatre on January 28, 1914, became fodder for suffragists across the country. Within two years of its presentation, which triggered further debate on equal rights, women in Manitoba achieved the right to vote in provincial elections, the first province in Canada to accomplish this.[2] And now, here I was, some eighty years later, sitting on the very stage where this significant historical event for women and politics had occurred. History could be made again, I thought. For the first time in the campaign, I allowed myself to imagine being the first female mayor in the history of the city of Winnipeg. Before I could think too far ahead, someone approached the microphone and directed a question at me. Back to reality...it was my turn to speak.

At the end of the evening, all of the candidates mingled with the crowd for a bit and then bid farewell. **As I walked towards the exit doors, I turned back to the stage where I had just stood. For a brief moment, it was almost as though I could hear Nellie McClung's voice: "It is <u>your</u> time, Miss Thompson...your time to turn a page for the women in our province...your turn to make history."**

Get "HER" Out of the Race

There is no doubt that there was a concerted effort to get me out of the 1992 mayoralty race. The three frontrunners were incumbents and made it clear that outsiders were not welcomed. Councillor Dave Brown was the current deputy mayor to Mayor Bill Norrie, Councillor Greg Selinger was a member of the Executive Policy Committee and the chair of the Finance Committee, and Councillor Ernie Gilroy served on Mayor Norrie's Executive Policy Committee in the late eighties and early nineties. They fought a tough campaign.

A number of groups supporting various candidates were formed during the 1992 campaign. One such group was "Winnipeg into the '90s," an alliance of left-leaning municipal politicians and

---

2 Information regarding Nellie McClung was obtained from the Nellie McClung Foundation website.

self-described progressives. Their candidate of choice was Greg Selinger. They also supported a number of incumbents for positions as councillor. The stakes were higher for councillors in this particular election, as a decision had been made to reduce the number of councillors from twenty-nine to fifteen. Those who won would be expected to become full-time politicians and would be paid correspondingly.

Another group that made its way into the 1992 election campaign was "The Committee for Good Government." This group was right-leaning and threw its support to Dave Brown, the current deputy mayor. They knew full well that my candidacy could have an impact on their campaign and very early on, they approached my executive team. The first visit from this "Committee for Good Government" was to tell my team to "get HER out of the race"...that I was impeding Dave's shot at winning. They further related to my team that if I didn't pull out of the race, they would ensure that I would be "frozen out of the money." My executive team did not bite and we carried on. A second visit ensued a few weeks later, this time with a softer, kinder message, suggesting that it would be best if I first ran for city council so that I could get some experience. They even suggested that when **THEIR** candidate won, he would appoint me deputy mayor. Again, we dismissed their attempts to get me out of the race. My team advised them that we had every intention of winning. From that point on, different sets of tactics were used — some were nasty and some were just downright untrue. I was accused of "stealing" other candidates' strategies, I was charged with having a platform based on "buzz words," I was "all fluff" and "no substance"...it went on and on. With all these accusations, my team was given a challenge to overcome the insurmountable odds of having media turn against us.

The media was quite taken by the fact that there was an outsider, who happened to be a woman, trying to take the city's helm. It was quite evident that the leading newspaper was supporting Greg Selinger, and in fact, they endorsed him as the candidate of choice. Anything and everything came out as to why I should not be mayor. Was I "tough enough" to do the job? Did I have the experience? Did

I understand City Hall? One of the most absurd questions from the media was who would be my date at official events should I become mayor. Really? Did that really matter? Would any of my male opponents have been asked the same question if they were single? In spite of the criticisms, my campaign team and I developed a solid platform and well thought-out policies that exceeded any of my rivals' platforms.

I was not tied to any political party and I made sure that this was expressed often during my campaign. I was neither left nor right. I was a centrist. Yes, I was fiscally conservative, but I was also socially committed. I appealed to many Winnipeggers because I had the experience of owning a small business (and therefore understood fiscal matters), because I was a woman (and polls told us that voters trusted women more than men), and because I wasn't part of the old regime. I was prepared to roll up my sleeves and effect change. The public saw this and was impressed with my energy and enthusiasm for the city.

Our motto was "It's Time for Change." My campaign material accentuated this by underlining the fact that our city was burdened in debt, lacking in leadership and vision, and that the civic government needed a new approach. My speeches emphasized the many changes I planned to incorporate if I won. I addressed four main concerns — leadership, accountability, economic growth, and quality of life. My policies included many significant changes, including the following:

- Freeze property taxes for the next three years
- Streamline the bureaucracy at City Hall
- Aggressively promote and market economic development for our city
- Implement employment equity in civic service
- Set performance standards and goals for city bureaucrats
- End duplication of services
- Join with the Province of Manitoba to market Winnipeg

I am proud to say that once I was elected, my councils and I implemented each of these policy changes in due course, and by the time my two terms were over, all of these strategies had been accomplished.

Election Night

The day began with tremendous excitement and anticipation. I recall being quite introspective when I first woke up. I knew that this day could be one of those moments in time when life changes on a dime. I had experienced them before — good or bad — the break-up of my marriage, moving to Calgary and then to Montreal, the day my father told me he had cancer. In the next twelve hours, I was either going to be the mayor of Winnipeg or go back to selling cowboy boots. Suddenly the weight of the world (or at least of the city) was on my shoulders.

Early in the day, I went to cast my vote. At the time, I was renting an apartment on the second floor of a house on Grosvenor, near Rockwood Avenue. As I entered the polling station, members of the media followed me and cameras captured me as I went to vote. While I was there, I took the time to thank all the volunteers — not just scrutineers for MY campaign, but ALL of them — for their time and dedication to this election. I have always found Winnipeggers to be very generous. Many volunteers are required to successfully pull off election campaigns and it impresses me to this day that so many people are willing to give of their time for this and so many other causes. I chatted with the volunteers, the returning officers and poll clerks, and the general public as they came in to vote. I received well-wishes from friends and neighbours as I made my way back to the car.

I then headed over to our campaign headquarters. Since we were in the same building, I first took the opportunity to meet with my staff at Birt Saddlery. I thanked them for managing the place without me for the last six weeks. I then told them that if I lost, I would be back at work in a few days, and if I won, I would be in on the weekend to plan how things were going to work while I had dual roles. In actual fact, I was not able to re-engage with my staff for at least six months.

I had completely underestimated the demands that would be put upon me immediately after the election...I suppose I had anticipated more transition time...and so once again I had to rely upon my terrific management team, especially Beth Grant, to keep the business running as I established myself in my new role.

I then checked in with our volunteers. The campaign office was buzzing. Meryle Lewis, Beth Eva, and Kelly Spiring were coordinating the many volunteers required to get the vote out. They organized callers and drivers and made sure that there were enough scrutineers to cover every polling station in the city. I believe that we were the only campaign team to accomplish this, which was remarkable for a civic election. This is inevitably what helped us to post results so quickly later that evening. I met briefly with my key strategists and then left them to do what they had to do. Wally Hill was there setting up his elaborate system to tabulate the election results, and the rest of my management team was there going over the final details of the day and evening event at the Holiday Inn.

Close friends Gayle, Marla, Beth and Eileen were incredibly supportive in my campaign and in my life.

I then went to the Westin Hotel, where I had reserved a room for the night. Close friends and members of my family checked in there as well. We had decided that it would be best if we all stayed close by one another and have a place to gather together to watch the election results. The Westin was also close to our headquarters, only two blocks away. About a mile away on St. Mary Avenue was the Holiday Inn, where my volunteers and supporters were to gather. This would become "Celebration Central" should I win.

My sister Barbara was in town from Peterborough, Ontario and we thought it would be nice if we took our mother, who was in a senior's home at the time, to an early dinner well before the polls closed. We went to Dubrovnik's on Assiniboine Avenue and asked for a private table at the back of the restaurant. We managed to stay inconspicuous, even though Mother proudly wore a pin that said "Susan Thompson for Mayor." We had a lovely dinner, then took Mother back home and proceeded to the Westin Hotel to prepare ourselves for the evening ahead.

As I got ready, I recall being calm and happy. I was grateful for my incredible campaign team. I felt that we had done the most that we could do to share our message. I was confident that the citizens of Winnipeg recognized that it was time for a change at City Hall and I felt as though they had connected with my vision for a better political atmosphere. I had met many great people throughout the campaign and had a good feeling that many were supportive and would vote for me. I thought of the many volunteers who came forward to support me and remember thinking how blessed I was to have such a dedicated, incredible team. I was optimistic that the results would reflect the hard work. I waited for the results with great anticipation.

I was sequestered in a hospitality room with close friends and family. We were all fairly quiet but there was an undercurrent of pure excitement. We watched television and listened to the radio for early results but soon realized that the results from my headquarters were coming in much quicker. Early returns had me leading, but I wasn't about to get over-excited until I received more substantial numbers. I do remember Paul Labossiere working with me on two speeches — one was an acceptance speech should I win, the other was a speech, should I lose. I remember making sure that in either case, I would adequately thank the countless people who took part in this momentous campaign.

Meanwhile, an enthusiastic crowd consisting of volunteers, friends, family, and supporters was gathering at the Holiday Inn. Jim Carson, my good friend Gayle's husband, had set up a projector and a large screen and was able to connect the hotel's cable signal through this, so that guests could see the television coverage as it unfolded. Our results were coming in quicker than the city's tally, and as they came in, periodic announcements were made on the PA system. As unofficial results were being announced, anticipation began to build (so I was told). At first, numbers trickled in slowly, but then gained momentum, and once they started to pour in, it was evident that I would likely be the next mayor. At that point, apparently, the crowd was electric.

A few members of my campaign team were adamant that I not go to the Holiday Inn until the major candidates had publicly conceded. Two of the main candidates — Dave Brown and Ernie Gilroy — did so quickly. My team felt strongly that we needed to be absolutely confident of victory before heading over to "celebrate my win" and therefore we waited for the third major candidate — Greg Selinger — to concede. CJOB Radio, Winnipeg's premier local news station, declared me the winner at 9 p.m. CBC and CTV local television affiliates declared me the winner shortly thereafter. We waited and waited...well into the evening...still no communication from Greg Selinger's team. Finally, shortly after ten p.m., my team decided that we'd best head over to the Holiday Inn. We knew that the newspapers had an eleven p.m. deadline and we wanted to try to accommodate them. On the other hand, we hadn't heard from the runner-up, therefore we were in precarious territory. We could not be seen as proclaiming victory when it wasn't official. We quickly changed portions of my speech, focusing more on "thank you" than "victory" and headed over to the celebration event.

We literally "raced over" and pulled up in front of the Holiday Inn. I can recall entering the hotel and immediately hearing the sounds of boisterous supporters on the mezzanine level above. Ken Stuebing, my friend Eileen's father-in-law, piped me in as we headed past the foyer and up the escalator to the second level. Media followed and

I had cameras and bright lights glaring in my face. Once members of the crowd saw me, they started to shout "Susan! Susan!" It was mayhem. As I reached the top of the escalator, supporters lined both sides of a very narrow path into the hall. The first person I hugged was Eileen's mom, Lenore Roper. This could not have been more special! Serendipitously, that hug was captured by both newspapers and appeared on their front pages the next day. From there, I received congratulatory remarks, pats on the back, and hugs and kisses from many, many people. I couldn't begin to tell you who they all were... family, friends, acquaintances, volunteers...it was all so exhilarating. I could feel myself smiling from ear to ear and many photographs were being snapped; hence the start of "my famous smile." It took quite a while, apparently close to half an hour, before I could make my way to the podium. We had underestimated the size of the crowd and the hall was filled to capacity.

At last, just before eleven p.m., I stood before the crowd. The noise was excruciatingly loud. By this point, it was sheer pandemonium. As I watched the throngs of people on their feet, clapping, cheering, and smiling, I could not help but be humbled by their joy. The chanting continued for a few solid minutes before I was even able to utter a word. At that split second, just before I spoke, it occurred to me... my destiny had been reached... I was the mayor of Winnipeg...I had been elected to represent the citizens of our great city...all the people in this room supported me, and now they expected me to represent them with honour and integrity. I then began to speak and told them that I would do just that. I wasn't able to declare victory that evening because the results weren't "official," but that turned out to be a gift. Instead, I spoke about the people...the countless volunteers who gave their time and effort to help me with this election. I told them that the culmination of all their hard work appeared to have been rewarded. I also spoke of my father and told the crowd that I felt his presence. I could hear him saying, "No excuses, Susan. Just get in there and get the job done."

After visiting and celebrating with many people in the room, we headed back to the Westin. Friends and family continued to celebrate and many recall it to be “quite the party.” I was exhausted and headed directly to my room. As I finally lay my head on the pillow that night, it occurred to me that life was indeed a great journey. This was a lesson that I had learned before and here it was again.

October 28, 1992 will go down as one of the most spectacular days of my life. **My destiny had come to fruition.** After 118 years, the citizens of the city of Winnipeg elected their first female mayor. I don’t know that I realized the challenges I was about to face at that point, but I certainly understood the magnitude of this accomplishment. **History had been made.**

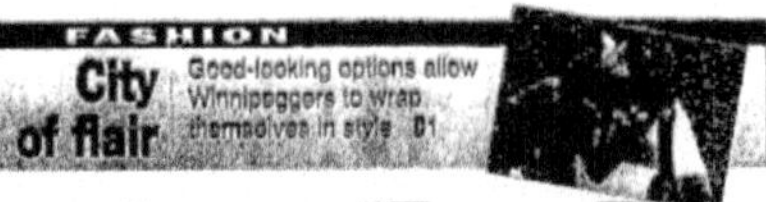

LOCAL
Grit gulf
Referendum rift widens party split B1

FASHION
City of flair
Good-looking options allow Winnipeggers to wrap themselves in style B1

MONEY
Show and tell
Trade shows are cost-effective exposure B8

60 PAGES

Winnipeg Free Press

50¢

Thursday, October 29, 1992

Her Worship, the mayor

Silva expects to be courted

By Nick Martin and Bruce Owen
Staff Reporters

EXPECT WIN members to be wooing Amaro Silva in a big way.

Of course, the independent newcomer in Daniel McIntyre ward pointed out last night, "I would expect a lot of people are going to want to talk to me now."

Winnipeg in the Nineties came out of last night's election without its mayoral candidate Greg Selinger, but the civic reform coalition took five of council's 15 seats, barely led a sixth that's expected to go to a recount, and had a "WINdependent" ally in a seventh.

"I will not align myself with any group," Silva said as he savored his triumph over veteran WIN councillor Donovan Timmers.

But, Silva said pointedly: "My platform was quite in tune with the WIN platform."

St. Vital victor Al Golden is a true independent, a councillor who could never be predicted to align himself with anyone over the past three years.

Golden said it's a more balanced council between WIN and the vestiges of the former Gang of 19, but cautioned: "The gang is in control again. There's more brains on the gang side."

There'll be only two new faces on council — Silva and Mayor Susan Thompson — along with one new-old face.

But the new council will feature the largest proportion of women in Winnipeg's history.

Thompson and four WIN women councillors make up 31.3 per cent of council, compared to the previous record of 20 per cent in the outgoing council.

Even if the expected recount in Mynarski unseats WIN's Gloria Mendelson, there'd be 25 per cent women on the new council.

The WIN councillors include Glen Murray (Fort Rouge), Lillian Thomas (Elmwood), Rick Boychuk (Transcona), Evelyne Reese (St. Boniface) and Sandy Hyman (River Heights).

Mendelson led Harry Lazarenko by a handful of votes in Mynarski.

Terry Duguid (North Kildonan) refused to join WIN and claimed independence, but has generally voted with WIN.

Thompson gets a victory hug and round of applause last night at her Holiday Inn headquarters.

Novice Thompson Winnipeg's first female mayor

By Gerald Flood
Staff Reporter

A POLITICAL OUTSIDER beat the odds last night to become the first woman elected mayor of Winnipeg.

Susan Thompson, a western clothing store owner who has little interest in horses, was first out of the gate and ran away with it in the stretch, relegating three high-profile male politicians to the ranks of also-rans.

"Being a woman didn't hurt — it's time," family friend Lenore Roper said.

But supporters said gender only partly explained Thompson's success. "She's no dumbbell," quipped Ken Stubing, who piped Thompson into a wildly enthusiastic crowd at the Holiday Inn last night.

Thompson radiated happiness, jumping in the air and punching the sky, hugging people, shaking hands and exchanging high fives.

"We love you Susan," a man shouted. Everyone went wild.

Thompson thanked her workers and paid tribute to her late father.

"His words are with me tonight: 'No excuses Susan, just get in there and get the job done.' "

She said the message in the election is clear: Hold down taxes and get Winnipeg moving again.

"It's a new direction, a common-sense direction. Most of all it's a positive direction."

"She has something new to offer," Ken Hunt said. "Give her a year and she'll get it done."

"I don't think it's a woman's issue," Leslie Bingham said. "She has a different perspective. She's a manager and if you're a manager you just go in and manage."

Hillery Van der Vliet, a fashion consultant, said that Winnipeg is tired of old-style politics. "We're fed up with political shenanigans and backstabbing. One thing to her advantage is that she was never involved before, so maybe she'll stumble and make mistakes, but if she gets a good steam together it will be good for the city."

Greg Selinger said Thompson's apparent victory indicated that people wanted fresh blood at city hall.

"People wanted a fresh face and a fresh change," the former WIN councillor said.

While refusing to concede defeat and noting all the results were not in yet, Selinger said he had predicted he and Thompson would run neck-and-neck.

He said his campaign had no glitches but was hurt by the fact that it couldn't match the funding of Thompson's and Dave Brown's campaigns.

He said he wanted to take time to spend with his family.

Meanwhile, losing candidate Ernie Gilroy told downcast supporters at his campaign headquarters not to be disappointed at his poor showing.

Dave Brown said, "We put out a clear message to the public. Obviously the people were in a mood for change.

"It's a lot tougher being a mayor than cutting hair. I won't have to put my business in a blind trust anymore.

"I'm out of politics."

■ Detailed coverage starts on B5

Your New City Council

MAYOR
Susan Thompson

COUNCILLORS

Bill Clement
Charleswood-Ft. Garry

Amaro Silva
Daniel McIntyre

Lillian Thomas
Elmwood

Glen Murray
Ft. Rouge

Harry Lazarenko/
Gloria Mendelson
(undecided)
Mynarski

Terry Duguid
North Kildonan

Mike O'Shaughnessy
Old Kildonan

John Prystanski
Point Douglas

Sandy Hyman
River Heights

Evelyne Reese
St. Boniface

George Fraser
St. Charles

Jae Eadie
(leading)
St. James

John Angus
St. Norbert

Al Golden
St. Vital

Rick Boychuk
Transcona

Old guard sings parting song

By Bruce Owen
Staff Reporter

LOSING INCUMBENT councillors were singing last night.

Singing the blues.

It was a sad song for incumbents who found themselves without council seats in last night's civic election.

A dejected Donovan Timmers, who lost in Daniel McIntyre to newcomer Amaro Silva, said he lost because a large segment of his vote abandoned him.

"What can I say? There were three strong candidates. (Catharine) Johannson pulled in a lot of NDP faithful. The NDP came out to vote for her in a significant way."

Incumbent councillor and deputy speaker Doreen Demare lost to Al Golden, who entered the race in St. Vital at the last minute.

Demare said she didn't want to talk about what she might do now that she's out of civic politics.

Veteran city councillor Don Mitchelson, a former deputy mayor, lost to rookie councillor Terry Duguid despite a vigorous campaign.

In Fort Rouge ward, in what was thought to be a close race, incumbent Glen Murray walked away with victory, leaving another incumbent, Roger Young, out in the cold.

Young, a human rights commission investigator, was unavailable for comment.

Other incumbents who faced elimination were Harry Lazarenko and Gloria Mendelson, who were fighting a seesaw battle in Mynarski.

The person I am hugging is Lolly Roper, my good friend Eileen's mother. Serendipity at its best. (Glenn Olsen/Winnipeg Free Press, October 29, 1992 Reprinted with permission)

Chapter 6 Early Days of being Her Worship

My First Day as "Her Worship"

Photo courtesy of A.D. McTavish

My first day as mayor-elect started very early on October 29, 1992 – 5:30 a.m. to be exact — with interviews on Winnipeg's local radio stations. I had barely slept the night before, if at all. As in so many of these kinds of occasions, the adrenaline had kicked in.

After the interviews, I returned to the Westin and joined my family and close friends for a celebratory breakfast. It was only when I returned to the hotel that I had a chance to review the election results in our local papers. The coverage was interesting to say the least. First of all, it confirmed the fact that I had won decisively; I received 14,620 votes more than my nearest opponent, in a total field of seventeen candidates. I was also pleased to see that the citizens of Winnipeg had become engaged in this election, and posted an incredible 58.4% voter turnout. This was the highest voter turnout for a civic election since 1971. It was great to be part of an election that created that kind of interest in the political affairs of our city.

The Roper/Stuebing/Stanton families were thrilled to see that the *Winnipeg Sun* ran a color photo of me hugging their mother on the front page. I was also delighted with this choice as I was very close to Eileen's mom and knew that she, too, would be pleased. We were all surprised however at what the *Winnipeg Free Press* chose to run. The front cover of their early edition had the headline "Her Worship, the Mayor" but chose to run a colour photo of the third-place candidate and his wife on the front page. I was astounded by the paper's decision to do this, as were my friends and family. In a way, I felt as though I had been denied recognition of the victory. The *Winnipeg Free Press* printed a second edition at 1:15 a.m., once they were able to develop a photo of me at my celebration headquarters. Unfortunately for the *Free Press*, the damage had been done and as soon as the early edition papers were delivered, the newspaper was inundated with calls from Winnipeg citizens asking why I hadn't been given proper coverage. The paper was accused of being a supporter of Dave Brown and this was just a way of "raining on my parade." (In reality, however, an editorial in the *Winnipeg Free Press* on October 23rd, three days prior to the election date, had actually endorsed Greg Selinger.) Others went further and accused the *Free Press* of not being supportive because I was a woman and because I was an outsider. To add insult to injury, one of the inside page headlines stated that Thompson was "the best man" for the job. I found this absolutely disgusting. Good heavens! Did the blatant discrimination really have to continue? If a man had won, would they have dared print, "He was the best woman for the job?" I think not. So my first day started out with controversy. Welcome to politics!

Mayor-Elect — Preparing for the Job

On Friday, October 30th, I headed over to City Hall to meet with outgoing Mayor Bill Norrie. We chatted briefly and I was shown in. After the "welcome and hand over," Mr. Norrie left. There I stood, alone in the mayor's office for the first time.

I distinctly remember, at some point, walking over to the window facing Main Street. I looked across the street to the Winnipeg Concert Hall, remembering that this was where the first Birt Saddlery store had stood, the very spot where I peered across the way as a child to see the "gingerbread building." **And now, here I was looking across from inside City Hall. So uncanny**!

Soon, my sister Barbara arrived with my eighty-two-year-old mother. It was an extremely proud moment for me to welcome them to the mayor's office. It was what happened next that will stay in my mind forever. I was about to ask them to join me on the chesterfield for a chat and some tea. Instead, my mother headed right for the mayor's desk and sat down. It was obvious that she was totally comfortable where she had chosen to sit, and she looked very much like she was ready to get to work.

I asked my mother if she ever thought I would become mayor. "Oh yes." she answered. "You come from a long line of politically-involved people."

I was startled. I did not know what she meant. In Part 1 of this book, we shared a quote "Sometimes you have to look back where you came from to see where you are going." Well, this was such a moment.

I had always identified with the Thompson side of the family. Yes, I knew my mother's family history — sort of — but both her parents had died long before I was ever able to get to know them. One died before I was born, the other when I was just two or three, so there was never a real connection.

My great, great-grandfather Thompson and his brothers were part of the starving Irish from County Armagh in Ireland. They had come to Canada in the mid-1800s, and through the generations, had become successful business people. Every generation was very hard working and self-made. Most of our family life revolved around my father and grandfather Thompson and our store, Birt Saddlery.

My mother's family name was Bellamy. Originally the "Belle Amis" from France, they fled to England in the mid-1700s and anglicised the name to Bellamy. My great-grandmother Lorinda Jane Bellamy and my great-grandfather Thomas Bellamy were pioneers in Edmonton.

My great-grandfather, Thomas Bellamy, was a successful businessman and served on Edmonton City Council several times. His son, my grandfather, Ralph Bellamy, was the first Rhodes Scholar from Alberta and represented the North West Territories at Oxford in 1903. He also served on Edmonton City Council. He was a school trustee for six years, an alderman for six years, and was a candidate for mayor of Edmonton in 1935.

It was my great-grandmother Lorinda Jane however, who was the powerhouse. She was a suffragist, the first president of the Edmonton chapter of the Woman's Christian Temperance Union (for seven years in the early 1900s) and a friend of Nellie McClung. She helped establish the YWCA in Edmonton and was its first president, serving for four years. She and my great-grandfather established the First Baptist Church in Edmonton. She was the first woman to stand on a public platform in Edmonton (at a missionary meeting) and founded the first mission circle there. She was absolutely devoted and committed to building Edmonton into a city.

So here I was, all these years later, Winnipeg's first woman mayor, having my mother remind me that there was a long history of political action and service on her side of the family. And so it goes... "Sometimes you have to look back to where you came from to see where you are going." **What a moment in time!**

Things moved very quickly from then on. At the municipal level, there is a five or six-day transition before the new mayor is sworn in. I met the mayor's chief of staff and was immediately asked to come up with a guest list for the swearing-in ceremony. I was briefed on details of the event and what I should expect. Local television media arrived, and I had another round of interviews and photo ops at City

Hall. It may have been at this point where I really felt a shift occurring...it was starting to sink in... I WAS the mayor.

The mayor's office staff consisted of a chief of staff, a receptionist, a secretary and office/finance manager, a scheduler, and a part-time clerk. All were city employees who had served other mayors, going back to Mayor Juba in the 1970s. All were very professional. Of course there was trepidation on both sides — we did not know each other — but in time we learned to work together. Through the years, changes and adjustments were made, but the core group stayed with me until the end of my tenure and we still see each other on occasion.

The next few days were extremely busy, as I met with the mayor's office staff, councillors that I was considering for the newly formed Executive Policy Committee (EPC), and the chief of the Board of Commissioners. As mayor, it was my duty to choose who would be part of the EPC and this had to be decided before the swearing in, which was just a few days away. I took it upon myself to meet individually with as many members of council as I could before the ceremony. I asked them to meet me at my Birt Saddlery office and asked each of them to bring along their three top priorities. I had initiated these meetings to discuss their appointment to the EPC. "Discuss" is a term I use loosely. One by one, these members came to my office, many with a "take it or leave it" attitude and made it clear to me that "they" were the decision makers when it came to City Hall and that collectively, they would make decisions about our city and that I only had one vote. It became evident as I met with them that most had been in discussion with each other and had already determined who should be on EPC. This was an eye opener as to how my council thought things were going to run. Being a political rookie, I knew that I needed to have members with political experience at the civic level. In the end, I chose Bill Clement, Terry Duguid, Jae Eadie, Glen Murray, and Mike O'Shaughnessy as members of the EPC. Bill Clement was also appointed deputy mayor and Sandy Hyman, a woman, was appointed acting deputy-mayor.

From Mayor-Elect to Mayor

You are cordially invited to attend the

Swearing In

of

SUSAN THOMPSON

as Mayor

and of

HER COLLEAGUES AS COUNCILLORS OF THE CITY OF WINNIPEG

on Tuesday, November 3rd, 1992 — 8:00 p.m.
Council Building — Civic Centre

—Reception to Follow—

On presentation of this card the bearer will be entitled to one reserved seat in the Council Chamber Gallery

Printed with permission, City of Winnipeg Archives

The inauguration was a celebratory event. On the evening of November 3, 1992, I was sworn in as the city of Winnipeg's fortieth mayor. Over 250 people were in attendance, including many close friends and family members. My inaugural address clearly declared that my priority was to work for the betterment of our city. I also made it known that I was going to follow the will of the people. Winnipeggers had made it clear that they wanted a change. I tried to emphasize this in my address: "A model of a well-run, forward-thinking city is one that nurtures its assets and pays attention to the needs of its people." The citizens of Winnipeg had clearly had enough of "old boys' club politics" and they were looking for a change. That is what I was elected to do and my mandate now was to follow through on my platform.

One of the best memories I have of my first week in office was how the mayor's office was transformed into a full-fledged flower shop. I received many, many beautiful arrangements from friends, colleagues, acquaintances, even complete strangers, all congratulating me on my win and sending me best wishes. The messages were heartfelt and joyful. I received countless cards and letters — even one from Prime Minister Brian Mulroney — and was quite touched by the overwhelming response from the citizens of Winnipeg. This of course was a great contradiction to what I was feeling from within the walls of city hall. Political gamesmanship was already starting to rear its ugly head, as councillors and senior administration began to let me know where they stood on my new role.

Once I was sworn in, my priority was to meet with my newly appointed Executive Policy Committee and get the ball rolling. I asked them to meet with me informally in my office. I purposely held it there in the hopes that my new team would get a taste of what I foresaw as regular informal meetings with this core group. I saw the EPC as the key leadership group for our city government. In recent polls, city councillors had received a ten percent approval rating on their performance from the citizens of Winnipeg. Clearly, I wanted to change that. I welcomed them to the meeting and thanked them for agreeing to serve on this committee. I emphasized how important it was that we should all work together to accomplish great things for our city. Over time, these informal meetings got better. I introduced a process whereby we could all discuss matters pertaining to the city in a confidential setting. These meetings were meant to give us the opportunity to discuss, deliberate and if necessary, vent. Eventually, my EPC became a much more cohesive group and they did become the leadership group for civic government and effected significant change. By the end of my six years in office, we had a positive and respectful relationship with each other.

Following the first informal EPC meeting, I invited all city councillors for lunch in a city hall meeting room. I personally paid for this luncheon so that there wouldn't be any criticism about spending city funds. My intention was to do a round table, with each council member sharing with me what they saw as the top three priorities they wanted to achieve. I saw this as an opportunity to listen and see what my colleagues thought. It started with a number of councillors refusing to eat lunch because I had personally paid for it and they weren't about to be "bribed" by the new mayor. Seriously! And it went downhill from there. Again...welcome to politics!

Settling In

Physically, the mayor's office was of significant size. It served as a reception area for dignitaries and guests, and also as a real working office. When I arrived, I found the area to be quite sparse. The walls were bare, the furniture was out-dated, and there was one plant in the entire office, and it was barely alive. The desk was very simple — no front privacy panel, more like a long table really — and it had a matching credenza. There was another credenza on a far wall, which housed a small television set. This is where we could watch council meetings in action, as they were televised at that time. In another part of the office, there was a sitting area, with a chesterfield and a few chairs.

My first priority when I saw the office was to get a conference table and chairs in there, so that we could hold meetings. I was advised that there was no budget available to acquire the basic necessities for the office. Thus began my quest to give the mayor's office a "historic" look. This initiative was spearheaded by MaryAnne Rudy, who was the manager for the City's corporate office and buildings. She was able to create a very eclectic look. She arranged to get various items donated from a number of City departments and over time, collected some of the City's most historic pieces. The Fire Department lent me a fabulous brass antique fire bell to hang on the wall. The Police Department lent me one of the original, solid-iron call boxes, which were used back in the day when officers also wore buffalo coats. Winnipeg Hydro lent me their first electric wall clock...a magnificent piece with all kinds of history. St. Boniface City Hall graciously lent me their original conference boardroom table. Local businesses also helped out. Air Canada lent me an antique desk from their vice president of Finance. A simple thing like a decent chair for the mayor's desk was solved by having one of my employees at Birt Saddlery take my office chair and wheel it down two blocks to city hall. I used that chair the entire time I was in office.

The historic pieces from the city's various departments gave visitors a definite feel that they were at city hall. As for artwork, there was one piece available, and it hung in the reception area. We had no budget, so we had to use some ingenuity to add items to the remaining walls. Again, emphasizing our goal to make the office a "people's place," we began to put up framed photographs of various city events and some of the many visitors to our city. In time, it became a people's photo gallery. Most of this collection of framed photographs now resides in the City of Winnipeg Archives. To further beautify the office, Wendy Mackie, the floral horticulturist from City Parks Department, came in and added greenery to our surroundings...no more nearly dead plants. In a few short months, we had transformed the mayor's office and city hall. With a lot of cooperation and help from local businesses and departments within the city of Winnipeg, we were able to make city hall more inviting for citizens, and more importantly, one that celebrated our history.

I was taken aback that no policy, research, or communications positions existed within the mayor's office. In due course, changes were made, and two additional jobs were created — research coordinator and communications manager. I believe these two positions still exist today.

It was shocking to find out that the mayor's office was not computerized, especially since other city departments were. Apparently, we were "on the list" for computerization. This may have been the first of many discussions I had with my chief of staff about the "state of affairs" in this important office. I made it abundantly clear that if we were to be effective, we had to have proper systems and equipment in place. Shortly thereafter, we were computerized. Over the next three years, members of my staff would be instrumental in developing systems, plans, and forms to make the mayor's office more efficient than it had ever been in the past.

One of the more peculiar things that happened came about when I was asked to sign official documents. Once a week, administration would send over a number of documents that required my signature. This is not so peculiar, but what was odd (to me at least) was that the documentation had "His Worship" printed to the left of where I was to sign my name. When I first saw this, I commented that this would now need to be changed. I was advised that there was a large supply. Clearly, no one ever conceived that there would be a "Her Worship" when formulating these documents. It was agreed upon that until the supply ran out, we would use these documents. However, I did improvise. **Many legal documents I signed until the supply ran out had "His" crossed off with a red marker and I added "Her."**

At the end of my first week in office, the reality of politics, power, and gamesmanship was more than evident. I didn't exactly get the welcome I thought I might get when I arrived at city hall. I do savour many happy moments in that first week, but I also remember the share of challenges presented to me as well. I do recall thinking to myself "Surely, it couldn't get any worse," but it did.

Getting down to Business

In council chambers with Deputy Mayor George Fraser and City Clerk Dorothy Browton (Photo courtesy of A.D. McTavish)

During my first month as mayor, I was often reminded of the words of the late Peter Lougheed: "Stick to your priorities and don't get off track." Within a week of the election, I felt as though I was being pulled in 100 different directions. From Day One, I was faced with a number of major issues that required my attention. The more critical priority was the city's annual budget. I had told voters that I would do my best to freeze property taxes. This issue alone proved to be a great undertaking and learning experience. I knew this was one of my main priorities and in those first few months, I tried my best to stay focused on this one important goal. That being said, I was presented with a litany of scheduled meetings, events, and trips. I went to Phoenix, Arizona just two weeks after the 1992 swearing-in ceremony to visit with their City Hall. A week later, I attended the 1992 Grey Cup in Toronto. The following week, I took part in the Canadian bid for the 1999 Pan American Games. I was briefed on a number of other upcoming events and quickly needed to get up to speed on countless projects and activities. The Mid Continent Trade Corridor, the Winter Cities International Conference, a new aboriginal centre, new bridge proposals...these were all extraordinary projects and I now needed to know absolutely every aspect of each undertaking. It was an enormous learning curve. I immediately began to ask for "bedtime reading"; files and folders filled with briefings of critical issues — items that I didn't have time to read or even look at during the day.

My election platform was developed with the recognition that a new approach was required to lead our city government. It was based on the belief that our future could be promising if we were prepared to make the necessary changes. I reviewed the four main concerns addressed in my platform: accountability, economic growth, leadership, and quality of life. As I moved from one decision to another, I ensured that every project approval was based on whether it was a positive move for the city. Was it financially viable? Would it enhance economic growth for our city? Did it fit the vision of our city? Would it improve our citizens' quality of life? Every decision made under my tenure was done for the betterment of the city of Winnipeg.

I had every intention of putting Winnipeg on the map and I knew intuitively that world-class events such as the Pan American Games and the World Indigenous Games would clearly raise our city profile to another level. The tourism benefits of hosting sporting events of this calibre cannot be understated. I was determined to promote and market Winnipeg as "the city of choice" when it came to choosing locations for such events. I recognized our strong volunteer base and our ability to attract sponsorships from local businesses. As the city began to win bids for these prestigious events, its citizens became more and more engaged. We became a city that began to believe in itself again and to this day, the city of Winnipeg continues to have the ability to attract world-class events. I am proud to say that during my six years in office, we won every bid we applied for, mostly sporting events. We also took part in many meetings and conferences to promote trade and planned talks surrounding the Mid Continent Trade Corridor. This led us to host a Summit of Mayors in 1998, part of the Mid Continent Trade Corridor initiative.

I had started this journey with a six-year timeframe in mind and I stuck to my guns, only running for two terms. Looking back, I probably should have run another term or two. It takes a long time to learn everything there is to learn when one becomes mayor, especially an "outsider." I underestimated the amount of time it would take to implement the various initiatives. I could have used the experience I gained to make better decisions and continued on the road to implementing new approaches for the betterment of our city. Nonetheless, I am proud of what I accomplished and honestly feel that I left City Hall in better shape than when I arrived. In the next few chapters, I will describe some of the more significant events and happenings from 1992 to 1998. All in all, it was an incredible ride.

A personal luncheon to thank my staff and special guests, to express my appreciation to those who helped make a difference to our city.

City of Winnipeg Mayor and most council members Christmas 1992 (both photos printed with permission from the City of Winnipeg Archives)

Aerial view of Winnipeg (Photo courtesy of Stan Milosevic)

Chapter 7
Getting down to Business

The State of the City

In 1992, the city of Winnipeg, like the rest of Canada, was confronted with some very tough financial challenges. Our country was faced with a struggling national economy, burgeoning national and provincial government deficits and debt, and a slow GDP growth. In fact, North America was in a recession and unemployment was on the rise.

Locally, we had our own set of problems. Winnipeg was a city in decline economically and financially. We had the highest property taxes and the highest per-capita city debt, and we had been dubbed the "murder capital of Canada."[3] We had an aging population and our growth was stagnant. We were not seen at all as a destination city. If anything, we were most often referred to as a "have not" city, as was our province. Plus, people thought it was funny to refer to us as "Winterpeg."

Certainly the biggest issue for Winnipeg taxpayers at that time was that we had the highest property taxes in Canada. For many years, property tax rates had been increasing slightly each year, and by 1992 – an election year — the citizens of Winnipeg had had enough. Frustration among Winnipeggers had started to develop in 1990, when the Manitoba government introduced amendments to the Municipal Assessment Act. In an effort to revamp the system to a more equitable one, the new laws deemed that property assessments

3 Information obtained from *Winnipeg Free Press* Archives

should be determined based on market value rather than replacement value. This was the first reassessment in thirty years and it caused a "skewing" of property values. In many cases, property taxes — residential and commercial — skyrocketed. The city administrators proposed a thirteen percent hike in property taxes. Of course, this caused uproar among the electorate and council eventually reduced the increase to eight percent.[4] Still, citizens were outraged. A large number of property owners, mostly commercial owners, were able to successfully appeal their assessment values and many were also granted refunds. The city was then obligated to refund a huge amount of money. This ended up costing the city hundreds of millions of dollars. From 1992 to 1993, assessment refunds doubled, which seriously affected the 1993 budget. This whole debacle was aptly dubbed the "reassessment fiasco."

Being a business owner myself at the time, I remember the dissatisfaction with our civic government very well. In fact, early in 1992, a group of Winnipeggers had staged a number of "tax revolts" at city hall. At one such gathering, led by local activist Marion Krause, more than 1,500 people showed up to vent their frustration with elected officials and the city's bureaucrats.[5] Their main concern was that the city had implemented yet another property tax increase, just as they had done every year for decades. The protests visibly showed that Winnipeggers were fed up.

During the 1992 election campaign, the discontent of Winnipeg citizens about taxes and the reassessment was loud and clear. Once I became mayor, I was shocked to find out what the actual numbers were. I first heard about the impact these refunds would have on the city's budget in early 1993. The refunds went way above what had originally been projected and our 1993 budget was severely affected. To deal with the reassessment fiasco, we made significant staff changes, and with the assistance of the city auditor and an outside auditor, we were able to address the situation. From this point on, reassessments were mandated to occur every three years. This is a "best business

4 Proposed increases obtained from the *Winnipeg Free Press* archives.

5 This information was also obtained from *Winnipeg Free Press* archives

practice" that I am proud to have implemented during my years as mayor, as it ensures that the citizens of Winnipeg would never have to endure a thirty-year gap again. With a disciplined system to adhere to, reassessments were done on a regular basis and never fluctuated as much from one assessment to another. Today, reassessments are done every two years. I believe that what we accomplished in the early nineties directly got the system back on track.

Other issues existed. When I talked to Winnipeggers during the election campaign, I found that many were just generally frustrated. They felt that the level of government closest to them — their city government — appeared to have forgotten who they were there to serve. They felt as if they weren't getting enough value for their tax dollar. An Angus Reid poll backed up these perceptions by revealing that fifty-four percent of Winnipeggers disapproved of city council's performance and forty-eight percent thought the City had a flawed system that needed to be changed.[6] What resulted from this study was that in the next election — the one in which I would run for mayor — council was reduced from twenty-nine councillors to fifteen. Each councillor would be responsible for much larger wards and the elected positions would move from part-time to full-time. When the existing council voted on this fundamental change in early 1992, they also agreed to an increase in their salaries and an augmented pension plan. In my run for mayor, I stipulated that I would only serve for two terms and I would not accept a city pension. I did not believe that I should be entitled to a lifetime pension paid by taxpayers after having only served two terms. I would have appreciated RRSPs for the years that I served, but that did not occur. On October 21, 1998, my last day as mayor, I left the office with my last paycheque, no pension, no RRSPs and no transition package...period.

I absolutely believed that the only solution to changing the way that Winnipeggers perceived their civic government was to implement major systematic changes. As soon as I began my first term, I

---

6 Taken from my 1993 State of the City Address to the Winnipeg Chamber of Commerce

worked on making significant changes as to how our city was structured and on ways in which we could improve our civic government.

Each January, the Winnipeg Chamber of Commerce holds a business meeting and luncheon that features a "State of the City" address by the mayor. I was barely three months in office in January 1993, when I was set to speak to the public at this event. For years, this address had been given by seasoned veterans of municipal politics, and for years, this address was prepared and written by the Board of Commissioners for the mayor. Though I took into consideration the Board of Commissioners' ideas on what should be included in this address, I had my own plan on how this needed to be presented. My perspective on this speech was that it was the first opportunity for the mayor to let the public know what was happening at City Hall. I saw the speech as an opportunity to begin to talk about the changes and introduce my new vision. I wanted to outline how these changes could be accomplished.

I distinctly remember my first State of the City speech. The chamber had advised me that there could be as many as 900 people there (a sold-out crowd) and they also told me that my speech would be broadcast live on a local radio station. As I entered the mezzanine level of the hotel, I was faced with a barrage of people, media, and some protesters. To say that I was nervous at this point would be an understatement. I knew that I had to set the bar and knock it out of the park. When I got to the podium, I realized I didn't have a glass of water. At this point, my mouth was dry and my knees were knocking. I had never done anything like this before. I did my best to hide my fears, and forged ahead. In the end, I got a standing ovation. It was a great success. It completely changed the status and importance of the State of the City speeches going forward.

In the following years, I implemented a much more expansive process in preparation for this annual speech. Over the years, between 1993 and 1998, the State of the City speech evolved. It was eventually changed to April of each year, rather than January. This was a much better time of year, as we were then able to report on a budget that had already been approved and implemented. The presentation became more focused on leadership, vision, and accountability. The venue was also changed to a location that could accommodate larger audiences.

Bringing About Change

The general public has a definite perception about bureaucracies; how they work and how they have their own distinct culture. Governments do work in a very different way from the private sector. That became quite clear to me almost immediately after I became mayor. Being the newcomer, my first course of action was to observe the way things were done. I needed to listen and learn. I did, however, recognize that I had been elected on a platform of change, and I had delivered the message loud and clear that if I were elected mayor, I would bring about significant systematic and cultural changes. I sought to tackle what was at the forefront of the minds of the citizens of Winnipeg and I did so by gauging what the electorate told me when I went door to door during the campaign.

Once I was elected, my top priority was to implement a property-tax freeze. Easier said than done! The development of the annual budget is a huge undertaking and I understood that it was a complicated process. It took a lot of input from citizens, the Board of Commissioners, and every city department. I also felt that it required more participation than had traditionally been given by the mayor and councillors. In my 1993 State of the City speech, I spoke of involving council in the budget process much earlier than had ever occurred before. Part of the reason for doing this was to allow ample time for the budget to be carefully considered. Since I was adamant about providing a tax freeze, council needed to have enough time to consider all implications concerning the budget. Having the elected members become more involved in the process took a while to achieve. The bureaucracy's attitude toward elected officials was not always welcoming, and I personally felt an attitude of disdain. I am glad to say, however, that with perseverance and determination, council succeeded in becoming more involved in the annual budget process. Each year, as we prepared annual budgets, we tried to find the right balance and do our best to freeze taxes while delivering services required to efficiently run our city. Some tough decisions needed to be made, including cuts to certain sectors. Certain recommendations were going to work and others were not. Each year, there was a lot of give and take and we stepped on a lot of political landmines, trying to balance the budget and not increase taxes. I did not deliver on my goal of a tax freeze until later in my tenure. By legislation, the City cannot run a deficit and with the reassessment refunds in the early nineties, balancing the budget without a slight raise in taxes was impossible. Success came by streamlining where possible and contracting out and through public/private partnerships. In 1996, the first property-tax freeze in decades was achieved through hard work by a dedicated and mutually determined council and it was a landmark achievement. We were also able to implement a tax freeze in 1998, my final year in office.

Accountability to the taxpayer was also of paramount importance to me. I knew before I became mayor that the civic government had a reputation of being controlled by (1) a powerful Board of Commissioners and (2) the unions. I soon recognized that city councillors were clearly frustrated by the lack of proper governance and I knew that we needed to change the way things worked at City Hall. Shortly after I arrived, I was "advised" by the senior administration that the business of the city had to be approved by nine votes on council and that as mayor, I only had one vote. I was also "advised" that as the new mayor, I most certainly did NOT have enough influence to garner nine votes on council, but the Board of Commissioners were certain that they did. In other words, THEY ran things. This piece of information that was so patronizingly shared with me began an incredibly unpleasant and difficult power struggle that lasted most of my tenure.

In my opinion, the leadership and effectiveness of a well-run city government belonged to the mayor and council; those who were elected by the citizens, and that is exactly how I intended it to be. Thus began a journey to change the administrative and political models at City Hall and council. The new model would incorporate a strong mayor model and the implementation of an administrative CAO model. This endeavour took much longer than I ever expected. I would need the majority of councillors to agree with me before I could ever move forward with the plan. The groundwork for this major change was unveiled in my first term, but it wasn't until my second term and the results of the "Cuff Report" that these changes started to occur. George Cuff, an Edmonton consultant, was hired as an independent contractor to assess the way City Hall worked and come up with recommendations to improve the way the city was managed. The key was to implement changes that would make our civic government more effective and accountable. The Cuff Report recommended new powers for the mayor and city councillors, replacing the Board of Commissioners with a chief administrative officer and five managers, eliminating a number of senior administrator positions and restructuring various city departments. Initially, a few councillors balked at the report, but it was evident that the Winnipeg electorate was very much on side. In time, both councillors and administration concluded that they had no choice but to accept the recommendations presented to them. By the time my six years as mayor were over, we had accomplished this very important goal... again a landmark achievement.

The success of this new model was dependent on two factors: (1) that best practices such as audits, evaluations, and performance measurements were followed by future mayors; and (2) that the citizens elected an ethical and hard-working mayor and council. It is important to note that this model still requires that the citizens of a city are the ultimate "choosers" of the mayor and city council. It puts the onus on the voters to pay attention to whom they choose to represent them and lead their city. Their choice of quality candidates is of utmost importance for this model to run successfully. When you vote for someone, you are giving that person your trust to operate with accountability, efficiency, and integrity.

A few months into my first term, I asked to meet with the heads of each of the unions representing city of Winnipeg employees — all of them — CUPE, WAPSO, police, fire, ambulance, transit — all at once

— representing 10,000 employees. My intention was to find common ground for an affordable and sustainable city government. It was my opinion that the wage, benefit, and pension levels in existence were completely unsustainable. As I reflect now, I realize how naïve I was in orchestrating one meeting with all union representatives at the same time. The meeting did not go well. I told the union leaders that Winnipeg was a city in financial trouble and we needed their help in implementing the necessary changes. I explained that Winnipeg had the highest property taxes in Canada and also told them that fifty-six percent of the city budget was in staff salaries and benefits. I sought their cooperation in finding solutions to reduce this expense. Hundreds of citizens had expressed to me that the wages and benefits of city employees were considered to be luxurious. While I strongly believed in fairness to our employees, I also realized we needed to pay attention to affordability and long-term sustainability. I was absolutely committed to providing fair remuneration, but it was clear to me that we could not sustain the benefits and staff costs that were currently in place. After my initial remarks, I asked the union leaders for their opinions and suggestions on how we could work together to be fair to our employees but also be fiscally responsible to our citizens and taxpayers. The language and the tone of that meeting resulted in an atmosphere of intimidation and antagonism. Collectively, the group of union leaders made it clear to me that they were a force to be reckoned with and would not back down on any of their demands. It ended on an uncomfortable note, to say the least. I then made the decision that going forward, I would only meet with them one on one.

Over the years, between 1992 and 1996, I did meet with each of the union representatives individually and we were able to achieve much better interaction, communication, and resolution. I hired Grant Mitchell, the best labour lawyer in Winnipeg, in my opinion, to negotiate with unions. In the end, both council and administration agreed that this was the best course of action we could have taken, and from that point forward, all negotiations between the unions and the city took place with our hired outside resource. I am pleased to say that in the six years I was in office, there was not one single disruption of labour.

Working towards Progress for our City

Winnipeg has always been known as the "Gateway to the West," the geographic heart of North America and in my world, the centre of the universe. Being the longitudinal centre of North America, Winnipeg has also been identified as the perfect location to promote itself as the northern terminus of a transportation corridor. Our Golden Boy,[7] the statue that sits atop of the Manitoba Legislative Building, faces north to signify that northern Manitoba is the provider of important natural resources and economic opportunities. Our forefathers recognized our province's northern location as an advantage many years ago. In the early nineties, discussions had begun with leaders of local government and the Winnipeg business community to market the city as a north/south corridor promoting trade and business opportunities across Canada, the United States, and Mexico. Through the efforts of Winnipeg 2000, an economic development agency, which is now known as Economic Development Winnipeg, a committee was established to further these interests. President Klaus Thiessen and Development Officer Greg Dandewich were tasked with organizing initial meetings with interested parties in the U.S. and Mexico . When I became mayor, the Mid Continent Trade Corridor (MCTC) initiative was just starting to get off the ground.

The Corridor concentrated on the recognition of existing highways and interstates in all three countries as a "Super Highway." These highways included: Highway 75 from Winnipeg to Emerson, Highway 29 from North Dakota to Nebraska, Highway 35 from Missouri to Texas, over the Mexican border at Laredo and down to Monterrey and Guadalajara, and all the way to Mexico City. The North American Free Trade Agreement (NAFTA), which the federal government orchestrated in 1994, further led the way to promote the transportation corridor, which would further encourage trade between our

7 Information obtained from Government of Manitoba website

three countries. The MCTC initiative then grew to market Winnipeg as an intermodal port of entry for air, rail, and vehicles. We had many major players on board, including the Winnipeg Chamber of Commerce, the Winnipeg Airports Authority, Winnport (now known as CentrePort), the University of Manitoba Transport Institute, the Manitoba Trucking Association, and Winnipeg 2000, the city's new economic development agency.

In 1995, I was part of a contingent that flew to Kansas City and Sioux Falls to promote trade and recognize Winnipeg as the northern terminus of a super highway. This first meeting was successful in that it confirmed interest from some very important players in the United States, including two U.S. senators. Most importantly, this meeting was the catalyst for a series of meetings among the mayors of cities along the super-highway route. The Winnipeg contingent spent three days "spreading the word" about our city and by the end of our trip, everyone we met knew "who and where Winnipeg was."

The first Summit of Mayors was held in Monterrey, Mexico in April 1997. Over fifty mayors from Canada, the U.S., and Mexico were in attendance. This meeting was very significant, as it was there that a number of mayors along the corridor signed an agreement to work together to promote trade along the north/south route. I was very proud of the Winnipeg delegation because we were all great at networking and presenting our case to get this initiative off the ground. Five other mayors were part of the founding committee — Dallas, Kansas City, Oklahoma City, Guadalajara, and San Nicolas de los Garza — and I got to know each one of them well. I thought this would be, yet again, an excellent opportunity to put our city on the map. I realized that tremendous lobbying efforts would be required for the MCTC initiative to work. Other mayors along the route were also keenly interested. At the meetings, discussions also took place with representatives from border services in all three countries, so that crossing the border could be simplified. One of the key challenges of the MCTC was the need to lessen delays when crossing into Canada. The initiative led the way in providing some much-needed funding for improvements at the Canadian border crossing into

Emerson in Canada. The U.S. Border Service at Pembina was also renovated and improved.

The second meeting of mayors was held in September 1997 in Kansas City, Missouri, with almost 100 mayors in attendance. This meeting was all about creating momentum and seeking specifics as to how to keep the initiative alive. Delegates, which included many other city representatives besides mayors, discussed ideas that could help solidify the iniative, such as the ability to find public funding for infrastructure, the inclusion of more cities along the route, the development of tourism, finding common trucking regulations, and discussing environmental policies. Mayor Emanuel Cleaver of Kansas City was amazed at the success of the conference, noting that it was difficult enough to get the mayors within one state together, let alone many states and two other countries. It was evident that Winnipeg was seen as an important ambassador in promoting the trade corridor. I was proud of our talented delegation and saw us as a central part of the process.

Winnipeg hosted the third Summit of Mayors in September 1998. The three-day event was packed with activities and included a forum on the final day, so that the mayors could be presented with a synopsis of every meeting that occurred. I was thrilled to host the summit in my own city and was pleased that more than 250 delegates attended. The third summit included the discussion of more specific issues. Five objectives had been established at the previous meetings — to create a partnership of North American communities linked by the corridor; to support investment in infrastructure, human resources, and techology to move the corridor from concept to reality; to develop marketing strategies to promote trade and public awareness along the corridor; to encourage expanded trade and economic development in each of our own communities; and to pursue the establishment of a commission to co-ordinate our efforts. I had asked each mayor to come prepared with remarks on these objectives, so that substantive conversations could take place. This made the meetings more focused and we were able to accomplish more.

By the time I was finished my second term, the MCTC initiative was in full swing and many cities in North America were aware of who Winnipeg was and how well it was situated to be the northern terminus of the corridor. The provincial and federal governments also got involved and the MCTC continues to be promoted today. Even now, over twenty years later, this initiative is growing and evolving, with the continuation of dialogue between countries and the establishment of organizations such as CentrePort. Trade has expanded exponentially between the three countries, particularly between Canada and the United States. Manitoba is still recognized as the logical location to connect Canada to a central North American market.

It is important to note that in Canada, eighty percent of our population lives in cities; Canadians are primarily urban dwellers. As well, the majority of our cities are close to the American border. As such, the civic levels of government have a critical role in ensuring that each city functions well. Decisions made by cities impact a large majority of our population. If you don't have a functional and livable city, then you don't have a functioning and livable province or country either.

I was glad to be associated with such a successful initiative. It is a great example of the power of teamwork. While other levels of government got bogged down with legal matters, the mayors were most anxious to get the job done.

Investing in Winnipeg's Future

My first State of the City speech in 1993 spoke of the changes I planned to implement at City Hall. We were in the midst of a difficult time financially, but I spoke of my firm belief that by the turn of the century, Winnipeg could be a viable, vibrant, and sustainable city. I was ready to work hard and engage others to ensure that this happened. The future of my city was of utmost importance to me.

In my 1994 address, I spoke of the changes that had already occurred within the internal workings of the city. The newly restructured and reduced size of city council was working well and beginning to take more ownership in broad-based decision making. City administrators were coming to grips with a "new view" of running the city, albeit not without a few hiccups. Heading into 1994, my priorities were to restructure, re-organize, find cost efficiencies, and look for innovation. I had found a quote from the *Globe and Mail* that reported that Winnipeg was the best city in Canada for business, and told guests of the Winnipeg Chamber about this accolade. City council, in consultation with its citizens, had created "Plan Winnipeg — A Vision for our City," and I extrapolated from this document the following vision: "To be a vibrant and healthy city, which places its highest priority on the quality of life for all its citizens." I truly believed that Winnipeg could be such a city and I told those in attendance that I had an unshakeable faith in the city of Winnipeg. I was sure that we were poised to make great strides in the coming years.

By 1995, plans were becoming reality. Goals were developed into action plans. For the first time in recent memory, the City's budget was finalized in December, rather than March. This was a landmark achievement. The administrative restructuring process was well underway and downsizing was beginning to occur. Works and Operations were amalgamated from six districts to one and Winnipeg Police Service was restructuring. Reforms were made to the election legislation and bylaws, greatly improving the system and saving approximately $600,000. The assessment department operations had been reviewed. Plans relating to the city's redevelopment were getting off the ground; the Winnipeg Development Agreement, CentrePlan, and Transplan 2010 were either up and running or being approved. Changes were taking place at the airport, as the local airport authority successfully negotiated with the federal government to privatize the Winnipeg International Airport and a development plan for the airport lands was underway. Business Improvement Zones were expanding, Sunday shopping was introduced to Winnipeggers, and photo radar was implemented.

What I was pleased to report in 1995 was the construction of two new bridges — the Charleswood bridge (now known as William R. Clement Parkway) and the reconstruction of the Main and Norwood bridges (now Queen Elizabeth Way). In my view, both of these bridges were significant in increasing interest in the city's landscape. Both were well-designed architecturally and structurally and both incorporated beautiful pieces of artwork. The River Arch on the Norwood Bridge was designed by Catherine Widgery. Sixty feet high, the stainless steel arch rises from the river and features two concrete pillars rising from stone bison bases. The top of the columns feature gold wheat sheaves, representing the origins of our wealth. As you enter the Main Street Bridge, there are six Tyndall stone bison heads designed by Helen Granger Young. The artwork on the Charleswood Bridge was designed by Peter Sawatzky and consisted of six bronze bison sculpted in flat silhouette form.

During the planning phases of both bridge projects, it became evident to me that more future planning had to take place when it came to projects such as these. I was determined to put in place better provisions for infrastructure and capital spending, and did this through increased reserve funds. This way, the City would have money in place when required. It was a fiscally prudent process. At the 1997 State of the City address, I outlined twenty-one reserve funds established by the city. These included funds for: general reserves, equipment replacement, future tax levies, recreation programming, transit bus replacement, concession equipment replacement, computer replacement, snow clearing, contributions in lieu of land dedication, land operating, water-main renewal, zoo animals, zoo purposes, combined sewer renewal, wastewater sewer renewal, water treatment, river quality environmental studies, and the Brady Landfill site rehabilitation. In total, more than $32 million was placed into reserve funds.

By 1998, when I delivered my final State of the City address, much had been accomplished and much had changed. Civic government had a new model and citizens were happy with this change. Major departmental restructuring was occurring, including the amalgamation of Fire and Ambulance Services, which had been initiated by Councillor Michael O'Shaughnessy. Every business and organization was looking at the implications of Y2K (remember that?!) and the city was Year 2000- compliant two years ahead of schedule. I was very happy to report that property tax revenues and the business tax rate were frozen in 1998. A downtown revitalization plan was proceeding and the Forks development was continuing to take shape. Centre Plan initiatives were getting off the ground and the Millennium Library project had been launched. Many other initiatives were on the go and I was so proud to have been part of the process in so many of these new programs. I was in awe of how, in just six years, our city was a well-oiled machine. Our city and our province were making tremendous progress financially and economically. Our economy was almost twice the national average in 1997. Our exports had doubled. Our personal income had increased exponentially. Our employment numbers were up. It was good to see the shift to prosperity occurring.

My mandate in 1992 was to bring about change. By 1998, my team and I had done what was necessary for the betterment of our city. This was a team effort. I thanked the members of my council and my Executive Policy Committee, who had the courage, perseverance, and commitment to drive the process of change. I knew when I gave that speech in April 1998 that I would not be running for office again, but I also knew that I was leaving the city in better shape than I found it.

The Re-Election... Being Both Mayor and Candidate

After going through the 1992 election and against all conventional odds, I thought I had encountered the most difficult challenges I could ever face. Then came the re-election and that was a whole new ball game.

In my first campaign, I was an outsider, a woman (God forbid) with no political experience and I was taking on the old boys. For the first time in my life, I was experiencing the inner workings of an election. The goals I had set for myself — to introduce a new culture and better accountability during an extremely difficult fiscal time for the city of Winnipeg — were deemed aggressive and provocative by many. To date, I had never faced such negativity.

The conflicts that ensued during my first three years in office tested my intestinal fortitude. Often, I was simply trying to survive the most hostile, dysfunctional, and adversarial situations I had ever experienced, and in between it all, I was trying to get things done. It was excruciating. It nearly cost me my sanity.

So for my re-election, I did sense that I could be re-elected, but I knew it was not going to be easy. The biggest challenge was the most obvious one — I was both mayor and incumbent. Trying to balance my day-to-day responsibilities and my candidate obligations during the election period was gruelling. Campaigns are tiring under any circumstances. Continuing my mayoral duties and campaigning at the same time was something else.

The election was held in late October of 1995. I had a potpourri of situations colliding around me during that time. My personal business was going under. In August of that year, I was one day away from losing everything. I then accepted an offer on the purchase of the Birt Saddlery building. This allowed us to pay the bank, taxes to the government, employees, suppliers, the accountant and the lawyer. We did our best with the money we had. The family and I got nothing. We closed the doors to Birt Saddlery and moved on.

In May 1995, the city had lost the Winnipeg Jets. Many citizens were still reeling from this event by the fall and some took to blaming politicians of all stripes on the loss. This spilled over on the campaign trail. The good news was that in August 1994, we had won the bid to host the Pan American Games, and momentum was starting to build as the city prepared for this huge event.

Because running for mayor was a calling and not an ambition of mine, I was always prepared to do what needed to be done. I chose to make tough decisions and not base things on what I needed to do to get re-elected. I accepted the fact that this could mean that I might not win again, but I did not let a second term colour me in any way. After three demanding years and far too many lessons learned, I absolutely knew what could be accomplished if I were to be re-elected.

The other major candidates for mayor in this election were:

Peter Kaufman — Peter was a former city councillor, serving from 1983 to 1986. His main passion was the Winnipeg Jets and he vowed to bring them back. He was a Conservative.

Terry Duguid — Terry was a current city councillor and a Liberal. He was chair of the Public Works Committee. I had appointed him to my Executive Policy Committee. I admired his environment knowledge and thought he had a lot to offer. I tried to work with him, but in my opinion, Terry had no use or respect for me. In early 1995, he expressed his desire to run for mayor. I suggested that he wait until the 1998 election, as I would definitely not be running a third term. He replied that Glen Murray, another city councillor, would be running for mayor then, and that he could not beat him. I assured Terry that he could not beat me, which I think he found most amusing. He then proceeded to run against me.

One of the main differences between the 1992 and 1995 campaigns was the media. Yet again, they were tough on me, but in the last two weeks, things began to change. Brian Cole, editorial chief of the *Winnipeg Free Press*, the city's leading newspaper, spent an entire day with me. A lot happened during our day together and we had an intense twelve hours. You get to know people under such circumstances.

The day began at seven a.m. at the Winnipeg Convention Centre for the L.E.A.F. (Legal Education Action Fund for Women) breakfast. Over 1100 guests, mostly women, were in attendance. This fundraising breakfast was held annually in support of women's rights. Brian didn't know that this event existed and therefore had never attended. I believe he was quite enlightened.

What followed was a very busy day. We went from one scheduled event to another, I made a few speeches that day, and we ended up at a neighbourhood gathering at Monica and Brian Wood's home. It was organized so that their neighbours could "meet the candidate." By late evening, I think it is safe to say that both Brian and I were exhausted. We both knew, however, that our day wasn't quite over, as both of us had to go to our respective homes to read background material and prepare for our next day.

A few days later, Brian telephoned to say that the editorial board of the *Winnipeg Free Press* wanted to endorse me. I was shocked. Having been on the receiving end of NOT being endorsed, I did not expect this at all. We had a great discussion about it. My view was that I didn't feel that newspapers should be in the business of endorsing candidates. Regardless, on Sunday October 21, the *Winnipeg Free Press* editorial, entitled "Choosing a mayor" went on to recognize that I had done as much as any mayor could to keep her promises. The paper credited my leadership to holding the line on property taxes, noting that "increases over the last three years were the lowest in a decade." It stated "Winnipeggers should grant her request Wednesday and provide her with a mandate large enough to ensure that everyone understands that she enjoys the support of a majority of the city's residents." I was quite taken aback and pleased by the endorsement. It went on to say, "Ms. Thompson's greatest strength, of course, is her dedication to hard work and enthusiasm for the city she seeks to serve. She brings an upbeat, positive approach to a job that, to a large degree, is all about shaking hands and promoting the city outside the province as a good place to live and do business. She also has a good grasp of the issues of the day and challenges that lie ahead. And, she has demonstrated that she is tough enough to handle the rough and tumble of civic politics, while still being able to build the political coalition required to get things done at City Hall."

Elections, however, always produce surprises and curveballs. So when I picked up the October 21 edition of the *Winnipeg Sun*, I saw a blazing, sensationalized headline that said, "THOMPSON IS TOAST." The article reported results of, in my opinion, an amateur poll that stated I was sitting in third place and on the brink of disaster heading into the election. The impact of this article, printed four days before the election, resulted in two things. One, it outraged my voters. People voiced their displeasure with the local tabloid and many wrote letters to the editor. Two, it helped solidify my vote. Those citizens who were sitting on the fence suddenly began to move in my direction.

The *Sun* went on to report that Duguid had 29.3% of the support, Kaufmann 23.2% and I was supposedly at 19%. My campaign team knew otherwise. What ensued was this. It cost my campaign over $10,000 to commission a new, independent poll. My team felt we had to provide Winnipeggers with more credible information. We felt the need to deal with this immediately, using a reputable, independent pollster and with transparency.

This entire last-ditch effort to discredit me was unpleasant, unfortunate, and costly. And the election proved that it was also highly inaccurate. In the end, I won with 38% of the votes. Peter Kaufmann came in second at 32% and Terry Duguid came in third at 27%. Over 83,000 citizens of Winnipeg voted for me.

All in all, my re-election campaign period was a blur. The fact that there had to be two of me — the mayor and the candidate — was exhausting. In addition to my regular duties, I had to attend mayoralty forums and many election events. I went door-to-door, made speeches everywhere to everybody, did media interviews, and did my best to meet as many people in person as I could. To this day, I feel that we ran an incredible campaign, thanks to a phenomenal team, to which I am most grateful. The 1995 campaign was co-chaired by Robert Gabor and Dennis McKnight, who were an integral part of my first campaign. They worked extremely hard and were brilliant. In my world, they are both geniuses.

Once I was re-elected, the media became somewhat more civilized and in my final year, a semi-honeymoon occurred. Media was more respectful towards me. They were more balanced in their reporting. There were more positive stories than negative one. It all seemed to have taken on the tone that I had "earned my stripes." I was suddenly acknowledged as a hard-working mayor and a person of substance who was producing results.

Another significant shift in my second term occurred within city council and the Executive Policy Committee. They accepted me... sort of... and in my opinion, this allowed us to make the most important and courageous decisions in well over twenty-five years. My re-election launched a highly productive three years, which resulted in:

- 124 consecutive years of a balanced budget;
- a new model for the city's bureaucracy;
- major departmental restructuring;
- a property tax freeze;
- a business tax freeze;
- major economic development initiatives, producing new jobs and growth;
- downtown revitalization plans continuing to take shape;
- the launch of the Millennium Library project;
- major safety, infrastructure, aboriginal and fiscal initiatives.

In my 1998 State of the City address, I pointed out that our economy had grown at almost twice the national average in the past year. Our employment was up, our exports doubled and personal income increased by more than five times the national rate. While it is most certainly understood that the city is but one of the partners in producing these positive outcomes, in a few short years, the city had come a long way from a most negative situation to one where I was confident in saying "Winnipeg's future looks promising."

The editorial cartoon ran in the Winnipeg Free Press depicting my farewell to City Hall (Dale Cummings/Winnipeg Free Press/Reprinted with permission)

Chapter 8
The Reality of Public Life

The Reality of Public Life

People in public life face incredible scrutiny... to say the very least. This is perpetuated by the general public's curiosity for personal information about public figures. Members of the media, be it television, radio, or newspaper, are always looking for a story and they are known to impose their own slant/bias. After all, their job is to sell newspapers and/or boost ratings. The more sensational, controversial, or dramatic, the better it is for them.

More often than not, politicians are the target. While I realize unequivocally that running for office is a choice and that candidates should expect that their lives will be subject to examination, I also know from personal experience that the degree to which this scrutiny is inflicted is far greater than one can ever anticipate. The constant and persistent public analysis of one's professional and personal life can be devastating. The immediate loss of privacy and the intensity of personal attacks cannot be understated.

As soon as I announced my candidacy, the majority of the local media exercised consistent negative spins on me as a candidate. They embellished my lack of experience in the political arena. It became clear that each media outlet had its candidate of choice, all of whom were existing council members. I was an outsider. I did not have any City Hall experience. I had never held public office at any level. I did not belong to any political party. Interestingly enough, these same qualifications (or lack thereof) were seen as a plus to many citizens in Winnipeg. Our polling indicated that people were fed up with the "old boys" at City Hall. They no longer trusted them and yearned for someone who didn't carry any baggage. Many voters told me during the election campaign that I offered a refreshing and credible change. I was told by many members of the general public that my experience in running a business during tumultuous times far outweighed my lack of experience as a politician. I had real-world experience and was not beholden to anyone or any party.

Another factor that the media insisted on expressing was that I was divorced. I was often referred to as a divorcee in articles and wondered why that had any pertinence to my being mayor. Male politicians were rarely singled out for being divorced. I soon realized that this was simply another way for the media to spin how they wanted to portray me. Their objective, it seemed to me, was to be negative.

I truly believe that women politicians are subject to an added layer of examination by the media and the public. They are often portrayed as being overly emotional and not equipped to handle the demands of public life. Personally, I was judged on how I looked, what I wore, and how my hair was coiffed. In general, women are subject to this type of analysis in the corporate and academic world as well. What makes it more difficult for women in politics is that personal attacks are splattered across newspapers or flashed on television screens for all to see. The degree and breadth of these attacks can sometimes be devastating. A very strong self esteem is a critical component for a woman leader.

The man of my dreams

Being a woman made for some peculiar questions when I was being interviewed by the media. I was once asked (on a live radio broadcast no less!) who my "escort" would be at public events if I became mayor. I was very surprised by that question. I simply could not comprehend why the question was even being asked, and in disbelief that the most important questions would not be about my various policies. I quickly recovered and immediately replied that my escort would be Tom Selleck, if he were available. I wondered quietly if a male candidate would ever get asked such a question.

My run for mayor brought to the forefront a whole barrage of issues surrounding equality and chauvinism. It had never occurred to me that discrimination would still be prevalent in 1992...but it was. I was depicted inappropriately and disrespectfully in many newspaper articles and cartoons over the course of the campaign. Some were more offensive than others. None are worth describing or repeating.

My personal opinion is that women generally make excellent politicians. I do not believe that women go into politics for power. I believe that women go into politics to make things better, to make a difference, to improve things, and to plan for the future. By nature, women are protectors. Their desire to protect their families and close friends gives them a competitive edge to "do the right thing." When they show emotion, to me, they show sensitivity...a trait that is essential for leaders. Unfortunately, still today, women who enter the political arena often receive unfair, biased treatment from the media and have to endure personal attacks on themselves and their families.

A former editor of the *Winnipeg Free Press*, Margo Goodhand, once wrote an editorial on the viciousness of media toward women politicians. She gave scathing examples of how women have been portrayed by the media, pointing out that women reporters and columnists were no less sympathetic. She went on to say that pioneering politicians, such as former Prime Minister Kim Campbell, Canada's first (and so far only) female prime minister, have "helped to design a whole new landscape" for women of this generation. I hope that my six years as mayor of Winnipeg have contributed in some small part to this landscape.

It can be said, most certainly in recent years, that many politicians bring on negative criticism themselves by making inappropriate remarks or exhibiting bad behavior. I recognize this and am the first to say that if one wants to be treated with fairness and respect, one must exemplify fairness and respect. Unfortunately, articles written about public figures, particularly elected officials, often reflect a lack of balance and misinformation. Transparency is a big buzz word for reporters as they constantly look to expose the "truth" in every story. As such, reporters often inflict an abrasive style of interviewing to capture a story. They pick up on any controversial remark or allegation and expand on it. They prey on the most vulnerable. You can be rest assured that they will feel for your soft underbelly.

Once I was elected, the onslaught of offensive comments and crude depictions of me in newspapers and on radio and television continued. I was described as a woman with no substance, as someone who was too emotional to lead a city and as a person who couldn't get along with others. The spin put on most news reports about me and my new role were almost always full of negativity. They dissected my political platform and scoffed at my goals, such as my plan to freeze property taxes. This initiative was a major achievement. Once passed, it marked the first time in twenty-five years that city of Winnipeg property taxes were frozen. Once adopted, the freeze remained in place for fifteen years. "No substance, indeed!"Are you kidding me?

Barely a week would go by without seeing cartoons of me overemphasizing my weight, my teeth, my hair, and my smile. Everything was fair game. I learned the lesson that nothing is off the record. A former Liberal MP and cabinet minister Iona Campagnolo once said, "The media simply builds you up just to tear you down." That perspective helped me and I never forgot her words. I always tried to take the high road, never indulging in negative politics or attack ads. I was sometimes criticized by my advisors who urged me to "take the gloves off." I would not. At times, it really felt like it was a "blood sport" and I was the one being bloodied and bruised.

The most unconscionable of any report ever written about me occurred just fifty days after I was elected, right after the death of my mother. The last day of my mother's life happened to be the day of my first city council meeting. My day started with an Executive Policy Committee meeting that ran until eleven a.m. As soon as I returned to my office from that meeting, my assistant rushed to my side to tell me that my mother was in the hospital and in critical condition. Unbenownst to me, she had been rushed there from her nursing home earlier that morning. My brother had tried to handle the situation without telling me, but by mid-morning, my mother was in intensive care and he knew that I needed to know. I needed to get to the hospital.

I'm not entirely sure how I did it, but I drove myself to Grace Hospital. Along the way, I thought back to how my mother had looked just two days earlier, when I had dinner with her. At eighty-three years old, she was still in relatively good health and fairly independent. It was uncanny that things could turn for the worse that quickly.

As soon as I arrived at the hospital, I rushed to Intensive Care to see my mother. She was still conscious and in great pain. Her face was ghostly white and her eyes were dark and piercing. She looked at me with the most desperate look in her eyes, in absolute fear and said, "Susan, help me." Never in my life had I ever felt such helplessness. I let her know that I would do everything I could to make sure that whatever could be done to help her was being done. I was in disbelief that she was in such a state and had no idea how long it would be before we would know what caused this, and whether she would survive the day.

I met with her doctor soon after I arrived. She explained to me that they hadn't detected what was wrong at this point but had ruled out a heart attack. She cautioned that Mother was very ill and that the next twenty-four hours were critical and would tell us whether she would make it.

The council meeting was set to start at one p.m. The agenda included some major decisions and the meeting could not be postponed. Though I understood fully the importance and significance of these decisions and my duties as mayor weighed heavily upon me, I also knew I could not bear to leave my mother's side. If possible I thought...if Mother showed signs of stabilizing...I could head over to city hall for a short time to be present for a few crucial votes. I was frantic.

I spent the remainder of the afternoon at the hospital, either at my mother's bedside or in a private room the hospital had arranged for me to use, telephoning my siblings and keeping in touch with City Hall. This was pre-cell phone days, so I had to use a hospital land line. I was running on adrenaline and kept up a hectic pace. I kept my emotions in check, but inside, I felt as though I was being torn apart.

By four p.m. the doctor told me that Mother had stabilized. She had been given some pain medication and this seemed to have helped. Her doctor advised that I could go back to city hall if necessary, but that I should return as soon as possible. However, upon our approach to my mother's bed, I could immediately see that something was terribly wrong. "She's gone!" I shouted. Doctors and nurses rushed in with resuscitation equipment and literally brought her back to life before my eyes.

By six p.m, Mother had stabilized. I asked the doctor whether I should leave. Her instructions were, "Go, and get back quick." I appreciated that it was very clear that time was not on my side. I made the decision to return to city hall, arrived in time for an important vote, and immediately returned to the hospital. I will never forget the horrendous drive back to the hospital...this was December in Winnipeg...there was already snow and ice on the roads and the weather that day was miserable. Thank goodness my good friend Gayle was with me.

I quickly returned to be with my mother, along with my brother, sister-in-law, and other family members. We spent the evening in vigil and shortly after midnight, my mother passed away. The next few days were spent making funeral arrangements, picking up my sisters at the airport, and removing mother's belongings from her personal care home. As anyone who has lost a parent knows, these are always trying times.

Two days later, an editorial appeared in the *Winnipeg Free Press* with the headline "Leading from Behind." The article criticized me for arriving late at the council meeting and not taking part in most of the decisions. It referred to me as a "*neophyte mayor naturally unable to grasp immediately the implications of one choice or another.*" Naturally unable? How patronizing and demeaning could one get? The article went on to say that the people of Winnipeg did not vote for an "*absentee mayor.*" What an absurd comment! On that same day, in the same newspaper, in the local section on page B1, there was a small write-up reporting that my mother had died.

Leading from behind

Mayor Susan Thompson, as the one civic official elected by the whole city, should be leading the council and the public toward a coherent policy on financing the municipal services in 1993. This is done by writing a city budget, which is one of the things mayors and councils have to do.

This week, the council had to decide what to do with the utility rates, which are one source of city funds. The city commissioners want to raise the rates a good deal faster than inflation, but the power to set those rates rests with the elected officials — fifteen councillors and Mayor Thompson.

The mayor, however, arrived late for the council meeting and did not take part in the vote on utility rates. The rates were raised as the commissioners proposed.

When the mayor fails to lead, the city is run by the board of commissioners. On tough decisions like raising the bus fares and the water and sewer rates, elected officials are often tempted to duck, to let others take the flak for the unpleasant decisions.

Mayor Thompson's specialty is beaming her radiant smile on pleasant social gatherings. A radiant smile, however, does not pay the bills. That can only be done by making the tough choices about revenue and expense.

The councillors have agreed that they should reduce the number of council meetings that intrude on their private time with their families. Having done so, they should have the decency to attend the few meetings they do hold.

When the budget is being written, the mayor should be there. She should have a direction and a policy and she should do her best to persuade councillors to agree with her. She should take part in the budget votes. Sometimes she will be on the losing side of a vote, but at least the record will be clear and her policy will be understood.

A neophyte mayor naturally is unable to grasp immediately the implications of one choice or another. But she did run for the office of mayor starting now, not starting sometime later after she has had a chance to think it over.

When her hand is not on the controls, the municipal machine switches to automatic pilot: the city commissioners take control. Ms. Thompson's electoral mandate can be interpreted in many ways, but the people certainly were not voting for an absentee mayor who would leave it to the board of commissioners to write the budget.

New mayor's mother dies in hospital

Eleanor Thompson, the mother of Mayor Susan Thompson, died in hospital Wednesday night. She was 83.

Thompson, a longtime St. James resident who recently made her home at Golden West Centennial Lodge, died in her sleep at Grace General Hospital.

Born in Edmonton in 1909, Eleanor Thompson moved to Winnipeg in 1934. A widow, she was married to William Maurice Thompson for 54 years.

She left behind four children: Lenore, Norman, Barbara and Susan. She had six grandchildren.

A memorial service is set for Monday at noon at St. Bede's Anglican Church. A reception follows at the parish hall.

Winnipeg Free Press, December 18, 1992. Reprinted with permission

On that same day, in another section of the same newspaper, on page C10, was my mother's obituary. This smarmy reporting could not have been more cruel to me and my family.

The following day, a ridiculously small paragraph titled "Unwarranted" appeared in the editorial section, explaining why I had not been at the entire council meeting. It was not an apology. It was not a retraction. In my opinion, it was unacceptable bad behavior and highly unprofessional. For the editorial reporter to say that he didn't know where I was on that day, in my opinion, was untrue and deceitful. What planet was he on? He had sat in the public gallery for the entire council meeting. Everyone else there knew what was going on and he didn't? Give me a break!

Unwarranted

Mayor Susan Thompson missed part of a city council meeting on Wednesday on account of the critical illness of her widowed mother, who later died. Mayor Thompson quite properly stayed with her mother at that moment of need and nonetheless managed to attend part of the council meeting and to vote on one of the major issues before the council.

Ms. Thompson deserves sympathy and support in her time of sorrow. Criticism of the mayor for her absence from the council meeting, in an editorial on Friday, was unwarranted.

All Winnipeggers will wish her hope to brighten her grief and strength to bear it.

Winnipeg Free Press, December 19, 1992. Reprinted with permission

The *Winnipeg Free Press* did eventually offer an "apology" on January 8, 1993. It was written by Maurice Switzer, who was the publisher of the paper at the time. He admitted that the newspaper "goofed" (as he put it) on much of the coverage relating to my campaign and my early days in office. I thought the word "goofed" was quite flippant, considering the seriousness of the situation. He offered me a "sincere, unmitigated, abject apology" but then went into a negative spin about my credentials and stood by the paper's editorial position on my candidacy. Nice apology! Suffice it to say that the remainder of the column had nothing to do with an apology and did nothing to right a terrible wrong. Unfortunately, it was just the beginning of crude and biased reporting, and I was subjected to personal attacks for the next six years.

Thompson deserves apology for FP articles

Publisher

Maurice Switzer

PERCEPTION IS reality.

If you look like a duck, walk like a duck, and act like a duck, people can be expected to call you a duck, even if you are a pigeon in disguise.

Since before last November's municipal election, supporters of new mayor Susan Thompson have accused the *Free Press* of being a duck.

This newspaper's editorial board determined that we would endorse a mayoralty candidate other than Ms. Thompson and published a pre-election editorial explaining our reasoning.

From her election night victory to the present, some of Ms. Thompson's supporters have been extremely vocal in expressing their perception that the *Free Press* has not treated the mayor fairly.

It began with our morning-after election edition, the front page of which carried a photo of one of the losing mayoralty contenders instead of the victorious Ms. Thompson.

Our excuse was that the winner did not make herself available to the media on election night until after our deadline.

But couldn't we have published at least a "mug" shot of Winnipeg's new chief magistrate?

We goofed.

Stories in subsequent weeks about the new mayor's redecorating of the city hall office long occupied by predecessor Bill Norrie were criticized as being petty, as were local media reports of her acceptance of the perk of a chauffeured car provided at taxpayer's expense.

The *Free Press* did not belabor those stories, but felt justified in reporting them since candidate Thompson's main campaign plank had been containment of the taxpayer's cost of running this city.

In mid-December, as one critic wrote, our newspaper "hit a new low".

The *Free Press* reported that Mayor Thompson arrived late for a Dec. 16 council meeting, and didn't vote on the package proposing fee hikes for everything from bus fares to sewer rates.

An editorial the following day said her action brought her leadership abilities into question and indicated that "her hand is not on the controls".

What our staff did not report or comment on was the fact that Mayor Thompson missed the start of the Dec. 16 council session to be at the side of her mother, who died in hospital later that evening.

Free Press reporters failed to make note of a council motion granting the mayor leave of absence due to her personal family situation, and also failed to report that the mayor voted for the rate increases at an Executive Policy Committee meeting immediately prior to the city council meeting.

When editors became fully aware of the circumstances, it was too late to issue a correction until the edition of Saturday, Dec. 19.

A brief editorial said that our criticism of Mayor Thompson's absence from part of the Dec. 16 council meeting was "unwarranted". We wrote that "Ms. Thompson deserves sympathy and support in her time of sorrow."

She deserves more than that.

This newspaper owes Susan Thompson a sincere, unmitigated, abject apology for our sloppy reporting that creating the impression that she was not doing her job.

Coming when it did, our poor performance had the effect of being insensitive as well as unprofessional.

This is perhaps an appropriate time to clarify our newspaper's editorial position.

The *Free Press* did not think Susan Thompson possessed the credentials necessary to lead the municipal government of a major Canadian city through what promises to be a period of formidable economic and social change.

We endorsed a candidate who had more experience and who we felt possessed the leadership potential that will be required to effect the coalitions necessary to move our city through the trying times that lie ahead.

If another election were called tomorrow, we would endorse the same candidate for the same reasons.

But, despite the fact she was not our choice as Winnipeg mayor, the *Free Press* certainly hopes Susan Thompson succeeds in her new office.

To wish bad luck on any political leader — be they Susan Thompson or Brian Mulroney — smacks of suicide, because nobody benefits when managers fail.

If the *Free Press* is fulfilling its role properly it will fully and accurately report on Ms. Thompson's actions as mayor, and be quick to comment on what we perceive to be both her failures and successes.

For example, she should get full marks for having the courage to say the city's police force would have to be operated with the same funds next year as it did last year.

After a big initial brouhaha by opponents and police union spokesmen, it was fascinating to hear that civic administrators think they can meet Mayor Thompson's objective by, as this newspaper reported, "trimming expenses for new office equipment and keeping an eye on overtime".

We hope Mayor Thompson is successful in "keeping an eye" on what happens to taxpayer's money.

And we will continue to keep an eye on her performance.

There is nothing we would like better than for Mayor Thompson to force those who didn't endorse her candidacy — 60 per cent of local voters and the *Free Press* editorial board — to admit we were wrong.

Winnipeg Free Press, December 19, 1992. Reprinted with permission

And here is another reality of public life. I returned to work almost immediately after my mother's memorial service. I knew I had been elected to do an important job and I felt that I could not allow myself the proper time to mourn. I virtually parked my grieving until I was no longer mayor, six years after my mother's death.

I am including the details of this painful part of my life in this chapter because I think it is important for people to know what leaders go through when personal tragedy confronts them. The media does not go away. In fact, they are more likely to increase their coverage in the face of personal adversity. There were times from 1992 to 1998 where I was relieved that my mother and father were not alive to witness the misinformation being spread by the media. It would have broken their hearts. I was also grateful that two of my siblings lived outside of Winnipeg, as this shielded them from much of the negative reporting. During those days, I sometimes wondered how high profile politicians with spouses and children sheltered their families from such media reports.

I don't want to paint all local media with the same brush. I do want to emphasize that there were some local reporters who were respectful and diligent in reporting accurate information. It is important to note that Winnipeg's leading local newspaper, which had spent a great deal of time trashing me from 1992 to 1995, endorsed me in my run for a second term. Go figure! Not all members of the media were vicious. In fact, I can honestly say that there are some who have become good friends.

On the whole, national media was very good to me. During the 1997 Flood of the Century, the International Winter Cities Conference in 1996, and throughout the development of the Mid Continent Trade Corridor, the reporting was very positive and frankly, personally encouraging. In 1994, Chatelaine Magazine recognized me as one of the fifty most influential women in Canada. This was a tremendous honour.

In the twenty-plus years since I was mayor, media coverage of public figures has escalated even more. The addition of social media has intensified the scrutiny to the point where nothing is private in the life of a public official. I really wonder how this is going to play out going forward. How do we as a society recruit, support, and nurture our leaders? Who is going to want to subject themselves and their families to such intense examination? It is a huge concern that we need to pay attention to as a society.

The "Old Boys" Network

At city hall, I was faced with negativity as well. The entire atmosphere felt toxic...councillor against councillor, councillor against administration, administration against the mayor's office. Right from the beginning, I felt actual physical effects whenever I entered the building. People were tense. Everything seemed to be moving in slow motion. Any effort to get something done seemed to take forever. The amount of political control maintained by the administration was a real eye-opener. I was not aware until I got there just how powerful the Board of Commissioners had become. Clearly I had my work cut out for me.

There was a fierce competitiveness amongst city councillors as well. Power grabbing and grandstanding were the norm at meetings, particularly council meetings. I found the conduct between some elected officials to be offensive and vicious. Often, they would throw insults at each other and lacked public civility. Then when the TV cameras would turn off (council meetings were broadcast in those days), they would all be buddy-buddy. I was speechless. One councillor once commented on the importance of being captured by the media saying, "As long as you're in the paper and they spell your name right." I completely disagree with that type of thinking. In my world, you have to be held to your word and to your actions, on and off camera.

When I became mayor, the "old boys network" was in full force and everyone from councillors to administrators did or said what they could to complicate things for me. Whether it was a lack of appropriate protocol shown to me as mayor, something as simple as a welcoming chair at the Board of Commissioners' meeting, or being unavailable for a first meeting between a mayor and chief commissioner, a clear message was being sent to me immediately that I was but one vote in the approval process at city hall and nothing more.

It was fascinating to observe the meetings that took place right outside my office window in the courtyard. Almost daily, I could see one of the councillors talking to one of the members of the Board of Commissioners in this courtyard. Almost certainly, the discussion was how business would get done at city hall. The "boys" would also meet informally in the councillors' office. I swore they drew straws as to who would "tell" me how things were going to be done, according to them.

Another archaic reality of city hall in 1992 was the lack of women in management roles. Out of thirty departments, twenty-nine had male department heads. Over the years, I worked very hard to encourage women to apply for positions within the city's administration. By the time my second term was completed, many had succeeded, and the majority of the city's civic departments were managed by women. That included the most senior job of chief administrative officer, who at the time was Gail Stephens and the first woman to be city auditor, Carol Bellringer.

The obstacles I faced each day required that I exercise sheer perseverance and faith. What kept me going through this litany of challenges were the citizens of Winnipeg. In general, the people I met at events, be they private or public, were kind and considerate. I was constantly greeted with friendliness and compassion. In fact, I learned very early on that my best days at city hall were when we had visitors. And so, I began to invite citizens.

I wanted the mayor's office to become a welcoming place for guests — a people's place. We offered tours to various groups, both adults and children. I had discovered the joy that children could bring to city hall when I became involved in the "I love to read" sessions, whereby prominent Winnipeggers would visit local elementary schools to read to children. I went to an inner-city school and distinctly remember reading, *If You're Not From the Prairie* by David Bouchard. I loved to see how curious and honest young children could be. I was impressed by how genuine they all were. They were our future and seeing them on a regular basis reinforced that part of my work as mayor was to help build a better future for them. Throughout my tenure, I continued to invite children to city hall and loved how they inspired me. These young people, our future, helped to transform the physically sterile world of city hall to a friendly place filled with energy, laughter and enthusiasm.

The Dark Side of Public Life

When I made the decision to run for mayor, I anticipated that public life would have its ups and downs. I expected that I would have some loss of privacy, though I probably never knew to the degree this would evolve. I tried to make light of any loss of privacy, whether I was at a restaurant, shopping establishment, or grocery store. In fact, for the most part, I enjoyed meeting the citizens of Winnipeg as I went about my errands and social activities. What I didn't expect was the negative side of citizens knowing who you are and where you live.

I must reiterate that most people I met in public while I was mayor were a breath of fresh air. I loved meeting and talking to people. It was important for me to hear people's concerns. I even enjoyed the odd banter with people who had opposing views from me. I was not prepared, however, for people who were clearly unstable, which resulted in threats to my well-being. In one such incident, a disgruntled citizen decided to take it upon himself to let me know that he did not approve of the cuts City Hall was making on a particular budget. He displayed this by spray painting, "Suzy Scissorhands" across the outside wall of the Birt Saddlery business building. While I had braced myself for criticism because I took a tough stand on issues, I never expected physical damage to my property. It brought an entirely new set of circumstances and rage of emotions to the forefront.

The most harrowing experiences I ever had to face personally were the death threats. One in particular was a specific bomb threat to my residence. I remember being in an Executive Policy Committee meeting when the chief of police entered the room. I must say at this point that this rarely happens. When the chief of police interrupts a meeting, you know that something is up. He asked me to step outside of the meeting. He told me that someone had called to say that a bomb had been planted in my apartment. At the time, I lived on the second floor of a house on Grosvenor Avenue in River Heights. On that particular day, I happened to have a friend visiting from Toronto and she was staying at my apartment. I immediately called her and told her that a police squad car was waiting for her and that she had to leave. Police scoured my apartment, sniffing dogs and all, and determined that there was no bomb. They told me they had completed their investigation and my apartment was clean. I was told I could return home.

That evening, when I stepped into my apartment, I was understandably experiencing very high anxiety. "What if the police missed something? What if I were to turn on a light switch and it would trigger something?" I sat myself down on a living room chair. It was at this point that I began to shake uncontrollably. The fear was gripping me. I decided right then and there, however, that I was not going to let this psychologically destroy me. Though this incident shook me to the core, I would not let it define me. From that day on, I did not succumb to fear when threats came my way, but I certainly realized that the depth of commitment required by me to this life in public office had become most serious in each and every way.

Unfortunately, there were other threats. City hall received other bomb threats, but more often, threatening letters and abusive telephone calls. At one point, I witnessed a despicable act — a likeness of me burning in effigy, right in front of the main window of the mayor's office in the city hall courtyard. Imagine a crowd surrounding a likeness of yourself, with a noose around its neck, set on fire and burned. This act was hurtful and yet again, it shook me to the core. I sometimes wonder if these same threats would have occurred if a man were at the helm. Were these threats being made because the thought was that as a woman, I would react with fear? That it would force me to retreat?

A while back, I was asked to write a foreword for a book about women in Canada who dared to enter politics. Its title, *Dancing Backwards: A Social History of Canadian Women in Politics*, published by Heartland Publications, was based on the following quote by Ann Richards, former governor of Texas: "Being a woman in politics is like being Ginger Rogers. You have to do all the same dance steps as Fred Astaire, but you have to do them backwards and in high heels." In the foreword, I went on to write about some of the personal struggles I faced in breaking the proverbial glass ceiling. I gave examples of the "culture" I found at City Hall when I first took office. I described some of the discrimination I faced and how I responded. As does any other woman who enters the political arena, I faced barriers and dealt with the challenges as they came up. While I prefer not to dwell on the negativity that evolved when I became mayor, it is a reality, and a story that must be told to help women going forward.

In total, I spent 2,190 days in public office. In each of those days, I was willing to wholly commit to my duties. I was willing to work 24/7. I was prepared to persevere. I was not prepared to succumb to the threats of a few unstable people.

For years, I felt both physical and psychological effects from my six years in office. My strength, my character, and my tenacity were all tested. At times, I felt that my soul and my spirit had been violated. I survived because of my deep faith and determination to overcome all adversities. I honestly believe that there was a greater force at work.

Then again, I learned some great lessons being Mayor. City Hall taught me patience. I survived seventy-two council meetings. City Hall taught me perseverance. I learned how to try different approaches to get things done and eventually, I realized that my time would come when I could get done what needed to be done. Eventually, the system worked and when it did, my team and I savoured the moments.

I also saw the best in people. So many times over the course of six years, I saw the citizens of Winnipeg shine. Whether it was to volunteer for one of our many significant events or to assist with flood efforts, the people of Winnipeg showed me how wonderful they could be with their selfless spirit and boundless energy. When my decision to leave politics was announced, I received some absolutely heart-warming letters from some Winnipeg citizens expressing sadness that I was leaving. They thanked me for my six years of service and praised me for my accomplishments. Each time I read the kind words written to me in those letters, I am touched. To this day, I remain honoured and privileged to have served this great city as Winnipeg's fortieth mayor.

To anyone who is considering a career in politics, I offer a few words of advice on how to deal with public life. When faced with criticism, be it from the media, your colleagues, or your electorate, confront it and focus clearly on what has been said. Some criticism is just better left alone. Also, keep a sense of humour. That is often easier said than done, but it is very important. Finally, do not be afraid to cry or to swear. Keep it short, maybe ten seconds, but experience the emotion and then get on with the job. Political life is not easy for anyone and is especially difficult for women, but it can also be extremely rewarding. Focus on the positive, savour the moments when things go well, and believe in your innate abilities as a leader.

Aerial view of the Flood of the Century (Photo courtesy of City of Winnipeg Archives)

Chapter 9
The 1997 Flood of the Century

Over 10,000 years ago, the land where Winnipeg stands was the centre of a huge glacial lake. Lake Agassiz was hundreds of thousands of square miles and covered most of what is now Manitoba, North Dakota, and parts of Minnesota, northern Ontario, and Saskatchewan. The lake flowed from its southern basin, north to the Nelson River, and into Hudson Bay. Over the course of many centuries, Lake Agassiz drained, mostly to the north and into the Arctic Ocean. Eventually, it receded completely, leaving thousands of smaller lakes and a few winding rivers. One of these rivers, the Red River,[8] starts in western Minnesota, flows north through eastern North Dakota and up into Manitoba. Just over 800 kilometers (approximately 500 miles) long, the river winds its way through a few urban centres — Fargo, Grand Forks, Emerson, Morris, Winnipeg, and Selkirk. In Winnipeg, the Red River joins forces with the Assiniboine River, meeting at a historic site aptly called The Forks. The Red then continues to flow north where it eventually drains into Lake Winnipeg.

The land on either side of the Red River is presently known as the Red River Valley. Much of it is fertile soil used to grow wheat, barley,

8 Red River and Red River Valley information obtained from Province of Manitoba website and Wikipedia.

corn, and much more. This rich, agricultural land is famous for its #1 hard wheat and is an integral part of the food supply system used to feed the world.

It has always been a historic fact that the city of Winnipeg is situated on a floodplain. I knew it as a child growing up in St. James, on the banks of the Assiniboine River. Our civic government knew it, and understood all too well the destruction that could occur when a river overflows its banks. There had been catastrophic floods in the 1800s along the Red River Valley. Two major ones, in 1826 and 1852, temporarily turned much of the province into a massive lake once again. The most devastating for Winnipeg in the twentieth century was the 1950 flood, when eight dikes broke and most of the city was covered with water. Many thousands of people needed to be evacuated and many of the city's bridges were damaged and needed to be rebuilt. As a result of this catastrophic event, the Red River Floodway[9] was built to protect the city from rising waters going forward. Construction began in 1962 and the building of the floodway was six years in the making. Notably named "Duff's Ditch" after Premier Duff Roblin,[10] whose government spearheaded the project, the artificial waterway is forty-seven kilometres (thirty miles) in length and diverts the Red River just south of Winnipeg around the perimeter of the city and then releases the flow back into the Red River at Lockport, through a lock and dam system. It is said that over seventy-six million cubic meters (nearly three billion cubic feet) of dirt was excavated, more than what was moved to build the Suez Canal. The building of the floodway initially had its share of naysayers. At the time, it was thought the plan was too elaborate and overzealous. Time told a different story, however, and the endeavour was justified as the floodway was used many times to prevent flooding in the city. For the city of Winnipeg, the floodway is our saving grace. That being said, both the city and the province are still very much aware that they must never let their guard down each spring when the melt occurs. Both

---

9 Red River Floodway information obtained from Wikipedia.

10 Premier Duff Roblin was the Province of Manitoba's fourteenth premier, from 1958 to 1967.

levels of government continue to have processes in place to monitor river levels and calculate flood forecasts.

The catalyst for the 1997 Flood of the Century[11] actually began in the winter of 1995-1996, when Winnipeg experienced heavy snowfall throughout the winter and well into the spring. We set a record that year – 170 days in a row with snow on the ground. This unprecedented amount of precipitation was almost certain to cause a late spring melt, making the possibilities of flooding that year very real. Flood officials were preparing for the worst. Some flooding did occur in southern Manitoba, but no homes in Winnipeg were directly affected. The Red River crested at 5.9 meters (19.4 feet) that spring, which was at least three meters (ten feet) above normal levels.[12] This resulted in a high water table across southern Manitoba, which could only recede with a hot, dry summer. Unfortunately, the summer of 1996 was one of the wettest summers ever. Once again, we broke records, this time for most rainfall over the course of one summer. This resulted in a higher than normal water table when the land began to freeze that autumn.

Coincidentally, in the fall of 1996, Winnipeg's economic development arm, then called Winnipeg 2000, was hosting a contingent of mayors and reeves along the Red River Valley. This particular group represented the northern portion of the Mid Continent Trade Corridor and included the elected civic officials from Fargo, Moorhead, Grand Forks, Pembina, Emerson, and Selkirk. Among those present were Fargo Mayor Bruce Furness, Grand Forks Mayor Pat Owens, Pembina Mayor Hetty Walker, Emerson Mayor Wayne Arseny, and Selkirk Mayor Bud Oliver. The purpose of this meeting was to discuss trade opportunities between Canada and the United States. We did however take some time to discuss flood management and what each of us had experienced in the spring of 1996. Not long after the meeting, on November 6th in fact, a gigantic snowstorm hit

11 The term "The Flood of the Century" was originally used to describe the 1950 flood in Manitoba.

12 Information/statistics regarding snow and rainfall from City of Winnipeg — Flood Facts

Winnipeg. At the next meeting with this group, though the focus was still on trade between our two countries, we discussed how the significant amount of snowfall early in our winter season could affect flooding the following spring. By the time we had our next meeting in January 1997, the conversation shifted almost completely to flood management. We all knew that we were in for something big. I must give acknowledgement and credit to this specific group of people. Their collective leadership, knowledge, and experience served all of their citizens in an incredible manner. Their instincts were extraordinary. They knew the river. They knew the damage it could cause. They did everything in their power to prevent it from destroying their towns and cities.

Snow precipitation during the winter of 1996-1997 in Winnipeg was once again much higher than normal. Over sixty-two centimeters (just over two feet) of snow fell in November 1996 alone. An accumulation of over fifty centimeters (nearly twenty inches) of snow fell in early 1997. These weather patterns were being felt south of us as well, particularly in North Dakota, right along the banks of the Red River. As such, river levels were extremely high and the soil throughout the Red River valley was saturated.

Then on April 5th, 1997, the entire area was hit with an extreme blizzard. In Winnipeg, a record thirty-seven centimeters (just over a foot) of snow fell over the course of three days, clogging our city streets, knocking down power and telephone lines and closing our airport.[13] City Hall had to deal with clearing the streets as quickly as possible to get the city moving again. I was in Monterrey, Mexico at the time, meeting about the trade corridor. Just as we were about to head back home, we were told about weather conditions in Winnipeg. We flew to Dallas, Texas and were informed by airline staff there that it was not possible to get to Winnipeg for at least three days. Telling them that I was mayor of that city and that it was important for me to get home did not change anything. It was critical for me to return to Winnipeg as soon as possible, so we opted to fly to Toronto instead, thinking that we would have more options if we were in Canada. We

13 Snowfall amounts taken from Environment Canada archival website information.

were then able to arrange a flight from Hamilton, Ontario and arrived home the next day.

Given the massive amounts of snow in this latest storm, it was now evident that the river levels would be much higher than originally forecasted. It was a "perfect storm" situation. Prior to this storm, predictions by Alf Warkentin, the province's flood forecaster, were that the river would exceed 1979 flood levels. After April 5th, Mr. Warkentin anticipated things would not only be worse than 1979, they would be worse than 1950. The 1979 flood was almost as devastating as the 1950 flood, but the province and city were better prepared in 1979 due to improved dykes, flood systems, and the Red River Floodway.[14]

As we looked to our neighbours to the south, residents of Fargo were already fighting flood waters. Their city had built a dike to protect them, but levels were expected to be at least four feet higher than the dike.

In Winnipeg, we were on high alert and extremely worried. We knew we were beginning to face a most serious situation and significant variables had to be considered. It was becoming increasingly difficult to anticipate water levels. As the city's leader, I couldn't help but worry about what was still to come. What if we were hit with another snowstorm? What if we had significant rainfall in April and May? Would the dikes built throughout the Red River Valley hold? Were the floodgates at top operational performance? Would the pumping stations be able to operate with such a volume of water? What would we do if we had a significant breach? Did we have sufficient manpower? These were all questions that had to be considered and discussed at this early stage.

Planning and preparation for what could be the city's worst flood in a century escalated. Key members of city council, those whose wards were directly impacted, and each member of the Board of Commissioners, assisted in leadership roles to fight the flood. The Public Works Commissioner at the time was Bill Carroll, and he gathered a team that included Barry McBride, a director from the city's

14 Information from "A Red Sea Rising" published by the *Winnipeg Free Press*

Water and Waste Department, and Doug McNeil, Land Drainage and Flood Protection Planning Engineer. The Emergency Preparedness Committee, made up of the Executive Policy Committee and a number of bureaucrats, was put into operation and the Emergency Operations Centre was activated to manage the flood efforts for the city. Everything had to kick into high gear and this now involved all departments at the city. One of the most critical components was to properly analyze the information we were given and anticipate our needs. Our motto became: "Plan for the worst-case scenario; hope for the best-case scenario." Everything from the erection of dikes, to safety issues, to communications, to sandbag supply had to be reviewed and revisited.

Earlier in the year, the city had ordered sandbags in anticipation of the rising waters. In 1996, just over 300,000 bags had been used. I distinctly remember asking what we had in stock in early 1997. We had 50,000 on hand. Call it gut instinct or woman's intuition, and that is putting it mildly, I recommended that we order more...many more. This would be a year where it would be better to be safe than sorry. By the end of February 1997, the City had 500,000 sandbags ready to be used, more than 200,000 than the previous year. While other municipalities were scrambling for sandbags, Winnipeg kept ahead of the curve, and throughout the spring of 1997, always had enough supply to keep up with demand. By the end of the crisis, over 8,000,000 sandbags were filled and used.[15] Lined up end to end, this would be the equivalent of a line from Winnipeg to Vancouver.

City workers began to fill sandbags early in the year, and immediately sought volunteers to assist with this enormous task. The city owned a sandbagging machine (invented by a Manitoban — Guy Bergeron from Elie). It was soon necessary to invest in another, and by the end of the crisis, the city owned four sandbagging machines. These machines filled more than four million of the eight million sandbags used. The remainder were filled by volunteers, by hand.[16]

15 1997 Flood Facts, The City of Winnipeg website

16 1997 Flood Facts, The City of Winnipeg website

A flood hotline had already been established in the spring of 1996 to deal with the many calls from concerned citizens. In 1997, this team was ramped up from nineteen employees to nearly 300. The Emergency Public Information Team (EPIT) was responsible for receiving all public and media calls relating to the flood situation. They set up a call centre and fielded tens of thousands of calls every day over a three-month period. This dedicated group of individuals provided a critical link to the citizens of Winnipeg. People called with questions about how the flood could affect their neighbourhood and where they could pick up sandbags. Others called in to volunteer their services. Countless volunteers from all over the province became involved. I had personal friends from Treherne, Manitoba — George and Leslie Stanton — who would drive nearly two hours to Winnipeg every day to help out, along with many others from their town. Many rural Manitobans, those who weren't in jeopardy of losing their own homes to flooding, found ways to help those who were. People came in truckloads. Some helped with sandbagging or building dikes; others took to the telephones at the call centre. Amidst the angst of what was to come, it was touching to see that so many people cared.

Overall, the volunteer efforts as the crisis evolved were outstanding. The City alone, through the EPIT Centre, placed more than 70,000 volunteers. People young and old came out in droves to help wherever they could. Businesses allowed their employees to volunteer time with pay and high school students were permitted to sandbag instead of going to classes. All 10,000 City employees, 3000 directly, helped with flood relief efforts. Many non-profit organizations rose to the challenge — the Red Cross, the Mennonite Central Committee, and the Salvation Army. As well, countless Hutterite colonies contributed to the flood effort. It was really incredible to see everyone pitch in and take on such daunting tasks. Thousands of people were trained to build dikes and countless others learned how to fill and use sandbags. It is estimated that over 200,000 volunteer days (a day being an eight-hour shift) were donated to the flood effort in Winnipeg. The spirit and generosity of Manitobans was inspiring.

People pulled together in a most heroic manner and I was never so grateful to the citizens of our great city and province.

Forever etched in my memory was the television news capturing the devastation in Grand Forks, North Dakota. On Friday, April 18, 1997, the Red River broke through their main dike and most of Grand Forks and East Grand Forks was under water. Then, the following day, a fire in the city's downtown area destroyed eleven buildings over a three-block area. The footage was difficult to watch as we saw a city ravaged by both water and fire. I had met Pat Owens, the mayor of Grand Forks on a number of occasions in the past year. She was elected in 1996 and she, too, was the first female mayor of her city. We had a lot in common and had hit it off when we first met, and I was most anxious to speak to her. We had exchanged cell phone numbers at the last meeting of mayors, so I called her right away. I knew that there was nothing I could do to ease the pain but I wanted to offer her my support. Understandably, she was devastated. Losing the city to the floodwaters and the subsequent fires felt like a death in the family. We talked about the chaos her city was in and she gave me some words of advice. "Do not trust the numbers, Susan," she told me, citing that their numbers were wrong by five feet. The National Weather Service had estimated that the river would rise to forty-nine feet above the bed of the river. Grand Forks had built levees to withstand rising levels to fifty-two feet; the crest reached fifty-four feet. We kept in touch as often as we could over the next week as the river's crest approached Winnipeg.

I followed news from U.S. television stations, so that I could see how Grand Forks was handling the aftermath. As I watched Pat Owens, this tiny woman with unwavering strength, speak almost daily to the media on television news, I felt such compassion for her and her city. It also occurred to me as I saw her that I could be in that exact situation in the next week or so. Though I knew we were protected by the floodway, the thought of any breach was terrifying. I cannot recall getting much sleep from that point on. My anxiety level had been high prior to this; now it was over the top.

The devastation in Grand Forks was an eye-opener for everyone north of the border. Reality set in for many that what happened there could also happen here. Southern Manitoba towns were on high alert and preparing for their own fight. It was inevitable that a large portion of the Red River Valley would be flooded. The land is so flat in southern Manitoba, and as such, the water just spreads out. There is nowhere else for it to go. By April 24th, mandatory evacuations were implemented. This was a difficult time for many people in southern Manitoba, as so many were forced to leave their homes.

A reception centre for flood evacuees was set up in an arena in south Winnipeg. Many families from towns in southern Manitoba took refuge there. The centre was set up to register all evacuees and provide them with resources, including a children's play centre and a library. This was also where volunteers coordinated efforts for evacuees to find places to stay. The city's public health department was also on hand for medical assistance and counselling.

Meanwhile, each day at city hall, I was relentless in double checking our numbers and asking every possible question I could, based on the information I was given. Plans were continuously being reviewed and revised. A medical plan was devised to evacuate hospitals and nursing homes and some facilities were put on alert. Creeks in the city were also filling to capacity, raising new concerns. There was even a plan to bring the animals at Assiniboine Park to higher ground if need be; this was aptly dubbed "Operation Noah's Ark."

As mayor, I wanted to ensure that Winnipeggers understood exactly what was coming our way and be prepared for it. I thought it was important during this unstable time to keep our citizens informed, but it was also essential to manage any misinformation. The last thing we wanted to do was create panic. At the city and provincial levels, a decision was made to give live press conferences on a daily basis. This would allow us to inform the public with up-to-date and accurate information. It was my position that, as leader of the city, I was responsible and accountable to the public and therefore I should lead the city's press conferences. Leadership is important at all times, but at a time of crisis, it is absolutely essential.

One of the many news conferences that occurred during the 1997 flood (Photo courtesy of City of Winnipeg Archives)

The first televised news conference occurred on Monday, April 21st. I went in with a one-page news release, a document that could be read in about a minute. We had an hour of air-time to fill. Thanks to a wonderful group of city staff who sat at this first conference with me — Doug McNeil, an engineer from the Department of Water and Waste; Mark Bennett, Emergency Services Coordinator; and Bruce Taylor, a superintendent from the Winnipeg Police — we filled the time with everything from details on river levels, to security issues, to lessons on how to build a dike and how to fill a sandbag. Representatives from the provincial government — Larry Whitney, Emergency Flood Spokesperson, supported by Alf Warkentin, Larry Neufeld, and Steve Topping — reported on various issues such as forecasting updates and the building of a new dike. For roughly two weeks, these press conferences were our way to inform the public and the system was widely successful. It was a real team effort and provided our citizens with a lot of great information.

Our local cable stations, Videon and Shaw at the time, televised each of the press conferences and played them continuously on their channels. In fact, both companies went as far as to provide twenty-four-hour coverage of the 1997 flood over a sixteen-day period. Every day, they showcased each of the press conferences in their entirety and filled the rest of the time with news footage, interviews, and informational pieces. This extensive coverage drew an audience of roughly seventy percent of television viewers, outdrawing all the three local television networks collectively during this period. It also won both Shaw and Videon a national award in public service broadcasting.

Each day, as the swollen river approached our province from North Dakota, representatives of all three levels of government met. In addition to receiving day-to-day statistical data on water levels, we also received best-and worst-case scenario updates. We were made aware of the many scenarios that could go wrong. There could be a malfunction of the flood-gates, a breach of the dikes, or a shutdown of our pumping stations. Mother Nature could have taken another run at us. Wind could also play havoc, creating waves on the swollen river and breaking down the dikes. These were all real possibilities and each of these scenarios could have resulted in catastrophic events. We knew that our pumping stations were tested to withhold a level of 19.4 feet above normal. We were expecting 24.5 feet. Our volunteers were exhausted. It was time to bring in outside help.

On April 21st, in the biggest deployment since the Korean War, 7,000 members of the Canadian Army, Navy, and Air Force came to our aid. By invoking the Emergency Measures Act, the Canadian government was able to pitch in both physically and financially. Our Canadian Forces personnel were instrumental in winning this fight. These young men and women helped in so many ways; building dikes and providing patrol services to evacuated areas. It is my personal belief that if they had not been brought in when they did, our city and province would have had a major struggle to keep up with the work that needed to be done. The intelligence provided by our military during this critical time in Manitoba's history was exceptional. They flew helicopters from Winnipeg to Emerson each and every day to study the approaching waters. They referred to the Red River as "the advancing army." General Rick Hillier gave daily military briefings at 17 Wing, Winnipeg's branch of the Royal Canadian Air Force. It was extremely interesting to see how the military worked.

Once the military arrived, I invited General Hillier to join our press conferences. This forum provided an opportunity for the military to update the public on the enormous service they were providing to our citizens. Winnipeggers were so grateful for their presence. As an aside, these press conferences also provided the military with an opportunity to assess their own communication strategies during a disaster. General Hillier recognized the value and importance of the city of Winnipeg's communication model and was instrumental in helping shape a communications policy for the Canadian Forces in national disasters.

I was given the opportunity to fly over the flooded areas with military personnel. I had the privilege of meeting Major General Jeffries on one of the helicopter flights to Emerson. It was overwhelming to have a firsthand look at acres upon acres of flooded land from the sky. The Red River had become the Red Sea, stretching over fifty kilometers (thirty miles) across the province. It was evident from this vantage point that not only was the river a threat but overland flooding was adding to the volumes of water. It was an interesting observation that, as the waters rose, so did anxiety levels.

From left to right: General Rick Hillier, City of Winnipeg engineer Doug McNeil, Major General Jeffries, City of Winnipeg Commissioner Bill Carroll and Brigadier General Robert Meating (Photo courtesy of City of Winnipeg Archives)

I found the relationship our city and province had with our military during this difficult time to be outstanding. I was most grateful for the arrival of the Canadian troops and most respectful of their presence. The public was also grateful for the military's presence and let military personnel know whenever they saw them. A tremendous bond formed between the soldiers and our citizens.

On April 22nd, the province of Manitoba declared a State of Emergency in southern Manitoba, putting 20,000 people in that area on alert. This meant that at any given time, provincial officials could force residents from their homes. This was also the day that a Winnipeg boy was swept into an open culvert and drowned. Fourteen-year-old Adam Young was near a ditch with a few school friends when he and a younger boy fell into the water. Unbeknownst to them, the swirling water was heading to a culvert without a cover. Mercifully, the younger boy was saved. Sadly, the older boy was not. Adam's body was found a week later. His death was a profound tragedy that brought the reality of the flood's danger to the forefront. What made it even more tragic for the city of Winnipeg was that Adam was the son of one of our city councillor's executive assistants, Rob Young.

On this sad day, April 22nd, a number of flood officials, bureaucrats, and politicians visited the floodway gates just south of Winnipeg, to assess the predicted water levels. Officials maintained that the crest would arrive on May 1st at a level of 24.5 feet above normal. The floodway would protect Winnipeg to 27 feet. I remember staring down at the swirling waters — in fact there was a photo of me in the *Winnipeg Free Press* the following day doing just that — and I recall thinking how much damage these ravaged waters had already caused...and now a death. At this point, I could only hope and pray that we were doing all we could to prevent any more flooding and that the extent of the damage was behind us.

On April 23rd, I declared the city a state of local emergency. This meant we could respond more quickly to flood-fighting efforts and carry out mandatory evacuations if necessary. As the flood forecasts were being revised, it was evident that some homes inside the city limits would have to be evacuated. Mandatory evacuations were ordered for certain areas.

The mobilization of citizens as the waters approached Winnipeg became of foremost importance. The threats were very real and as a city, we had to be prepared to handle whatever came our way. We were keenly aware that the number of evacuees could exceed 20,000. Already, many residents of southern Manitoba had fled their homes, headed to Winnipeg and they needed a place to stay. Displaying Winnipeg's true spirit of generosity, many citizens opened their homes as temporary shelters, welcoming strangers, relatives, and friends. Of the approximately 20,000 evacuees, the city provided shelter for 2,100 of them.

The last week of April, we were alerted that there was a good possibility that the La Salle River, which feeds into the Red River just north of the floodway, could spill its banks, causing serious flooding within the city limits. As a result, St. Norbert, a suburb at the extreme south of the city, was in danger. The city began to construct an earth dike in St. Norbert and more sandbagging was organized for that area. Meanwhile, in order to prevent overland flooding to reach the La Salle, the province took on the huge task of constructing a dike about thirty kilometers south of the city, which would run from the towns of Brunkhild to Domain. It became known as the Brunkhild dike but was also called the Z-dike, as it was shaped like a Z over a stretch of many acres of land. Government workers, private contractors, and the Canadian military helped to build this massive embankment. Farmers also lent a helping hand, using their own equipment to get the job done. The dike was constructed of crushed rock, clay, limestone, and sand. Time was not on the side of building this colossal dike, and crews were forced to work extremely long hours to get it done. Though it technically took three weeks to complete, most of the work was done in three days. The work site was open twenty-four hours a day. The military provided lighting at night, using flares and hovering overhead in helicopters. Hundreds of people worked brutally long hours. The area had the appearance of a war zone. Once built, the Brunkhild dike was forty-two kilometers (twenty-six miles) long and eight metres (twenty-six feet) high. It was a huge undertaking.

In what could only be described as another devastating blow, the small Manitoba town of Ste. Agathe was overcome by water on April 26th. This was a horrendous situation for the many residents of this small community. A number of circumstances contributed to the flooding of this town and to this day, the issue is still controversial. Bob Stefaniuk was the reeve at the time. He could not have fought any harder to save his municipality.

Plans for a worst-case scenario continued to evolve. Other towns just outside the city's perimeter — St. Germain, Vermette, and Grande Pointe — were also in jeopardy. The city purchased two additional sandbagging machines and thousands more bags were filled. A second mandatory evacuation was ordered for some residents living close to the river and in the suburb of St. Norbert. Many others within the city's limits were put on twenty-four-hour notice. Outside the city, at the floodway and near the dikes, bales of straw were being dumped on the banks to absorb moisture and curb erosion. It was simply fascinating to see and hear about the various strategies used at this late stage.

Throughout the crisis, drama unfolded "behind the scenes." While I don't think it would serve any purpose to regurgitate the details surrounding these issues, suffice it to say that we faced additional challenges during this crisis, which can only be referred to as "political." For example, in the middle of the chaos, we were advised that negotiations were taking place for a new national funding formula for states of emergency. This resulted in delays in having our city and province declared national disasters. Until the federal government officially declared a national state of emergency, we would receive no federal financial aid. There was no way that the Province or the City could possibly afford this national disaster. To be in a position of having to deal with negotiations at this particular time was, to me, mind-boggling. As mayor, my position was that the historic funding formula (which was eighty percent federal / twenty percent province and city) had to be honoured. In the end, the cost of the flood to the city was somewhat aligned with the historic formula.

The other political factor in play was that a federal election was called during the spring of 1997, for an election date of May 6th. According to the information I received, the river's crest was to be in Winnipeg prior to this day, so I was not opposed to the federal election. The fact remains, however, that many Winnipeg citizens took offence to having an election at such a challenging time.

On May 1st, the crest of the Red River finally passed through the city. Alf Warkentin's prediction that it would be in the range of 23.5 to 24.5 feet was correct. It was apparent at this point that all the hard work that had been done to protect the city appeared to have worked. As the waters headed through and around the city to Lockport, where the river would once again become one continuous flow, everyone in Winnipeg remained optimistic but cautious. Finally, the flood levels seemed to be flattening. We were, however, absolutely aware of the danger still being felt in the municipalities north of Winnipeg and the city of Selkirk and aware that they would be the next area likely to be impacted by this enormous flood.

On May 6th, for the first time in 1997, the floodgates were lowered slightly, slowly allowing the Red River its normal flow. It was a sign that the worst was now behind us. This may have been the first time in two months that I and most others in Winnipeg breathed a sigh of relief.

One incident that did occur around this time was that the forty-year-old Provencher Bridge, originally a lift bridge, had to be shut down. The high water level was causing the ballasts to fill with water and the bridge was beginning to lift. The bridge remained closed for a fair amount of time and structural damages had to be dealt with long after the flood threat was over. Years later, this bridge was completely rebuilt and its stunning new look has become the iconic landmark for the city of Winnipeg.

The 1997 flood was the biggest flood in a 100 year period. The Red River, normally less than a tenth of a kilometre (.062 mile), widened to fifty kilometers (over thirty miles) at its peak. At its crest, the flow of the Red River approaching Winnipeg was 138,000 cubic feet per second, enough water to fill Winnipeg's Pan Am Olympic Pool once every second. Approximately 8.1 million sandbags were filled and delivered by the city and 600,000 cubic meters (800,000 cubic yards) of clay was excavated for earth-dike construction. This was enough earth to fill the Winnipeg Football Stadium to a height of a twenty-storey building. The city's thirty-four pumping stations were in full operation and a total of 134 flap and positive gates in Winnipeg's sewer system were checked and operated.[17] The Red River Floodway was used to its absolute peak potential in 1997, triggering an eventual upgrade to the system many years later.

The generation who experienced this event firsthand will always refer to it as the Flood of the Century. For me personally, this was absolutely the most catastrophic event I had ever experienced. I witnessed unbelievable courage during a very difficult time. It was reinforced that Winnipeg is a resilient city whose residents can work together, tackle whatever is in front of them, and accomplish the impossible. I was never as proud of the citizens of Winnipeg as I was when I saw how they could rise to the occasion in a crisis situation. I was also touched by the generosity of my fellow Canadians. Response from across the country was overwhelming. People sent food, clothing, household and personal items, and cash.

Many entertainers scheduled to come to Winnipeg in the spring of 1997 shared part of their earnings for flood relief. Celtic rocker Leahy and the band KISS sold T-shirts at their concerts dedicated to flood relief. Local broadcaster Peter Warren spearheaded a campaign to raise hundreds of thousands of dollars for flood victims. A number of benefit concerts were organized, including a CBC national radio broadcast that was heard around the world. One of the largest events was held at The Forks in Winnipeg, organized by Tom Jackson. It also featured Susan Aglukark, Bruce Cockburn, and our very own Chantal Kreviazuk, Burton Cummings, and Randy Bachman. It was attended by many thousands of Winnipeggers, who showed their appreciation

17 Information in this paragraph obtained from the City of Winnipeg website - 1997 Flood Facts

with thank-you signs and massive cheers, especially for our military. All in all, more than $4 million was raised for flood relief through these events.

The financial costs of the 1997 Flood of the Century are difficult to gauge. In Winnipeg alone, the cost was pegged at $51 million. The province had its own set of costs. Some estimates have the cost pegged at over $500 million, when one takes into consideration the damage done to private properties and farmland and the cost of the fight efforts. More than the financial costs, the emotional toll was greater. The devastation created by this flood still affects me to this day. I will never forget the destruction, nor will I forget what I witnessed in the strength of the people in my city and province.

Six years after the Flood of the Century, I met a woman who had immigrated to Winnipeg from Argentina with her family in 1997. They arrived on April 5th, the day before the great blizzard. They were brought to their new home — an apartment complex in downtown Winnipeg. They arrived with no winter clothing and they had never seen a blizzard. When the storm arrived, their sponsors did their best to reach them with food and clothing. The family was frightened and despondent. And then the flood started...this crisis unfolding before their very eyes. They were glued to the TV set, trying to understand what was happening to their newly adopted city. Though they barely spoke any English, the family watched the daily televised conferences. That is where Marta Zylberman saw me, and began to refer to me as "her" mayor. There, they could see that people were trying to do something. They began to see countless volunteers helping to fill sandbags and build dikes. They saw people welcome evacuees into their homes. They saw people baking and cooking for people they didn't even know. They saw citizens working night and day to help protect and save our city. Marta, who is now a good friend, and who still calls me "my mayor," recounted to me once, "Susan, when we saw how the people of Winnipeg loved their city and would do everything they could to save it, we knew we had chosen the best city in the world in which to live. We were so touched by the dedication, commitment, and spirit of the people of Winnipeg. We have never looked back." Today, Marta and her husband Mauricio have successful careers, right here in Winnipeg, and are proud of their three grown children — a doctor of philosophy (and Rhodes Scholar), a gold-medal winning lawyer, and a doctor of psychiatry.

I have always loved the city of Winnipeg's motto, "One with the strength of many." I think it speaks volumes about our city and who we are. We are a city that pulls together and overcomes adversity with unwavering determination. The flood of 1997 showed exactly how much strength we had. Everybody did what they could to save our city...and we did save it...against enormous odds and Mother Nature herself.

A parade was held to honour our Canadian troops, who were instrumental in fighting the 1997 Flood of the Century.
(Photo courtesy of City of Winnipeg Archives)

The original cauldron of the flame for the 1999 Pan American Games is now located at The Forks in Winnipeg.

Chapter 10
The 1999 Pan American Games

So much can be written about the 1999 Pan American Games held in Winnipeg. The entire story really merits a book on its own. What I have attempted to do in this chapter is share in some highlights based on my own experiences. I added in some general knowledge about the games to put the story in context and also engaged in the help of many friends and colleagues who were part of this historic event.

The Pan American Games is the second-largest event to the Summer Olympics, bigger than the Winter Olympics in terms of athletes and larger than the Commonwealth Games in terms of the number of sports. In 1999, approximately 5,000 athletes from forty-two countries were involved. Over 20,000 people volunteered their services and the event had a budget of about $150 million. (Since 1999, the budget for the Pan American Games has risen substantially. In 2003, the Dominican Republic spent over $175 million. In 2012, the reported budget for the 2015 Pan American Games in Toronto was approximately $1.4 billion.[18])

When a country decides to bid for such an event, it is a huge undertaking. Financial backing from public and private sectors is required and many, many volunteers are counted upon to ensure

18 Information obtained from the May 11, 2012 press release from toronto2015.org, official website of the 2015 Pan American Games.

success. All three levels of government — federal, provincial and municipal — and corporations have to be on board. All said, it takes a lot of human effort and commitment. Luckily for Winnipeg in the early 1990s, it was a responsibility that a group of very dedicated people were most happy to take on and commitments from all levels were extraordinary.

Hosting the 1999 games in Winnipeg really began with our city having hosted the 1967 Pan American Games. Chaired at the time by William Culver Riley, a notable Manitoban with a great history in Manitoba sports, the 1967 games were an unequivocal success and set the stage for Winnipeg to take the honour of hosting again in the future.

Susan McMillan and I hosting two members of the Mexican soccer team at the 1967 Pan American Games in Winnipeg (Photo courtesy of City of Winnipeg Archives)

I remember the 1967 Pan American Games vividly. I was a student at the University of Winnipeg at the time and I wanted to get involved. Like so many other Winnipeggers, I decided to volunteer. I was assigned as a volunteer driver for some of the members of the Mexican soccer team...quite a thrill for a twenty-year-old girl living in Winnipeg. It was a lot of fun and I even learned to speak a little Spanish. I will never forget the pride I felt for all of Winnipeg and how much my world opened up as I met athletes from North, South, and Central America and the Caribbean. I remember thinking what a legacy these games were for our city and that if we were ever given the opportunity to do this again, I would want to be involved.

Years later, organizers of the very successful 1990 Western Canada Summer Games held in Winnipeg, began to discuss the possibility of a Pan Am bid. While organizing the summer games, they often asked, "How would we do it if we were hosting the Pan American Games?" As such, the legacy of the 1990 summer games was that it "laid the foundation" for the Pan Am bid and the eventual hosting of the 1999 Pan American Games. Don McKenzie and Barbara Huck became the volunteer co-chairs of the bid committee.

Don, a former junior hockey player who had played for the Winnipeg Rangers at age fifteen, was a dedicated volunteer in amateur sport. For many years, he coached hockey, football, and baseball, and served as director and president of both the Winnipeg Minor and Manitoba Amateur Hockey Associations. He served as president of the Manitoba Sports Federation and was vice-chair of the 1990 Western Canada Summer Games. His experience led him to be involved right from the get-go on the 1999 Pan American Games bid.

Barbara Huck, an award-winning journalist and broadcaster, was the first woman in Canada to win a national newspaper award for sports writing. Her volunteerism in local sports and her involvement in many sports events in Manitoba led her to play a major part in the 1999 Pan Am Games bid. Today, Barbara is a successful author and she and her husband Peter St. John are managing partners of Heartland and Associates, a local publishing firm.

Other members of the committee included Premier Gary Filmon and his wife Janice, Mayor Bill Norrie, and many dedicated Winnipeggers (too numerous to mention here) from the sports, business, and local tourism communities. When I became mayor, I was automatically a member of the committee, along with Mike Sterdan, manager of strategic initiatives with the city. We had an incredible team!

Even though I had just begun my first term, it was evident to me that Winnipeg needed to win this bid. It was important for the city to attract international attention. Hosting these games would certainly spur on some economic benefits for both the city and the province, and would also be a boost to the local tourism industry. On an internal level, the citizens of Winnipeg needed to feel better about their city...it was something to get excited about and instil pride. City Hall certainly recognized the importance of the games and prepared to invest both time and money, and do its part to make this event a huge success.

The Canadian Bid

In early December 1992, one week after the Grey Cup had been held in Toronto, and only one month after I was elected, the four city delegations were invited to make a presentation in Toronto to the Canadian Olympic Association (COA), who would ultimately choose Canada's representative to the Pan American Sports Organization (PASO). Who would have believed that twenty-five years after the 1967 Pan American Games, where I was a student volunteer, I would be the mayor of Winnipeg and a member of the 1999 Pan Am Bid Committee? Surreal! Yet here I was, just over a month since I had been elected in 1992, and I was on my way to Toronto for the Canadian bid. I was overjoyed to be involved at the ground level. It was the start of an amazing journey.

There were actually two bids required to host the Pan American Games. First, our city had to win a bid to be the only Canadian city to compete for the games. My first task as mayor was to be part of the Winnipeg delegation vying for this right. We needed to find ways to make Winnipeg the obvious choice to represent Canada in the bid for the 1999 Pan American Games, which was to be decided in the summer of 1994 in Guayaquil, Ecuador. The 1994 bid would involve forty-two countries including Canada, the United States, and Mexico, and a host of other countries in Central America, the Caribbean, and South America. According to the Pan American Games selection process, only one city per country is allowed to apply for the bid to host.

Four cities were in the running for the Canadian bid — Edmonton, Sherbrooke, Toronto, and Winnipeg. There were rumours that the provinces of Alberta and Quebec were putting all of their energy into bids by Calgary and Québec City for the 2002 Winter Olympics, so that left Toronto as our main competitor. Then in late November, Toronto hosted the 1992 Grey Cup, and it was not nearly as successful as this annual Canadian Football League extravaganza tends to be in other cities. Torontonians were unabashedly apathetic, the stands were half empty and there were fewer pre-game events than usual. They even cancelled the Grey Cup Parade. Fortuitously for us, Winnipeg had hosted the 1991 Grey Cup and it had been an overwhelming success. Despite the minus thirty-degree weather, the game was a sell-out. Our Pan Am bid committee believed that this would bode well for Winnipeg.

Over a two-day period, a number of breakfasts, dinners, and receptions were organized for the bid committees of each of the cities. All of these events were wonderful opportunities to mingle with members of the other delegations and the delegates of the COA. We arrived in Toronto late Friday evening. Each city had a "hospitality room" and on Saturday morning, we immediately set up the Winnipeg room. While our three contenders set up the typical "wine and cheese" format, Winnipeg went for something a little different. A few weeks before the bid, members of our committee had asked many bakeries in Winnipeg if they could create a special dessert for us to bring to Toronto. What transpired was nothing short of extraordinary. Over thirty bakeries responded and off we went to Toronto with boxes of cakes and pastries, some with the city logo, one with the

Province of Manitoba crest, others with our Pan Am Bid Committee logo, and all beautifully decorated and unique. Committee members hand-carried these decadent desserts, bringing them onto the plane on their way to Toronto. The committee actually purchased extra seats on the plane so that the boxes could be very carefully placed there and held by a seatbelt. Once at the hotel, they were placed on an outside balcony, where it was as cool as a refrigerator but not freezing. We had purposely booked a room with a balcony for this reason. After all, it was December. The cakes beautifully decorated our reception room.

Festival du Voyageur reps Marcelle and Gabriel Forest accompanied the bid committee to Toronto (Photo courtesy of City of Winnipeg Archives)

Our bid team proved to be excellent hosts. Our hospitality room superbly showcased our city and our province. One of our committee members, Harvey Nairn, had gone into the streets of Toronto to find a real Christmas tree, which we decorated for the occasion. We set up tables that featured all the decadent desserts and we waited in anticipation for the COA delegates to arrive. Each committee member wore a white, long sleeved sweater with our Pan Am Bid Committee logo imprinted on the upper right shoulder. All of us were in a cheerful mood and couldn't wait to greet our guests. Gabrielle and Marcelle Forest, representatives of the Festival du Voyageur, Winnipeg's annual French-Canadian festival held each February, joined us. They were in full voyageur dress and warmly welcomed every guest who came through our doors in both official languages. The COA held meetings all day Saturday. They were then scheduled to visit each hospitality room, once they had eaten dinner. We had heard that their dinner would not include dessert, so we were intent on bringing them into our room to sample our sumptuous cakes. Their meetings ran a little late, as did their dinner, and we were the last visit on their schedule, so we became concerned that they might not get to us. Spontaneously, Janice Filmon and I visited the Toronto hospitality room to see what was happening. While we were there, we decided to invite everyone — COA delegates and other bid city members alike — to the Winnipeg room for dessert. We specifically zeroed in on two delegates from Sherbrooke, Québec and brought them back to our hospitality room. We then proceeded to the Sherbrooke and Edmonton hospitality rooms and invited them as well. Soon after our visits, guests started to arrive. Within an hour, our room was full of people.

Though all our desserts were elegantly placed on a row of tables, no one seemed to be going there. We needed to take action. Janice Filmon and I got behind the table and started cutting up the cakes, putting them on plates and serving them to the delegates. It worked like a charm. Everyone was impressed by the delicious desserts and by our hospitality. At one point, we even had our premier serving drinks to our guests. We did what we needed to do to get the job done.

Guests from the other delegations noticed. One committee member from Edmonton standing at our door was heard saying, "No wonder everyone is here... Winnipeg knows how to have fun." Another delegate from Toronto was quite impressed to see both the premier of Manitoba and the mayor of Winnipeg at the event and quickly said to one of her organizers, "Get on the phone and get somebody down here." The important thing is that we had all these people from the other delegations in our room when the COA delegates arrived. Our team had the opportunity to talk to everyone and we built relationships with our competitors, which boded well for us in the final voting stages. By the end of the evening, I believe everyone was in the Winnipeg hospitality room. Some stayed as late as two a.m. It was a huge success.

Presentations were to be held early Sunday morning. We'd heard rumblings that Toronto had a lock on the win, but we hoped that we had the support of the delegates from Sherbrooke. I remember thinking at one point that I did not want to return to Winnipeg having lost the bid just a month after becoming mayor. Perhaps this inspired me to really try to make this happen, and I took every opportunity I could to influence the other delegates. I recall that as our team made its way up to front to make our presentation, one of the Québec delegates took my hand and wished me good luck. A kind gesture, I thought, and a good omen.

And then it was our turn to make our presentation. Premier Filmon and I addressed the COA delegates. We played a video that showcased our city and province superbly — in both official languages — in English by Janice Filmon and in French by Maurice Gauthier. The entire presentation was professional and spoken with passion and enthusiasm. We boasted about Winnipeg's capacity to host the games, our friendliness, and our tremendous community spirit, and assured the committee that our entire city would get involved, especially the corporate and volunteer sectors. The video included testimonies from many prominent Winnipeggers, including athletes, entertainers, and business people, about how Winnipeg was the best choice to host the Games. This was not a consultant-prepared bid.

It was a bid from the entire community and it demonstrated confidence, competency, and heart. All Winnipeggers and Manitobans would have been very proud of how we masterfully represented our city and our province.

Then we had to wait. There were three separate votes. The first voting results were: Toronto 17, Winnipeg 15, Sherbrooke 10, Edmonton 3. This forced Edmonton to drop out and another vote occurred...and yet another wait. On the second ballot, the vote results were: Toronto 21, Winnipeg 14, Sherbrooke 10. This meant that the Edmonton votes had all gone to Toronto and somewhere along the line, we lost one. Yikes! With Sherbrooke dropping out in this second round, we knew that we needed their support in the next round. Luckily, we had made some friendships with many of them over the course of the weekend and we felt as confident as we could, given the circumstances. The final vote occurred just before six p.m. Yet again we had to wait for the final decision. The adrenalin was just pumping inside everyone in the room. Our bid committee had done its best to make a case for Winnipeg, and just before seven p.m. we headed to the room where the press conference was being held. The front of the room was set up with a stage and a podium. As well, a table and three chairs were set up on the stage, where the actual signing of the Pan American Games bid document would occur. Towards the back of the room were four long tables, two on each side of a middle aisle, for each of the delegation teams to sit. The Winnipeg table was directly behind Toronto's team. The bid cities were ushered to their tables. The room was jammed with media, which included a lot of reporters from Winnipeg. After what seemed like an eternity, Carol Anne Letheren, who was the CEO of the Canadian Olympic Association at the time, walked into the room with the rest of the COA delegates. She approached the podium and began to speak. At this point, media moved to the middle aisle and began to swarm around the Toronto table, standing directly in front of us. I thought to myself, *Toronto obviously has this*, and then just a split second later I heard Carol Anne say, "...and the winning bid city for the 1999 Pan American Games is...WINNIPEG." Suddenly,

TV cameras literally swung around to our table and captured Gary Filmon and me giving each other a huge high-five. I am sure you could have heard my scream of delight all the way back in Winnipeg. What a moment! Before you knew it, Don McKenzie, Barbara Huck, and I were up on stage to sign the bid document. While I was up on stage, a member of the Winnipeg media came up to me and asked if I wanted to know the final vote count. Of course I did. He took a small piece of paper and pushed it towards me saying, "You will want to see this." And there it was. We had won by only one vote. Final results were Winnipeg 22, Toronto 21. This confirmed that most of the Sherbrooke delegates had come to us. At that point, all that mattered was that we had won.

The delegates from Toronto, Sherbrooke, and Edmonton, though disappointed, were very gracious in defeat. They all came to celebrate with us and wished us luck in the next stage of the process.

The entire process was very nerve-wracking but also extremely exhilarating. When it was announced that Winnipeg would advance into the next step in the bid process, the elation was felt by every member of our delegation. It was also a reality check. As one of our committee members said, "Like a sports team that wins their division, the celebration is short-lived when the realization sets in that this is only a step in the ultimate goal."* Being part of the bid process was a great opportunity. I was so honoured to be there in person when we won. After it was all over, it didn't take long to recognize that we now would have to do it all over again in front of the Pan American Sports Organization (PASO) in Ecuador in 1994. It was a challenge we were all prepared to take.

The Bid to Host the Games

No sooner were we back in Winnipeg and the quest to win the bid to host the 1999 Pan American Games was underway. We had eighteen months, from December 1992 to August 1994, to regroup, strengthen our structure, and create another successful bid. The core of the bid committee remained the same, but others were added in strategic areas.

The Winnipeg bid committee immediately arranged to meet with Dick Pound, who was an executive member of the Canadian Olympic Committee and one of only two Canadian members of the International Olympic Committee (the other being Carol Anne Letheren, who had "seen us in action" during the Canadian bid and was definitely on side). Our co-chairs, Barbara Huck and Don McKenzie met with Dick Pound in Montreal to seek his support and advice. This meeting was less than encouraging. Mr. Pound bluntly told them that chances were very slim that Winnipeg would ever be awarded the Games. He assured them that the Pan American Games were regarded as a "Latin American" sports event and he understood the two other countries in the running — Colombia and the Dominican Republic — had much better chances at winning than Winnipeg did. He basically told them to drop the bid. The organizing committee was not prepared to do that, and so we forged on, regardless of what Mr. Pound thought. I found out much later, years after the games were held, in fact, that he did eventually "get on board," supported us wholeheartedly, and did what he could to influence the delegates.

The next order of business was to meet with the President of PASO, Mr. Mario Vasquez-Raña, a very powerful and wealthy Mexican media mogul and a champion of sports. Mr. Vasquez-Raña was also the owner of a large Latin American newspaper business and through this affiliation, he had personally interviewed many heads of state over the years. From these conversations, he had written a series of books entitled *Dialogues with History*. Among the extensive list of leaders he had interviewed were Fidel Castro, Mao Tse Tung, Nikita Kruschev, and many, many more. When our co-chairs went to meet the chair of PASO at his office in Mexico City, they were accompanied by the Canadian Ambassador to Mexico. At this meeting, Mr. Vasquez-Raña indicated that he had never interviewed a Canadian Prime Minister and expressed an interest in interviewing Jean Chrétien. They then went on to discussing the matter at hand — the chances of Winnipeg being awarded the Pan American Games. Mr. Vasquez-Raña remained non-committal. Nonetheless, the visit proved to be successful. Through the Canadian Ambassador, Mr. Vasquez-Raña did eventually meet with Prime Minister Chrétien and was quite pleased that this was accomplished. This was an important and influencing factor in our bid for the Pan Am Games.

Some members of the bid committee: Michael Moore, Ken Faulder, me, Ron Paulson (barely visible) and Janice Filmon (Photo courtesy of City of Winnipeg Archives)

A very important aspect of the bid strategy was to make personal contact with each voting delegate in each country. Mike Sterdan clearly recalls a great piece of advice our committee received just after the Canadian bid. Roger Jackson, a representative of the Canadian Olympic Committee told us to focus on making friends with the members of PASO. He advised that Central and South Americans, in particular, were all about friendship and being comfortable with those with whom they associate. He further advised that handshakes went a long way and in some cases, formed agreements, and that we should focus less on technical information. This was a major mindset for us. Our committee was really good at detailing plans and competencies, but not necessarily comfortable hugging and kissing new acquaintances, as is common in the Latin culture.

Throughout 1993, the bid committee invited some of the PASO delegates to visit us in Winnipeg. We saw this as an important step, not only to extend our hospitality and friendship, but also to show them that our infrastructure was already in place and we were well-equipped to host the games. Having successfully hosted the 1967 Pan American Games, we knew their requirements. We knew what was needed and we knew we could accommodate. We had developed important relationships as a result of the 1967 Games and we had a good reputation among members of PASO. 1967 was a busy year in Canada. It was Canada's centennial and there were celebrations across the country. Montreal also hosted Expo 67 that year. Despite all the festivities, the 1967 Pan Am Games "held their own" and were most successful.

The organizing committee knew it was of utmost importance that the PASO delegates see Winnipeg's huge and highly effective volunteer capacity. Strategically, we invited them to come during Folklorama, the city's annual multicultural festival held each summer. This absolutely worked in our favour. Our extensive volunteer base was fully evident and the multiculturalism of our city shone brightly. It must be noted that Winnipeg is a very diverse city, like a mini world, with over eighty ethnic groups living in the city. This made delegates feel very much at home in Winnipeg. We ensured that each delegate was greeted by natives of their own country who were now living in Winnipeg, and they were spoken to in their own language. Many members, including Mario Vasquez-Raña, came up for a visit in August 1993. All of them were pleased and surprised by our hospitality and friendliness. It was in Winnipeg in 1993 that I first met Mr. Vasquez-Raña and we immediately connected. Perhaps it was because I waited at the private jet hangar for him five hours later than he was scheduled to arrive. His plane pulled up at two o'clock in the morning. We had a limo waiting for him and took him to his hotel. By then, only two bid committee members were left...me and Don McKenzie. Mario liked to call me Suzanna; I would call him Mario. I always felt that we understood and respected each other. I am certain he knew emphatically that I would do everything I personally could to make the Pan American Games an outstanding success if Winnipeg were to get them. Just prior to this visit, Winnipeg was experiencing a summer of torrential rains that had left the city with flooded rivers, streets, and basements and city hall was overwhelmed with calls for help. This circumstance required me to maximize my time with the PASO delegates to the best of my abilities. I only hoped that this unusual weather did not impede Winnipeg's chances of getting the games.

From left to right: Barbara Huck, Paquita Vasquez-Rãna, Mario Vasquez-Rãna, me, Don McKenzie, Hector Vergara and Peter St. John (Photo courtesy of City of Winnipeg Archives)

Next on the agenda was to lobby on their own turf the forty-two countries who were part of the Pan American Games organization. It was not possible to get every voting delegate to come to Winnipeg, and it was equally important that we go to them. The committee immediately went to work arranging trips to meet with PASO delegates. Over the course of a year and a half, approximately thirty members of our committee travelled in groups to meet with most of the nearly 300 delegates to seek their support. My assignment was to be part of the team that would visit PASO delegates in Poncé, Puerto Rico during the Central American and Caribbean Games in November 1993. I distinctly remember this trip. In all my travels over the years, this trip still rates as one of the most hellish I've ever taken. First of all, I had to take three planes over an eighteen-hour period to get to Puerto Rico. I travelled alone and I was to meet other members of the committee the next day. I flew in to San Juan in the late evening on the 500th anniversary of the founding of San Juan. You can just imagine the pandemonium.

Needless to say, it took a very long time to get to my hotel — near midnight by the time I pulled up to the hotel entrance. I could see right away that this was a most modest hotel. The lobby's décor consisted of a fluorescent-tube ceiling light above a small registration desk and two orange plastic chairs off to the side for guests. I checked in, hoping to catch a bit of sleep before meeting other members of my party for a very early morning ride to Poncé, which was on the other side of the island. I could think of nothing better than to sink into a nice comfortable bed and get some shut-eye after such a long travel day. Instead, when I stepped into the hotel room, I saw the carpet move. It turned out that the room I was to sleep in was infested with cockroaches. As quickly as I stepped into the room, I picked up my bags and walked out. I went to the lobby to see if another room was available. Unfortunately, there wasn't one, and they couldn't do anything about the state of the room at this time of night. I chose to sleep in the lobby, sitting in one of the plastic orange chairs, until my ride arrived. I barely slept of course and by this time, I had been in the same clothes for close to twenty-four hours.

At seven a.m. some members of the Winnipeg bid committee came to pick me up in a van with a Puerto Rican driver and we were on our way to Poncé. The ride there should have been no more than three hours. Shortly after leaving the outskirts of San Juan, the van broke down. The driver and the others in the van all stepped outside, looked under the hood of the vehicle, and had a long conversation, but nobody seemed to know what was wrong. I sat in the van — exhausted, dishevelled, and suffering from the sweltering heat. I had nothing to add. This was at a time when there were no cellphones and it felt like we were the middle of nowhere. Eventually, the driver got the van going and it sputtered all the way to Poncé. Just as we pulled up to the hotel, it died again. What did I care; we had made it. I frantically unloaded my luggage and literally ran into the hotel. Thank goodness for one of the committee members, who had arranged for me to have a room to "freshen up." Surprisingly, we were able to make our presentation to the Puerto Rican delegates on time at one p.m.

The bid committee spent a few days enjoying some of the festivities surrounding the Central American and Caribbean Games. Each of us was assigned to the PASO delegates in attendance and each of us prepared ahead of time and got background information on each delegate before we met them. We knew the importance of getting to know the delegates and our due diligence paid off. We left Poncé confident that we had impressed those that needed impressing. We all followed up as soon as we returned home with thank-you notes to each of the delegates that we had met.

We encountered complications on our return trip. We were to return via Air Canada from San Juan. Unfortunately, airline workers were about to go on strike and flights were being rerouted across the globe. Our flight from San Juan was cancelled. As fate would have it, a few of our committee members knew some people in high places at Air Canada, and after a few telephone calls and much negotiation, we managed to have a chartered plane diverted from Jamaica to San Juan to pick us up. We were sworn to confidentiality and told that if we were asked by anyone, this never happened. Thank goodness for Winnipeggers and their connections.

In each of these meetings with the PASO delegates, our strategy was simple — find out what we needed to do to get the votes in Winnipeg's favour. It was a highly political process and some of what we found out turned out to be quite shocking to us. We understood that we needed to prove to them that we had the infrastructure and the manpower to get the job done. What we didn't expect was the rumour that offerings of money and other "incentives" would be helpful in order to get the necessary votes. While this suggestion was made to many of us, we politely told them that would not occur. We did however find some creative ways to help some of the impoverished countries that had requested our aid. For example, a number of older, wooden desks from our local school divisions were donated to some Caribbean nations in need. These desks were transported there via a number of older school buses, which were also donated.

Another interesting side story about the Pan American Games is how rock legend Burton Cummings got involved. On one occasion, during one of Barbara Huck's many trips to Mexico and South America, she sat in the back of a cab and a recognizable song came on the radio. "That's Burton Cummings" said Barbara. "Isn't that interesting that we would hear one of his songs down here!" At once, the cab driver began to say loudly "Yes, 'gazoo'" and he repeated it two or three times. Barbara had no idea what the cabbie meant. The cab driver elaborated. "Burton Cummings," pointing to the radio, "is gazoo." What he was saying was the "Guess Who." The driver then went on to say that he liked the Guess Who "muchissimo." This would be the point in time when a decision was made to call Burton and ask him if he could help us with our bid presentation. The end result was that he was willing to write his own song. Burton wrote a great song called "Winnipeg — The Song for Pan Am," and it was a beautiful addition to our bid presentation video. He even sang in Spanish in some sections of the song...very touching for many of the PASO delegates. Burton was asked to join us in Ecuador for the presentation itself, but was unable to attend. He did however stay involved, and he was asked to perform at the Pan Am closing ceremonies once we won the bid. This performance ended up being a Guess Who reunion, a historic moment in Canadian music history. As mayor, I had the pleasure of hosting Burton and his mother Rhoda at city hall. This was to thank him for his contributions to the Pan Am Games.

When Mr. Vasquez-Raña's meeting with the prime minister was finally scheduled, Barbara Huck and I went to Ottawa to meet with Mr. Vasquez-Raña and the Mexican Ambassador to Canada at the time, Sandra Fuentes. A few events had been specially arranged for Mr. Vasquez-Raña and his wife. One was at the Mexican Ambassador's official residence. Ambassador Fuentes hosted a phenomenal dinner for twelve that even featured a mariachi band. We were out to impress him. His interview with Prime Minister Chrétien, which was originally only scheduled for twenty minutes, ended up lasting almost ninety-plus. Mr. Vasquez-Raña was very pleased. From that point on, we felt that he was much more supportive of our bid.

In July 1994, our Winnipeg delegation went to Guayaquil, Ecuador to present our bid for the Pan American Games. Guayaquil is Ecuador's largest city — over 1.5 million people in the city alone — and it had its challenges and dangers. Our time there was focused on the bid and a few special events. I was pleased to meet the mayor of the city, Leon Febres-Cordero, who had previously been the president of Ecuador. When I arrived to meet with him, I was told that their city hall had just been raided and their air conditioning units had been stolen. It was an interesting visit, to say the least. We had a nice visit but he was definitely preoccupied with other matters. Our delegation also attended a few private dinners on the days preceding the bid presentations.

At one particular dinner, I sat beside a delegate from Cuba, a country that held two votes. I asked him unequivocally if Winnipeg could have both votes. He told me that he could only give us one and elaborated that his country needed to split their vote to keep their relationships with other countries balanced. He considered all three countries friends of Cuba.

The evening before the presentations, each city once again hosted hospitality rooms. By then, we had found out that the hotel chef was from Canada, and though we could not replicate our dessert extravaganza in Toronto for the Canadian bid, we did have the Canadian chef create a cake for us with the Canadian Bid Committee logo on it and a beautiful ice sculpture of a maple leaf. This was equally impressive.

The day finally came when it was time to make our presentation. Once again, we had a highly professional oral and video presentation. We paid attention to every detail, including how we were dressed. Women wore red suits and white blouses; the men all wore suits with "Pan Am" ties. One by one, members of our team went up and made their case for Winnipeg. When I addressed the crowd, I couldn't help but tell the story of being a student at the University of Winnipeg during the 1967 Pan Am Games, of being a volunteer at that time for the Mexican Soccer Team, of being at the closing ceremonies with my father, both of us standing in the pouring rain, and thinking at that moment, *If I ever get a chance to bring the Pan Am Games back to*

Winnipeg, I will. And here I was twenty-eight years later, the mayor of Winnipeg, standing in front of 300 PASO delegates asking them to reunite our Pan American family in Winnipeg in 1999. **What a moment. Serendipity indeed.**

Our overall presentation was outstanding. Each and every member put his or her heart and soul into it. We turned on our "Winnipeg hospitality" all the time that we were there and we were recognized and complimented for our friendliness. We felt confident that we had won over a few votes from the many South American delegates we had met and courted in the last two years. At one point, Mario Vasquez-Raña announced that the city that had never hosted the Pan American Games before would likely get it. This cut us out of the picture. Then, moments later, the first vote was announced and Colombia did not garner enough votes to move on. After the second ballot, Winnipeg and Santo Domingo were tied. *Are you kidding me?* I thought. Welcome to politics! In my mind, there was no conceivable way that Santo Domingo could field the calibre of games that Winnipeg could. However, this was the situation we were in and we had ten minutes to lobby the room before the next vote. Immediately, I thought of the Cuban delegate I had spoken to the evening before. Would he be able to swing his second vote our way? I found this delegate and we had another conversation. I told him emphatically "I can't go back to Canada if we don't win these games." He said to me "Where will you go?" "Cuba," I replied. We had a good laugh and I felt that I had done all that I could do. I believe that in the end, Cuba gave us both votes.

I so vividly remember when Mario Vasquez-Raña finally made his way to the stage to make the final announcement. I was staring at him intently, not taking my eyes off of him for a moment. I am sure he felt the intensity of "my look." I'm told to this day that this "look" can be very daunting. In any case, I think he knew what I was thinking. He announced "Winnipeg," caught a glimpse of me and flashed his huge smile. Once again, we all rose to our feet and were absolutely ecstatic. It was pandemonium and a moment I will never forget. All the hard work over the last two years had paid off and we couldn't have been happier with the result. We knew we were ready and we could not wait to get home to start the real work...to create an event that would be the pride of our city, our province, and our country.

I truly believe that our warmth, trust and sincerity shone through and helped us to win the bid. Such virtues translate into any language. The PASO delegates got to know us and we got to know them. We impressed them. They trusted us. They believed us when we said we could do this. None of us knew what the final tally was; it could have been overwhelmingly in our favour or it could have been by one vote. All that mattered was that we could not be denied. After years of hard work, Winnipeg had won the right to host the 1999 Pan American Games. As a member of the bid committee and as mayor of our great city, I could not have been more proud.

After the Bid...and on to the Games

Sandy Riley, Mario Vasquez-Rãna and Don McKenzie visit City Hall to discuss the games (Photo courtesy of City of Winnipeg Archives)

Now the real work was to begin. We needed to find a way to produce the best games ever. Soon after we won the bid, a new committee was formed to work on the games themselves. I had the distinguished honour of appointing the chair for the Games. I appointed Sandy Riley (whose uncle Culver Riley, coincidentally, chair of the 1967 Winnipeg Pan Am Games). Sandy competed in sailing at the 1975 Pan

Am Games and the 1976 Olympics. I chose Sandy because he is as talented an organizer and as proud a Winnipegger as you can find. His prominence in the city could not be overlooked and in my mind, he was the best person for the job.

Those most closely involved in the bid continued on in some capacity on the organizing committee. Some became staff members; others continued in a volunteer role. The transformation was quite seamless. Shortly after Sandy was named chair, the Pan American Games Society was formed, and Don McKenzie became president and CEO. A number of business and community leaders became involved, chairing various committees. Management and staff were hired and the large task of organizing every aspect of the 1999 Pan American Games in Winnipeg began. I became less involved in the operational side, but always kept abreast of what was happening. My political role was to attend press conferences, receptions, and other official functions as needed. I did my best to be as well-prepared as possible and to represent the city of Winnipeg in a first-class manner.

In 1995, the resort city of Mar Del Plata, Argentina hosted the Pan American Games. Many members of the Winnipeg organizing committee went to these games, as an opportunity to observe and learn. The next games were to be in Winnipeg, so it was important that we examine what worked well. As mayor, I attended the closing ceremonies and took part in the traditional handing of the Pan Am flag from mayor to mayor. In a bizarre turn of events, the mayor of Mar Del Plata was under investigation and had just been recalled to Buenos Aires. Instead, Mario Vasquez-Raña, as the president of PASO, presented the flag to me.

By the time the Pan American Games occurred, I was no longer mayor, as I stayed true to my commitment to only run for two terms, which ended October 1998. The federal government appointed me as one of two ambassadors to the games. I spent most of my days at Canada House, which was situated in what is now the Manitoba Theatre for Young People at The Forks. This was a brand-new building and the Government of Canada had set up an exposition of sports memorabilia, specifically for guests of the games. I also spent some time driving guests who were in Winnipeg for the games. In particular, I spent a few days driving the then Mexican ambassador to Canada. I found it serendipitous that in 1967 I had chauffeured the Mexican Soccer Team and at these 1999 games, I had "upgraded" to the Mexican ambassador. I also spent some time at the airport greeting guests as they arrived and I attended a number of events, including the closing ceremonies. In his closing ceremony speech, Mario Vasquez-Raña was most gracious and respectful in publicly acknowledging my role in obtaining the Pan American Games for Winnipeg in 1999. I was most appreciative of his kind words.

My involvement in bringing the 1999 Pan American Games to Winnipeg will always remain one of the major highlights of my life. This highly successful event made Winnipeggers believe in themselves again. At the closing ceremonies, Mario Vasquez Rãna proclaimed, "These were the best games ever!" and they were...we ALL felt it. We became a "can do" city. We went on to host many other major events including the World Indigenous Games, the World Junior Hockey Championships, the Brier, the Junos...the list goes on and on. The 1999 Pan American Games is one of Winnipeg's greatest legacies. It did something to our city's psyche and it displayed our spirit to the entire western hemisphere. As Sandy Riley once told me, "The success of the games galvanized the corporate community and it reignited the spirit and sense of pride of Winnipeggers. It revitalized the downtown and strengthened our province's already strong ethnic heritage." I was most proud to be from Winnipeg and most honoured to represent my city during this historic moment in time.

46 PAGES

Winnipeg Free Press

50¢

Thursday, May 4, 1995

■ *Hockey love affair ends in tears, bitterness*

■ *City to feel pinch in lost revenue, jobs*

Gone!

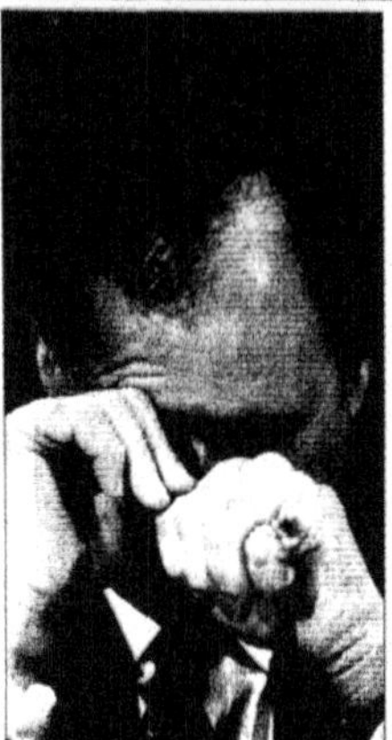

Shenkarow shows the strain of failed efforts to save Jets.

By John Douglas
Business Reporter

WINNIPEG'S 23-YEAR love affair with major league hockey ended yesterday in tears and recriminations.

Manitoba Entertainment Complex chairman John Loewen told an afternoon news conference, "This is going to hurt for a while but the facts are the NHL is not prepared to make hockey a viable sport in small-market cities like Winnipeg."

David McKeigan, 34, a fan who had put down $6,000 for two club seats next season, joined an impromptu protest at Portage Avenue and Main Street. "We've been stabbed in the back by rich people," he said. "I can't believe this. It's like someone died."

At the press conference in the ballroom of the Westin Hotel, 14-year Jets veteran Thomas Steen rushed from his seat, overcome with emotion.

Loewen, Jets president Barry Shenkarow, Premier Gary Filmon and Mayor Susan Thompson tried to put a brave face on the bleak news. Most blamed the National Hockey League and its trend to huge markets and huge payrolls. The league, they said, is too big for Winnipeg and cities like Ottawa, Quebec City, Calgary and Edmonton.

"We have reached the point where we are not prepared to pay the price, the NHL price," said Thompson as she choked back tears.

The city and the province stand to clear about $10 million each from the sale of the public's 36 per cent share of the club. That is offset by a loss of $21 million in direct taxes, $47.5 million in economic activity and 1,400 jobs the club generated.

Winnipeg has also lost the NHL draft in July. The week-long event would have brought about $16 million to the local economy.

When it came his turn to speak, Shenkarow was moved to tears.

Later, he said he has given two interested buyers 48 hours to put bids together to get the Jets into Minneapolis by week's end. Sources say the price is about $70 million US.

MEC spokesman Bob Silver said the deal to purchase the team and build a 16,000-seat arena was mortally wounded last week when NHL commissioner Gary Bettman set tough conditions for the sale of the Jets.

"The corpse was on life support after last Thursday but none of us were brave enough to pull the plug until (Tuesday)," Silver said.

Filmon faced the toughest questions, mostly from citizens who accused him of using the Jets to win votes last week.

"I voted for you, Gary, so you would save the Jets, I won't do it again," one woman shouted.

Filmon, almost overtaken by emotion himself, ignored the protests. He said that up until Tuesday, he was prepared to break his first election promise and put more than $10 million into the Jets-arena deal. The final provincial contribution could have topped $50 million.

"This is a day that I certainly never thought would come to pass and one that I certainly hoped would never come to pass," he said. But "the potential risk for the public and private sectors is too great."

He said he didn't know about the NHL's strict conditions, or the situation facing the MEC, until after the election.

Jets' fans and employees react to news that the Jets will be leaving Winnipeg.

As the dream perishes, a boy cries on his bed

By Randy Turner
Sports Reporter

LIKE ANY good eight-year-old hockey fan, Scott Mansbridge listened to the last Winnipeg Jets game on the radio, in the darkness of his bedroom, though he was supposed to be asleep.

That's what Scott always did, since the day a few years ago when he became a Jets junkie. But this was not like the other games.

Scott cried all the way through the third period.

"I was really sad," he said on the day the Jets died. "I don't want them to leave."

But leave they will, and it's a reminder of the hold this game of big business can have on little boys and girls, who dream in the dark of playing in the big leagues themselves some day.

They won't be dreaming of the Winnipeg Arena, however. Not any more.

"It's so much a part of their youth and so much a part of their upbringing," Scott's mother, Ellen, said. "It's like somebody died."

Scott was still wearing his Jets' jersey yesterday and his cap, too, after his parents told him the team was gone for keeps. They knew he'd take it hard, so they broke it to him gently.

"As a parent, your heart goes out when that happens," Ellen Mansbridge said.

But little boys were not the only Winnipeggers bemoaning the loss of the Winnipeg Jets.

"I almost feel like I've lost my best friend," said Brenda Thompson, one of 35 Jets' office staff who found herself unemployed yesterday.

A handful of young fans could be found at Portage Avenue and Main Street, where the Jets signed Bobby Hull before most of them were born, trying to ring out the battle cry — "Save our Jets" — one last time.

Nick Orford, 22, was bounding through the intersection, waving a Jets' jersey in front of passing cars like a bullfighter.

"These are the most loyal fans I've ever seen," said Orford, a former Vancouverite.

Winnipeg is in mourning, said sports psychologist Cal Botterill.

"The loss of the Jets is like ripping the heart and guts out of our community," Botterill said. "Hopefully our struggling society will pull itself up and get on with life."

Scott will, too. He plans to keep following the former Jets and his favorite player, Alex Zhamnov.

Wherever they may be.

Thompson sheds tear at yesterday's emotional news conference.

Hockey night in Winnipeg will return, promoter vows

By Dave Supleve and Steve Lyons
Sports Reporters

SPORTS PROMOTER Jeff Thompson promised last night there will be hockey nights to come in Winnipeg.

And Manitoba Entertainment Complex chairman John Loewen said his group will do all it can to see it played in a new arena.

Thompson, president of Woody Sports and a partner in the Winnipeg Goldeyes baseball club, said: "There will be hockey in Winnipeg. Whether it's the Western Hockey League, the International League or whatever, we will have hockey."

And Coun. Bill Clement (Charleswood-Fort Garry), past president of Winnipeg Enterprises Corp., said WEC will be meeting the IHL in the near future.

"I'm aware that there have been some conversations," Tim Bryant, IHL vice-president of communications, said yesterday, "but not to the point where anybody has put any money on the table.

"Serious interest is only when somebody puts the required $500,000 application fee in with the intent of putting something together in the next few weeks."

The IHL charged San Francisco and Orlando $6 million expansion fees to join the league for the 1995-96 season and Bryant said that price tag will likely jump to $8 million in the next expansion wave.

Other IHL entrance requirements include a population of close to one million, an arena with at least 10,000 seats, strong ownership, a good lease agreement and healthy corporate support.

"I suppose (Winnipeg) would be a possibility," Bryant said.

Clement said Winnipeg's population is no problem. "I can tell you, the IHL has no problem with the City of Winnipeg."

BOTH THOMPSON and Clement said it would be difficult to have a team for the 1995-96 season, and 1996-97 was more likely.

Up to this week, Thompson was working to bring a WHL major junior team to Winnipeg as a second tenant in a new arena. The junior club would have had ties to the Jets, just as the WHL's Calgary Hitmen will have with the NHL Flames.

"The intention never was to solely have a WHL team," Thompson said. "I had full intention of doing a WHL team in conjunction with the Winnipeg Jets. The circumstances now are obviously different. I think what we're going to do is re-examine the entire hockey situation."

A WHL expansion team will now cost $750,000, with additional start-up costs pushing the tab beyond $1 million.

Loewen said his group of 70 business people will continue to work toward building a new arena.

"We can't leave it up to the public sector to do everything," he said.

MEC member George Sigurdson said the group will meet after a brief period of "mourning."

"We are people who want to make this a better place, and we can't keep asking government to do it," he said.

TODAY

Quote of the Day

"They are forgetting the small amount of chicken feed that will keep alive the goose that could lay the golden egg."

– Hugh Campbell, a seed company owner and former farmer from Saskatchewan, wonders if the federal and provincial governments understand the benefits of shipping grain through Churchill.

Details on page B9

The Weather

Today: Morning showers then sunny. High 12. Low zero. **Tomorrow:** Mainly sunny and milder. High 15.

Sun Rises: 6:00 a.m. **Sets:** 8:50 p.m. **Moon Rises:** 9:20 a.m. **Sets:** 12:57 a.m.

Details on page C11

Inside

Lotto 6/49

5, 16, 17, 32, 45, 46, Bonus 10.

Winnipeg Free Press, May 4, 1995. Reprinted with permission (Photo of Susan taken by Phil Hossack)

Chapter 11
The Loss of the Winnipeg Jets

Winnipeg is a hockey city. It is steeped in hockey history. At the turn of the twentieth century, our professional hockey team was named the Winnipeg Victorias. This remarkably talented team played in the Stanley Cup finals eight times over a nine-year period and won three of those times – 1896, 1901, and 1902. Fast forward 110 years to our new and exciting current edition of the Winnipeg Jets. They are today known across North America for their incredible and enthusiastic fan base. From the Victorias to the Jets, Winnipeg has always had a deep involvement in the sport.

Our geographical location makes us a winter city, a winter province for that matter, and as such, winter sports dominate our days for a good portion of the year. Each winter, community centres across Manitoba are bustling with activity; predominantly hockey. Families pass on from one generation to the next the tradition of learning to skate, playing a winter sport, and supporting our local teams. Our cities and towns are known for their backyard rinks, their skating ponds, and their river trails. We may very well have invented street hockey. Many local artists have illustrated the sport in drawings or paintings. We are known for having been host to a remarkable number of amateur and professional teams over the years, who have made us who we are...a hockey city. It is part of our cultural fabric.

My personal interest with hockey started with junior hockey, played at the Winnipeg Arena. My childhood friend Gayle and I were very dedicated to our team, the Winnipeg Braves and attended many junior hockey games, at times up to three games per week. At first, our intentions may have been purely self-interest...we wanted to meet these fine-looking young men. We may have even had a crush on one or two of them. But over time, I got to learn a lot about the sport itself. It was fast-paced and exciting and I quite enjoyed watching the games just for the love of hockey.

Then, in the mid-1960s, Winnipeg was home to Canada's national hockey team. Many of the young men on this talented team were still students and most of them studied at either the University of Manitoba, the University of Winnipeg, or the U of W Collegiate. This is where I met and eventually got to know some of the players. Among the members of the team were Danny O'Shea, who eventually played for the Minnesota North Stars, Brian Glennie, who played for the Toronto Maple Leafs, and Fran Huck who played for the Montreal Canadians. Gayle and I became friends with Danny O'Shea, Harvey Schmidt, and Johnny Russell, and I have many fond memories about those days.

This was during a very exciting time in Canadian hockey history — the start of the Canada/Russia rivalry. Of course, it was exciting for all Canadians, and I remember it being such great fun for those of us attending the collegiate, especially when the team participated in the 1968 Winter Olympics in Grenoble, France. I remember going to see them off at the Winnipeg International Airport. They won the bronze metal. We were all so very proud of their accomplishment. They made our country proud; they made our city proud. All these years later, whenever I come across one of these former national team members, whether it is a chance meeting at a restaurant or at a public event, we recognize each other and share memories of this wonderful period of time when they played hockey in Winnipeg.

In 1967, there also existed a team named the Junior Jets, based out of Winnipeg. They were part of the Western Canada Hockey League and the owner was none other than Ben Hatskin, who later became the owner of the WHL Winnipeg Jets. Eventually the junior team was sold, renamed, and moved to another city. The Jets name, however, would remain in Winnipeg.

The Winnipeg Jets became part of a new hockey franchise, the World Hockey Association (WHA) in 1972. The team made a name for itself with the signing of Bobby Hull, a professional NHL player well known around the globe. Bobby was offered an unprecedented million-dollar contract and the ceremony took place at Portage and Main, the heart of Winnipeg's downtown. This move solidified Winnipeg as a major player in the WHA. The Jets conjured up much excitement in the city in those years, and our citizens' love of their professional hockey team was born. A few years after Bobby Hull's arrival, two Swedish players were signed — Ulf Nillson and Anders Hedberg — and that trio created one of the most powerful forward lines in the league. The Winnipeg Jets hit their stride during those years and won the coveted Avco Cup three times in the 1970s. In 1978, ownership changed hands to a group of eight businessmen who called themselves Hockey Ventures Inc. — Marvin Shenkarow, Barry Shenkarow, John Shanski Jr., Harvey Secter, Bob Graham, Dr. Gerry Wilson, Bobby Hull, and Michael Gobuty. By this time, many of the WHA teams were experiencing financial difficulties. The writing was on the wall that the same could happen to the Winnipeg Jets. The main goal of Hockey Ventures Inc. was to apply for entry into the National Hockey League.

In 1979, the Winnipeg Jets became part of the NHL. Now, we were in the big leagues. The 1980s saw our Winnipeg Jets team struggle through its first few years, as many of our original stars had either been traded or retired. We ended up in a very competitive division and found ourselves playing against strong teams such as the Edmonton Oilers or the Calgary Flames, who were quite dominant in those years. Nevertheless, Winnipeggers supported their team through and through. Then a young man named Dale Hawerchuk was signed and he brought much-needed talent and energy back to the team. Another Swede, Thomas Steen, (who loved Winnipeg so much he stayed after his hockey career was over), and Randy Carlyle (who later, at one point, was the coach of our Manitoba Moose) were added to the roster. The Jets now had some new life and made the playoffs eleven times in fifteen years. Unfortunately, none resulted in the winning of the Stanley Cup. During this time, my own career had taken me to Calgary and then Montreal, but I always kept track of how the Winnipeg Jets were doing.

Financially, the Winnipeg Jets, along with the other former WHA teams who had joined the NHL, faced significant struggles. The Canadian dollar was worth much less than the U.S. dollar, which made us a less attractive place to play. Player salaries were at an all-time high and there was no salary cap. Smaller clubs could not begin to compete with the larger, wealthier teams. The Jets organization also had the unique challenge of not owning its own building. The Winnipeg Arena was leased to the owners from Winnipeg Enterprises, a city of Winnipeg arms-length board, which oversaw major sports facilities. The building itself was getting old, out-dated, and in need of repairs. Adding to the challenges, less than capacity crowds at the Winnipeg Arena were the norm unless we were in the playoffs.

Talks began about the need for a new arena. This started well before I became mayor. In the early nineties, there were ongoing discussions and deliberations about the financial stability of the team. Talks then moved to possibilities of public ownership. Local governments were approached, but each proposal had caveats that the team's losses would need to be covered. Neither the province nor the city believed that this was appropriate use of taxpayer dollars. By the time I was elected in 1992, the league was just starting to talk about salary caps, which was encouraging. While I understood the city's role as one of the players in building a new arena, I also knew that we could not do it alone. Professional hockey had grown too large for any city to take this on by itself. A blend of private and public ownership would be the only solution going forward. We needed the commitment of private owners with deep pockets. I also took the position that any new building should be a multi-use facility that could be used year-round for sports, concerts, conventions, and trade shows.

Lastly, I envisioned a downtown arena, knowing the economic opportunities for the city in such a strategic location.

In 1993, the team acquired a rookie who would become one of the NHL's most successful players. Teemu Selanne brought excitement to the game and people embraced him. I certainly remember that his addition to the team gave our city hope that we could rise to the top once again.

By 1994, Barry Shenkarow had a solid offer from a few American millionaires to purchase the team and take it to a city in the United States. If hockey fans didn't think before this that losing our NHL team was a true possibility, this event hit the nail on the head.

Over a two-year period, four major initiatives were undertaken to try to save the Jets. The first was a feasibility study commissioned by the owners and spearheaded by Arthur Mauro, a well-known Winnipeg businessman. He and a committee of seven conducted a six-month study to determine what measures would need to be taken to keep the Jets in Winnipeg. The committee concluded that public support was necessary to keep the team alive. Recognizing the importance of keeping an NHL franchise in the city, and the economic benefits it provided for both the city and the province, Mauro encouraged politicians to come forward with plans to build a new arena and find innovative ways to publicly support the professional hockey team. He gave us a deadline of June 30, 1994 to come up with a plan to build an arena and we had until October 1993 to respond to his report.

I cannot speak for the province, but the city at that time was facing huge economic challenges of its own. I understood the importance of holding onto our NHL franchise, but I was also realistic enough to know that it was becoming economically impossible to do so. These were tumultuous times. The Canadian dollar was hovering around seventy cents U.S. during this time. To further complicate the issue, a new NHL commissioner had been hired earlier that year and from what I could see, he had his own agenda. Gary Bettman's vision was to expand the NHL to non-traditional markets, mostly new franchises in the southern United States. Time tells us that this may not have been the most successful of moves, but Mr. Bettman did make the NHL a bigger organization than most ever thought possible. Revenues skyrocketed under his tenure, but then so did salaries and team expenses. Small-market teams like Winnipeg were struggling. The NHL, under these circumstances, was no longer affordable for us.

During these years, I had the occasion to meet and speak with Gary Bettman. Some of these meetings were held in my office. In many of these conversations, we discussed the intensity of our city's passion for its hockey team. He was quite surprised that such extraordinary measures were being taken by our municipal and provincial governments to try to keep the team in Winnipeg. He was intrigued with the strategy to involve the entire community. In his mind, it seemed to me, owning a hockey franchise was strictly a business. I felt that he never quite understood that for us, it was part of our very being, part of our culture, and part of our identity.

In June 1994, a second report, the Burns Report, which was led by James Burns, a prominent and distinguished Canadian business leader, provided a model for the NHL franchise and a new arena, this one more specifically attached to the Winnipeg Convention Centre. Yet again, in the final analysis, it was determined that the provincial and civic governments could not use taxpayer dollars to cover losses on a team that was deeply in debt and likely to remain so for a long time.

A third report followed in August 1994; this one from a new organization — Manitoba Entertainment Complex Inc. (MEC). John Loewen, another well-known Winnipeg businessperson, headed this group. The MEC sought to find enough private financial backers to ensure construction of a new downtown arena in Winnipeg. At one point, they were called the Group of 44, as they had as many on board. It appeared promising and at first, many were optimistic that this group could actually save the Jets. Over time, however, elements of the MEC proposal began to generate disagreements and public outcries. The Jets issue was beginning to show real signs of divisiveness. Some Winnipeggers thought it was time for the Jets to go, that it was unreasonable and irresponsible for our governments to take on the debt incurred by the team. Hockey fans had the complete opposite opinion. They wanted their three levels of government to do everything in their power to ensure that the team remain in Winnipeg. In early 1995, after a lockout that wiped out half of the NHL hockey season, the Jets were playing what could very well be their final season. At this point, every looming deadline became more and more emotional.

May 3, 1995 was a very sad day for Winnipeg. On that day, a press conference was held to make a bleak announcement. John Loewen stated that despite the MEC's best efforts, "The NHL is not prepared to make hockey a viable sport in a small market like Winnipeg." Premier Filmon and I tried to put on a brave face and explained that the potential risk for private and public sectors was too great. Barry Shenkarow shed tears. I shed tears. Thomas Steen, who was there as a bystander, was overcome with emotion. It was an extremely gruelling experience for all of us in that room at the Westin Hotel, and for many, many Winnipeggers who just did not want us to give up the fight. Hundreds of devastated Jets fans showed up at Portage and Main. It was like a death in the family.

By June 1995, most Winnipeggers resigned themselves to the fact that our city could not sustain an NHL team...not at that time under the circumstances. A last-ditch effort was underway by Izzy Asper and Albert Cohen, two of the city's most influential businessmen at the time. They had major players in the city trying to raise $111 million. This group, too, failed to find a resolution. This effort was the most heart-wrenching. It caused crowds to gather at Portage and Main and at The Forks to rally support. It had little kids emptying their piggy banks. It had grown men crying. Local radio broadcaster Peter Warren rallied citizens in an unprecedented way to "save our beloved Jets." It was an outpouring of community spirit that went from euphoria to devastation. Inevitably, it was not to be.

Our Winnipeg Jets gave our city a tremendous sense of pride. Along with the status that an NHL team brings to a city, they also brought joy and inspiration for many of its citizens. One of the last words I ever said to Gary Bettman was, "We'll be back." I didn't know when, I didn't know how, but in my heart of hearts, I knew that Winnipeg would once again be an NHL city. And in true Winnipeg spirit, thanks to the tenacity of True North Sports and Entertainment owners Mark Chipman and David Thomson, the NHL is back. Accolades need to be given to Former Mayor Glen Murray for his hand in the building of Winnipeg's new arena, the MTS Centre. Most importantly, the citizens of Winnipeg need to be recognized for making our Winnipeg Jets a very successful revenue-generating franchise. In its first season in 2011, 13,000 season tickets for the Jets sold out in seventeen minutes. Winnipeg's exuberance for its favourite sport is alive and well. Winnipeg's hockey history forges on.

A surprise hug for the notorious Peter Warren. Peter is a well-known personality in Winnipeg, having hosted the longest-running radio talk show in Winnipeg's history. He is also the longest running open-line radio host in North America. He now lives in B.C., still in broadcasting, and is also a private investigator. (Photo courtesy of City of Winnipeg Archives)

Chapter 12
Extraordinary People

One of the privileges of being mayor is the opportunity to meet many people from all walks of life. During my two terms in office, I met an unbelievable cross-section of individuals, from royalty, dignitaries, and military generals, to politicians from all political levels and stripes, to athletes, actors, and entertainers. In total, I met four members of royalty, four presidents (from various countries), two prime ministers, most Canadian premiers, mayors of all major Canadian cities, many U.S. governors, and mayors from many cities in the United States and Mexico. Most importantly, I was blessed to meet so many citizens of Winnipeg and the province of Manitoba — seniors, children, and everyday people. In many instances, these encounters became much more than a typical "meet and greet." A few became special "moments in time" in my life and memories that I treasure to this day.

Extraordinary Winnipeggers

I cannot start this chapter without paying tribute to the many extraordinary Winnipeggers I had the occasion to meet from 1992 to 1998. Whether they were volunteers for community events, people who worked for the city, or concerned citizens who attended council meetings, these people went out of their way to make Winnipeg a better place to live. I was so often in awe of the dedication and commitment. Winnipeg is full of people who care deeply about their city and I enjoyed meeting each and every one of these special people. I would like to mention three exceptional local citizens who made my journey as mayor especially wonderful.

The Richardson family is without a doubt one of the most prominent families in Winnipeg. James Richardson and Sons, a grain export business, was founded in the 1850s and the business expanded to Winnipeg in 1923. In 1926, James A. Richardson founded Western Canadian Airways, which later became Canadian Airways and was instrumental in creating a transcontinental air system that was eventually incorporated into the fledgling Trans-Canada Airlines. In 1939, Muriel Richardson, the family matriarch, took over the family business after the death of her husband, and eventually her children also became involved in different aspects of the business. Kathleen Richardson, one of James A. and Muriel's four children and one of two daughters, was devoted to the arts, particularly the Royal Winnipeg Ballet. She was hugely involved in the philanthropic endeavours of the family and remains so to this day. I first met Kathleen in the early 1980s when I returned to Winnipeg to run my own family business. I was involved with many community organizations such as the Winnipeg Chamber of Commerce and the United Way, and sat on the boards of the Winnipeg Symphony Orchestra and the YM/YWCA. Kathleen was also involved in many community organizations. When I first met her, I was completely in awe of her many talents and skill sets. It was evident that she was wholeheartedly devoted to our community. Never wanting to be in the spotlight, she would quietly go about her generous work and was very private about her generosity. I enjoyed working with her as a business owner over a number of years and learned so much from her. I admired her quiet and unassuming ways. When I decided to run for mayor, I knew that involving Kathleen Richardson would be a wise thing to do. Historically, women in politics had difficulty raising money and I knew that I needed an excellent fundraiser. I knew that it was important to have someone from the Richardson family supportive of my campaign and Kathleen was the one I wanted involved. So I called Kathleen and asked her if she would support me. She said that she had to consult with her family first before accepting, which she did, and called me shortly thereafter. I will always remember what Kathleen said to me when she called back. "Yes, I will support you Susan, and I will be pleased to help you wherever you need me." I thought that was such a generous offer. Kathleen became co-chair of my fundraising committee and an integral part of my team. She was my friendly counsel and my voice of reason. Then, and all the way through my life since, she has been nothing but supportive and encouraging. We still keep in touch. Kathleen Richardson is one of the pillars of the Winnipeg community and the city is extremely lucky to have her.

The second person I'd like to mention is former Mayor Stephen Juba. I first met Mr. Juba in the summer of 1992. When it was certain that I would be running for mayor, I thought it important to meet with the city's longest running and certainly the most popular mayor in recent history. How could I not take the time to meet with him and pay him my respect? I looked forward to chatting with him about his years at the helm. On a warm summer day in July 1992, I drove up to Petersfield, Manitoba where Steve Juba and his wife lived. His wife welcomed me and led me to his studio. This is where he had spent much of his time since he'd retired, making Ukrainian pottery. We were supposed to meet for an hour — we met for four hours. He spoke about everything under the sun. He was a straight shooter and wasn't afraid to speak his mind. When I was about to leave, his parting words were, "Well it was nice to meet you but you are not going to win!" I was taken aback by his comment and left thinking that I was sorry he felt that way. I did not, however, let his words deflate my expectations. Then, two weeks before the election, an article appeared in the *Winnipeg Sun* with the headline "Juba: Time to elect a woman." I immediately called him and asked him if he really meant it. He said yes. He said he had been keeping track of the polling results and he was quite certain that I had generated significant support. From that point on, Steve would connect with me on a regular basis. Once I won the election, he in many ways became my guardian. During the first four months of my first year, he called me every Friday just to touch base. He mentored me in my early days. He was livid at the Board of Commissioners for the way they treated me. In fact, at one point, he was so angry that he wanted to come down to city hall and "straighten things out" with the city bureaucrats. I appreciated his comments as they reinforced the perspective I had developed about the situation. His weekly calls were very supportive. He called me to express his condolences when my mother died only six weeks after I had been elected. Then, in April 1993, the calls stopped. The former mayor's health had taken a turn for the worse. On May 2, 1993, Juba died at his home in Petersfield. I was very saddened by his death. His genuine concern for me is something I will always hold very near and dear.

Metropolitan Bzdel on one of his many visits to the Mayor's Office (Photo courtesy of City of Winnipeg Archives)

The third person I'd like to mention is someone that I would describe as a truly holy man. Metropolitan Michael Bzdel was the Ukrainian Catholic archbishop of Winnipeg from 1992 to 2006 and along with his appointment as archbishop, he automatically became one of four metropolitans for Ukrainian Catholics in Canada. He was a member of the Canadian Council of Catholic Bishops and served on several committees and commissions. He was a hardworking and compassionate man. One day, early in my career, Metropolitan Bzdel arrived at the mayor's office unannounced. He was greeted by my receptionist and asked if he could meet with me. He said that he realized I was likely occupied, but he only wanted a few minutes of my time. I was in a meeting, but my receptionist thought it was important enough to interrupt. She whispered in my ear, "The Metropolitan Archbishop of the Ukrainian Catholic Church is here to see you. He is insistent on seeing you and says he will only take a minute." I was puzzled as to what this was about, but my instincts told me that I needed to respect who he was and meet with him. I asked the people in my office to step out for a few minutes and Metropolitan Bzdel was led into my office. I can still recall him coming in. He was dressed in a black cassock with a burgundy sash and a clerical collar, and he wore a chain around his neck with an image of the Virgin Mary, which was made of porcelain. What happened next turned out to be what I can only describe as a profound moment. Metropolitan Bzdel had come to offer me a prayer of leadership and a blessing. We both stood facing each other and he immediately took my hands in his and asked me to bow my head. I was completely taken aback but I knew that I needed to trust him. He asked God to bless me and give me strength. He was so strong in his belief and his convictions, that I felt his words to my very soul. This was at a time when a lot of negative things were happening to me — power plays with city council members and the bureaucrats, and unwarranted attacks by the media. When a public figure is faced with so much criticism, having someone like a metropolitan archbishop show up unannounced to bless and nurture you can only be described as a wonderful kindness and gift of caring. The timing could not have been more perfect. I'd never had anything like that happen to me before and I was thankful that the metropolitan recognized the vagaries of public life enough to know that I needed him to do this for me. Throughout my tenure, I had regular visits from Metropolitan Bzdel and I really felt his prayers and his support helped me get through some of the darkest moments I faced at city hall. Sadly, Metropolitan Bzdel passed away in April 2011. He was a remarkable man and I will always remember him with reverence and respect.

The Strawberry Dinner: Feeding one of Canada's Billionaires

One of the most extraordinary people I ever met was Jimmy Pattison. I would describe him as a person born with a heightened sense of curiosity...about people, things, and places. A Canadian business magnate and philanthropist, Jimmy Pattison owns the Jim Pattison Group, one of the largest privately-held companies in Canada. He is one of Canada's richest people. From his humble beginnings in rural Saskatchewan to his current day empire with worldwide assets, Jimmy is tireless in the work he does. What is most genuine about this man is that though he is a billionaire, he takes the time to meet and talk with ordinary people.

I first met Jimmy while I was mayor. He had come to Winnipeg for a renaming of one of his new businesses. From the moment I shook his hand, it was clear to me that this was a man of action. He was also very inquisitive. He would ask a lot of questions and continued to ask questions until he got an answer, or until you decided that you did not have an answer. One of the first things he asked was, "How can I help you?" He had just met me, yet he extended his hand in friendship right from the start. He was always interested in how Winnipeg was faring financially, politically, and culturally, and was very concerned about local aboriginal issues. It was a matter often discussed between us and several times, he attended meetings at city hall and personally tried to help to make a difference on this issue.

Jimmy was quite concerned that I had opted out of the city pension as part of my election platform. He advised me on a regular basis to put aside as much as I could in RRSPs. I appreciated his concern and did the best that I could. In hindsight, I should have listened better.

During my six years in office, Jimmy kept in touch with me by telephone on a regular basis. He came to Winnipeg once in a while and we would sometimes meet in person. On one occasion, when he called to say he was coming to Winnipeg and asked if I was available to meet him for dinner, I suggested that he come to my home. I knew that Jimmy spent five days a week flying all over in his corporate jet. I lived in a charming, restored 1912 fire hall at the time and thought it would be far more enjoyable if we could have a normal home-cooked meal. I assured him that I was a pretty good cook. He agreed. I had read somewhere that he really liked one of our famous, longstanding local steakhouses — Rae and Jerry's — and especially enjoyed their well-done steaks. A steak dinner would be simple, or so I thought.

I picked up Jimmy at the private airline hangar in my Volkswagen Passat. We drove directly to the fire hall and I started to prepare dinner. I placed the steaks under the broiler, put the vegetables on low heat and served up before-dinner beverages. I returned to the living room, and as always, Jimmy and I got into an animated discussion about one subject or another. The next thing I knew, I could smell the beets. OMG...they were burning. I rushed into the kitchen to rescue them. The water was just starting to evaporate, but I thought I had recovered them. They looked fine. I then focused on the steak. When the smoke detector went off, I should have realized that was an omen. Instead, I invited Jimmy to the dining room table and served the meal as I intended. Jimmy began to cut into his steak, and as he did, I thought his entire plate was going to slide across the table. He took one bite, tried to chew it, but it was not to be. In fact, it was just awful. He didn't have to utter a word. I was so embarrassed. He then moved onto the vegetables. He took one bite of the beets and simply said "Hmm... they're a little smoky" and then set them aside. By then, I just wished I could have evaporated so as not feel any more embarrassment. We ate our potatoes and then I served dessert — a big bowl of fresh strawberries. He loved them. In fact, he loved them so much, he asked if he could take them back with him on the plane for his pilot and crew. "Of course" I replied, hoping this might make up for the disastrous dinner I had just served him. So immediately after dinner, we hopped back in my car and I drove Jimmy Pattison, big bowl of strawberries in hand, back to his private jet. He was so gracious about the whole thing. I was sure that I would never cook another meal for him, and I don't think I ever did, but we did remain in contact with each other and he never again mentioned what turned out to be "my strawberry dinner with Jimmy Pattison."

Famous Athletes

Teemu Selanne, in his rookie year with the Winnipeg Jets (Phil Hossack/ Winnipeg Free Press, March 25, 1993. Reprinted with permission.)

I was glad to see that our city had a program that paid tribute to athletes when they accomplished the extraordinary. During the 1992-1993 NHL hockey season, Teemu Selanne had joined our own Winnipeg Jets, and had an outstanding rookie season. He broke two NHL records, one for most goals scored in one season by a rookie and one for most points in one season by a rookie. He also broke a number of Jets records, including most hat tricks in one season, most consecutive games with a goal, and most goals in one game. He was an impressive young man and I felt the city would be remiss if we didn't recognize him in a special way. Hockey is a sacred sport in Winnipeg and I understood that. Even before the regular season ended, we arranged for Mr. Selanne to come down to city hall for a special presentation. We presented him with a "Golden Boy" statue in recognition of his accomplishments. It was a pleasure to invite him to city hall and I think he was pleased to have this award bestowed upon him. He took it all in stride and didn't let his overwhelming success get to his head. For such a young man (he was twenty-two years old at the time), he was mature, modest, and polite.

Wayne Gretzky was honoured with the Health Sciences Foundation Laureate of Excellence Award in 1993 (Photo courtesy of City of Winnipeg Archives).

Later that same year, another hockey superstar graced our city. Wayne Gretzky was in Winnipeg to receive an award at the Health Sciences Centre Foundation Celebration of Excellence dinner. This was an enormous event held on the third floor of the Winnipeg Convention Centre. Many, many people paid the hundred-plus dollars to meet "the Great One" in person. In fact, at the event itself, people began to line up at the head table just to get his autograph. Eventually the organizers put a stop to this, and explained that Gretzky was there as their special guest, not to be signing autographs for hours on end. With all his fame and fortune, he did not appear to be comfortable in large crowds. When you observed him, he appeared to be shy and reserved. Prior to the dinner, in a separate room for VIPs, a photographer was snapping photos of Wayne with various guests. A long line of special guests waited for their turn to get a photo with him. After all, it really was the chance of a lifetime to be photographed with such a celebrity. My role was a dual one — I was to welcome him on behalf of the city of Winnipeg and I would also present him with an Honorary Citizenship. By the time it was my turn to greet Mr. Gretzky, he was visibly tired. I already knew that this would be one photo that would go up on my "people wall" back at the office and I wanted to ensure that the photo turned out. Just as he and I were about to be photographed, I told him that as a recipient of the Honorary Citizenship, he would not have to pay taxes if he ever lived in Winnipeg. He immediately asked "Really?" and I immediately replied, "No, of course not. I just wanted to see you smile." And he did. The photo on the wall at city hall looked great; both of us smiling from ear to ear. Yet again, another person I was very pleased to have met.

Throughout my tenure, I made it a point to salute our local athletes, our world champions, and our Olympians. I particularly enjoyed bestowing recognition awards on behalf of the city to speed skater Susan Auch and cyclist Clara Hughes. In 1994, Susan Auch won a silver medal at the Lillehammer Winter Olympics. She repeated this four years later, winning a silver medal at the 1998 Olympics in Nagano. Clara Hughes was a local cyclist and in 1996, she won two bronze medals at the Olympic Summer Games in Atlanta. Of course, years later, she began competitive speed skating and won four medals in three winter Olympic Games — a bronze medal in 2002, gold and silver in 2006, and bronze in 2010. She is an outstanding Olympic athlete and a huge source of pride for Winnipeggers. I had the pleasure of meeting both Clara and Susan while I was mayor — two amazing young women — and found them to be not only committed to their sport, but to their city and country as well. They were such good ambassadors for Winnipeg and Canada, and positive role models for our youth. I always enjoyed meeting all of the talented, hard-working young athletes who graced the steps of city hall. They persevered in their chosen sports and made our city proud. I was pleased to present them with their awards.

Garth Brooks

Garth Brooks...a true gentleman

One of my roles as mayor was to promote and market our city to the greatest extent possible, to as many people as possible, in as many places as possible. Presenting an Honorary Citizenship to guests of our city was a platform to welcome some of the world's most accomplished people in a way that would honour them and give them an experience that would have them remember their visit to Winnipeg in a positive manner.

One of the first Honorary Citizenships I presented was to country singer Garth Brooks. The young Garth was at the height of his career in 1993. I saw this as a great opportunity to promote our city to him. After all, he had a worldwide reach. It was our intention to make his experience in Winnipeg positive and one he would always remember. We embarked on an exercise of "my people" speaking with "his people" and from what I can recall, there was a lot of back and forth going on. In fact, so much so that we didn't confirm until the day of the concert that I would be invited to attend his press conference prior to the event. Though Garth's priority that afternoon was to rehearse, he did agree to a short press conference whereby I would present him with his Honorary Citizenship. So off I went to the Winnipeg Arena on the afternoon of the concert. His team had set up a small podium with a table, a microphone, and two chairs, and the room was just big enough to hold the various media to set up their cameras. This was in the basement of the old arena...it was all pretty sparse. At the beginning of the press conference, I presented Garth with his framed certificate. Of course, being the owner of a western clothing store, I wore cowboy boots and a cowboy hat. Garth gave me a big smile when he saw me, kissed me on both cheeks, (which I swear I didn't wash for two weeks), took my hand and led me to the table on the small stage. He asked me to sit beside him (which of course, I was thrilled to do). Naturally, every question by the media was directed to him, making it the easiest press conference I had been to in a long time. I just sat there quietly, gazed at him, and smiled. I found Garth Brooks to be such a down-to-earth person. He was charismatic, but also considerate and sincere. He had a sparkle in his eye and it was a real pleasure to meet him. Later that evening, our city welcomed him with open arms and the reviews of his concert were incredible.

Roger Moore

Dennis McKnight and I with Roger Moore, the best James Bond ever!

Actor Roger Moore, aka James Bond (certainly THE James Bond of MY era) came to Winnipeg in June 1996 to attend a fundraiser celebrating UNICEF's fiftieth anniversary. Mr. Moore was a Goodwill Ambassador for UNICEF, a position once held by Audrey Hepburn. He and Ms. Hepburn were good friends and she was the person who got him involved with UNICEF. The dinner was held at the Winnipeg Convention Centre. Mr. Moore was pleased to be in Manitoba, one of only two provinces (the other being Prince Edward Island) to be graced by his presence for UNICEF. Prior to the dinner, the usual VIP reception occurred and a local photographer had been hired to take individual photos of Mr. Moore with the invited guests. When my turn came to be photographed with him, the photographer recognized me and referred to me as "Your Worship." Immediately, Roger Moore turned to me and said "Your Worship??" to which I said "Pardon?" Oh, I had heard him, I just wanted to hear him say it AGAIN. After all, who wouldn't want to be addressed by "James Bond?" It was such fun! Later that evening, just after dinner, Roger Moore went up to the podium to give his remarks to the crowd. He began by addressing the head table and when he got to me, instead of saying Mayor Thompson, he repeated and emphasized "Your Worship." Between his big smile and his suave voice, he had me feeling like a young girl meeting her teenage idol. His remarks were very eloquent, his stories very personal, and the evening was lovely. I was proud to have been a part of it.

Sir Peter Ustinov

Greeting Sir Peter Ustinof at a Winnipeg Art Gallery fundraiser (Photo courtesy of City of Winnipeg Archives)

Sir Peter Ustinov, an extraordinary person and Oscar-winning actor, visited Winnipeg in 1996 and spent a week in our city giving a lecture at the Centennial Concert Hall, attending a retrospective of six of his films, story-telling to children under twelve, and being guest speaker and special guest at a Winnipeg Art Gallery fundraiser. He had also recently authored a book and signed autographs at a book-signing event. This is what the newspapers reported about Mr. Ustinov's visit. What wasn't reported was that his arrival in Winnipeg was an immigration nightmare. Mr. Ustinov was flying internationally. Canadian Customs and Immigration did not recognize him and began questioning him on why he was in the country. Was he being paid for the events? Did he have a working visa? They kept him for a substantial amount of time, so much so that Michel Chef, director of the art gallery, who was at the airport to pick him up, assumed he had missed his flight and left to find out where he was. This was "pre" cell phone days and Mr. Chef thought it best to go back to the office and start making some calls. When Mr. Ustinov finally emerged, he was completely alone in the Customs arrival area. His next issue was to find someone who could convert his money to Canadian, so that he could have a “loonie” to pay for a baggage cart. Those of you who have ever been at the International Arrivals area at the old Winnipeg Airport would know that in between flights, this area was like a ghost town. Poor Mr. Ustinov had to find his way to another level of the airport, several bags in tow, and no baggage cart. I’m sure his first impressions of our fine city were not very positive. He finally arrived at the hotel, just in time to put on his tuxedo and head to the fundraising dinner in the ballroom of the hotel. Winnipeg Art Gallery management, who had arranged his appearance in Winnipeg, were upset when they found out what had happened. Everyone who knew of the incident apologized to Mr. Ustinov and wished him a better time in our city going forward. I was fortunate to be seated beside him at the head table. During dinner, the mishaps continued as a young waiter accidentally spilled a tray of soups on one of our head-table guests. Jack Fraser, a prominent Winnipeg businessman and husband of Val Fraser, who was the chair of the board of the Winnipeg Art Gallery at the time, was the recipient of a full bowl of hot soup right down his back. It was such an unfortunate incident. All of us at our table, including Mr. Ustinov, were horrified. Jack Fraser was ever so gracious. He quietly got up, left the table, and returned all cleaned up within an hour. During dinner, Mr. Ustinov mesmerized the guests at the head table with his words of wisdom. This man was not just an actor. He was an author, a director and an excellent speaker. He had some interesting stories to share. I remember that he and I spoke about travelling, living in Switzerland, and his twenty-year marriage to his wife Hélène.

Gregory Peck

Gregory Peck receiving his Honorary Citizenship
(Photo courtesy of City of Winnipeg Archives)

Gregory Peck also came to Winnipeg in 1996 to do a one-man show called, *In Conversation with Gregory Peck* at the Centennial Concert Hall. I had arranged to meet with him prior to the show to present him with an Honorary Citizenship. He was accompanied by his wife, Véronique, and a family friend. He told me that he was touched to receive such an honour and immediately turned to his wife and shared this award with her. It was evident that he cherished their partnership. I found him to be an absolute gentleman. He was polite and had a presence about him.

During his show on the main stage of the concert hall, he sat in a director's chair. This was the only prop on the stage. It was profoundly simple...black floor, black curtain, the chair, and a simple spotlight on Mr. Peck. It created an intimate and personal ambience. He spoke about how he had met his wife and again, it was obvious that theirs was a beautiful love story. They met just prior to his filming the 1939 classic movie *Roman Holiday* in Italy. Véronique was a Paris news reporter and had interviewed him about the movie. He also spoke of his valued friendship with Audrey Hepburn and gave us some insights into life in Hollywood. His deep, manly voice was spellbinding and one couldn't help but listen intently to every word he said. After the lecture, there was a reception and he was kept quite busy meeting many people in the room. I spent most of the evening talking to Véronique. She was intelligent, interesting, and charming. By the end of the evening, we had developed a nice bond. It was so nice to meet both of them.

Lauren Bacall

Posing with Lauren Bacall (Photo courtesy of City of Winnipeg Archives)

In 1997, the *Winnipeg Free Press* presented a series entitled *Unique Lives and Experiences* whereby well-known, highly accomplished women shared stories about their lives in a conversation setting at the Winnipeg Concert Hall. These women were excellent communicators, leaders, political activists, and philanthropists. Knowing the extent of their reaches, I was most grateful to meet with them on behalf of the city of Winnipeg, to welcome them, and to provide them with a positive experience.

Lauren Bacall was one of the first to make a presentation for this series. One of my staff had read that Humphrey Bogart often gave her orchids, so we thought that she would appreciate an orchid plant as a welcoming gesture. I attended Ms. Bacall's presentation, which was candid and touching, and had the opportunity to meet with her privately to welcome her to Winnipeg before a larger VIP reception. Immediately following her presentation, I headed to her dressing room. As I walked in, I noticed the beautiful orchid sitting on her dressing table along with a card that said, "Welcome to the City of Winnipeg." It definitely improved the look of the room, because the space was so drab and sparse. I was introduced to her as Winnipeg's first woman mayor and she was immediately drawn by that. She rose, gave me a big hug, and quickly engaged me in conversation. She asked me what it was like to be a woman mayor. I asked her about her experiences as a woman in the film industry. At one point, one of her handlers walked in and advised that we had best head over to the VIP reception in another room at the concert hall. Ms. Bacall turned to her handler and said, "No, this woman is quite interesting and I want to continue to talk to her." We talked for another ten minutes and then she asked me about when she would receive the Honorary Citizenship award. I was shocked! All I could do was ask her, "How did you know about this?" She was a close friend of Gregory Peck and he had told her that if she went to Winnipeg, she would receive this award. I was pleased that Gregory Peck had mentioned it to her and I was also pleased that she was excited about getting one. I assured her that we would get a certificate prepared for her and have it sent to her office in New York first thing the next morning. She was delighted. By the end of our conversation, I considered myself most fortunate to have met Lauren Bacall. She was very much "her own woman," a survivor, and acting to her was a lifelong professional commitment. She understood her profession and credited her success to sheer determination. As we left the room together and headed to the reception, I couldn't help but think how lucky I had been to meet her and how fortunate the people in the next room would be as well.

Sarah Ferguson

A few months later, the next scheduled presenter was Sarah, The Duchess of York. When Sarah did her presentation, I was struck by her candour. She spoke of her life choices and didn't shy away from any of the decisions she had made. She was open and honest about her failed marriage and acknowledged the mistakes she had made along the way. She explained that in her first year of marriage, Prince Andrew was gone the majority of the time and this had a huge impact on their marriage and her adjustment to being a royal. She expressed her sincere love and respect for the queen and for Prince Andrew. She mentioned her close-knit friendship with Diana, Princess of Wales (who at that time was already divorced from Prince Charles). She spoke of the challenges women face when they are thrust into the limelight and how that unpreparedness can cause challenges and embarrassment. I understood what she meant by that, having learned the fragility of being in public eye myself since I had become mayor. When she spoke, she had a very definite openness about her and people felt that.

I was able to meet Sarah Ferguson privately in her dressing room after her presentation. I was struck by her beauty and found her to be very gracious. I remember thinking how terrible it was that the British media constantly ridiculed and belittled her. It was shameful. We visited for a short time. She was such a down-to-earth person and very open. We then heard a knock at the door and she was told that she needed to go to the VIP reception. She turned to me and said, "I want you to stand beside me." She insisted that I be by her side and I was honoured that she asked me to do so. What resulted was that I was able to introduce her to the many Winnipeggers in the room. It was a moment of pride for me to do these introductions and it made it much more personal for the invited guests. When the event was coming to an end, she was quickly whisked away. A few minutes passed, the entrance door re-opened, and in came Sarah, heading directly towards me. She wanted to apologize for not saying goodbye. I was touched that she had come back just to say goodbye to me. How very kind of her. She asked me to walk back to her car with her and we talked briefly. This was just after the height of the 1997 flood and we were discussing the devastation our city had faced. I mentioned to her that our military was being recognized at an event at city hall the next day — we were having a farewell parade in their honour — and

I invited her to be in the reviewing area but she declined. She felt that the focus at this time should be on our military and she thought it wise for her not to be there. I walked away from meeting Sarah, Duchess of York with a sense that she was someone who was kind, humble, and really trying to do the right thing. Three months later, Princess Diana died and I sent Sarah a card of condolence. Not long afterwards, she sent me a lovely letter. In it she said: "I feel alone and isolated in a big world without my friend...if I feel this, then what on earth can William and Harry be feeling?" She then shared a beautiful prayer, which I would like to share with you:

"We give back to thee Oh Lord
Who gavest them to us
As thou did not lose them in giving them to us,
We did not lose them by giving them back to thee."

Prince Edward

Growing up, I was a definite royal watcher. In 1959, I remember lining up on Portage Avenue, just at the top of Douglas Park Road in St. James, to catch a glimpse of Queen Elizabeth and Prince Phillip as they made their way towards Assiniboine Park. They drove by in a big convertible and we all waved our flags as the car passed by. When I was a little older, I dreamt of meeting Prince Charles...after all he WAS the Prince Charming of my generation. So when I became aware that as mayor, I would be part of a welcoming committee for royalty when they visited Winnipeg, I was honoured. The first royal I ever met was the young Prince Edward in March 1993. He was in the city to present the Duke of Edinburgh Awards to deserving students from Manitoba, Ontario, and Saskatchewan. I had the good fortune of sitting at his table during a dinner at Balmoral Hall, a private school for girls. He was a bright young man who knew a lot about Winnipeg. He had obviously "done his homework." It was evident that he was dedicated to public service. He was also an incredible conversationalist. What I learned from him that evening was the importance of trying to engage everyone at your table. He understood the art of conversation. I felt privileged to be seated at his table and took note of his social grace. Everyone at our table felt a connection with him. After that evening, I tried to follow his example whenever I was at public functions and used his methods to try to engage everyone at my table in conversation. It is a lesson I learned early in my political career — the rules and responsibilities of being a good guest — and it has served me well.

Prince Charles

In the spring of 1996, Prince Charles came to Manitoba to open the Wapusk National Park in Churchill. He then headed down to Winnipeg for a visit. I first met him on the front steps of the Manitoba Legislative Building, where there was an official welcome by dignitaries. We were lined up by protocol on the outside staircase and he was given a 21-gun salute. Since this was largely a ceremonial event where the military would be in full dress, I asked if it would be possible to have a police officer in full dress uniform to accompany me. Ron Johannson of the Winnipeg Police Service attended with me. When Prince Charles approached us, the premier at the time, Gary Filmon introduced me, saying, "This is the mayor of Winnipeg," but before he had a chance to hear my name, Prince Charles proceeded to shake Ron's hand. Ron politely told him that he was not the mayor, that I was, for which the prince apologized. He and I had a light-hearted moment around the situation and the prince moved on up the steps. Following the welcoming, there was a reception in the rotunda inside the Legislative Building. I was able to chat briefly with the prince once again at this reception. After this second event, I had to quickly go home and change for yet another event, a gala dinner at the Westin Hotel. When the prince arrived, he was once again greeted by a small group. When he approached me, he chuckled and said, "Oh, you again!" to which I replied, "Yes, Your Royal Highness. There is only one mayor." It was another nice light moment. For the dinner itself, there were two head tables on a platform beside each other. Prince Charles sat with the premier and his wife Janice and other notables. I sat at the table next to the prince and we sat facing each other, just at a slight angle. Now being mayor has its advantages, and one of these was that I could sometimes choose what I wanted to eat at such events. I had been to three previous dinners at this hotel in the last week alone. By now, the serving personnel at the Westin knew me well and were always very thoughtful. Eric, the banquet manager, approached me discreetly and whispered, “Madam Mayor, we are serving Cornish hen again this evening. This will be the third time this week we are serving you this dish. Would you like us to make you something else?” I thought about it for a moment and then said, “Yes. I would like to have a cheeseburger and fries...onions on the burger, no ketchup on the burger but I will need some for the fries.” He looked at me in astonishment and said, “This may take about ten minutes to prepare. Are you sure you want this?” and I replied, “Yes.” Ten minutes later, a waiter brought me my order. Just before taking my first bite, I happened to look up and caught the eye of the prince. He gave me a big smile and a “thumbs up.” Such fun!

After dinner, Prince Charles addressed the audience. I found him to be self-deprecating and I thought that was sad. This was at a time in his life when he was going through difficult personal times. Throughout his adult years, I had always thought that the prince had been unfairly criticized for his stand on certain matters. I recall thinking that he needed to be more comfortable in his own skin. He had accomplished so much. During this particular visit alone, he had visited aboriginal children at a new school and patients in a palliative care centre, and he had a knack for making people feel special. I appreciated his visionary positions on many projects, including the environment (he staunchly supported organic farming) and architecture (he thought London should maintain more stringent rules regarding new architecture, so that the city could maintain its architectural history). I admired him for his total devotion to being the first in line to the throne. He clearly understood his responsibilities and was totally committed to them. At the end of his visit, I was proud and honoured to have met him.

President Jimmy and Rosalynn Carter

Former U.S. President Jimmy Carter in Winnipeg in 1993 to assist in building houses for Habitat for Humanity (Photo courtesy of City of Winnipeg Archives)

Former U.S. President Jimmy Carter and his wife Rosalynn came to Winnipeg in July 1993 to take part in a Habitat for Humanity project named in his honour, which involved the building of eighteen homes for needy families. Both were deeply involved with this organization in the United States and they had decided to expand their volunteer services internationally. The Winnipeg Habitat for Humanity affiliate had applied for funding from the "Jimmy Carter Work Project" and was lucky enough to be chosen. The Carters' visit generated much media attention and garnered major support for our local Habitat for Humanity organization. Prior to beginning their work for Habitat in Winnipeg, President and Mrs. Carter had planned a little getaway in Manitoba's north. Both avid fly fishers, they scheduled a few days at a fly-in fishing camp. They made a brief stop at the Winnipeg International Airport before heading on their mini-holiday. I was asked to be part of the welcoming committee when they would first arrive in Winnipeg and I gladly went. When I first met them, they asked me if I would be joining them on the fishing trip and I told them that I was not, but that I would definitely spend some time with them when they returned to Winnipeg. Though I had been invited to take this private trip, along with six or seven other guests from our province, I had chosen not to go. It being my first year in office, the media scrutinized every decision I made and had been highly critical of places I'd chosen to go on behalf of the city. I couldn't bear the thought that if I accompanied the Carters on their trip, the media focus could switch from a positive story about them to a negative one about me. It is a decision that I now regret. This was an amazing opportunity to spend some private time with two remarkable people...a chance of a lifetime.

When the Carters returned from their fishing trip, they immediately went to work for Habitat for Humanity. And work they did! Both were extremely diligent. They were as hands-on as any of the hundreds of volunteers who came together for this project. President Carter even wore a carpenter's belt throughout the entire project. I was at the building site every day to volunteer in one capacity or another, which gave me some time to meet with the Carters for either breakfast or lunch. In doing so, I got to experience each of them on a personal level. At one point, President Carter told me to go grab a hammer. I assured him that I was not the person he would want doing that activity. We both had a good chuckle over that. The more I chatted with Mrs. Carter, the more she opened up to me. We had many nice, private moments with no media around to capture our every move and I appreciated that she felt comfortable enough to confide in me.

As the week went on, I was struck by how completely hospitable they were to everyone they met. He was a true "people person" and she was friendly and charming in a quiet unassuming way. I noticed almost immediately that theirs was an incredible partnership. They were extraordinarily close and treated each other as equal partners with mutual respect. They were truly a team. There is only one other couple that I have observed and can honestly say has that strong partnership, and that is former Manitoba Premier Gary and Manitoba's current Lieutenant Governor Janice Filmon. The week flew by and before I knew it, the Carters were preparing to leave our city.

The evening before they left, there was a large fundraising dinner at the Winnipeg Convention Centre held on their behalf, with proceeds going to Habitat for Humanity. Over 1700 people attended this dinner on the third floor of the convention centre.

My role was to thank the former president and his wife for coming to our city for such a worthy cause. I also presented President Carter with an Honorary Citizenship. He came up to the podium, kissed me on the cheek, and the crowd cheered. It was all such fun. I really felt a sincere moment of friendship when he accepted the honour. Later that evening, President Carter made a point of inviting me to Atlanta to visit the Carter Centre for Peace. He also suggested that as mayor, I would be interested in visiting the Atlanta Project, a neighbourhood revitalization project that eventually became the catalyst for the Main Street Project in Winnipeg. Overall, President and Mrs. Carter's visit to Winnipeg had a major impact on our city. My visit to Atlanta was fortuitous, as not only were we shown a model for downtown redevelopment, but our delegation also had a chance to meet with members of the police and security forces who were in charge of the Atlanta 1996 Summer Olympics. Winnipeg was preparing to host the Pan American Games in 1999 and this meeting allowed us to learn about how security was managed during the Olympics. Many things were learned by this experience and it was extremely helpful for organizers of the Pan Am Games. I wasn't able to meet with the Carters when I visited Atlanta, but they certainly opened some doors for me for which I was grateful.

President and Mrs. Carter, volunteers and members of Habitat for Humanity at the Manitoba Legislature (Photo courtesy of City of Winnipeg Archives)

President Kuchma of Ukraine

In October 1994, the Canadian government selected Winnipeg to host a G7 Conference on the Economic Future of Ukraine. This was a significant event for our city to host, and a wonderful way to boost our city's international profile. It was also a very exciting time for Ukrainian Canadians as well, mainly because Ukraine's new leader was going to be in attendance. President Leonid Kuchma had just been elected leader of the Ukraine in June 1994, only the second leader to be democratically elected to represent the newly independent country. A day before the meetings were to begin, President Kuchma arrived in Winnipeg and a special dinner was held at the Westin Hotel. Ukrainians around the world celebrated his election and Canadian Ukrainians were delighted about his visit to Canada. It must be said that there is a sizeable Ukrainian community in Winnipeg, and because of this, there was an overwhelming show of support and emotion when President Kuchma arrived. Ukrainian Canadians living in Manitoba were so proud to welcome him here, and many drove from all over the province to attend this special dinner. I had the privilege of sitting at the head table, along with many other dignitaries. In fact, this was by far the longest head table I had ever seen. Everything was very structured and rehearsed. When we were led into the ballroom, we were instructed to stand by our chairs and remain standing until the president and his wife had passed by. Every chair was pulled back from the table far enough so that there was room for each of us to stand and still allow room for them to walk to their places. Protocol was to be adhered to and security was tight. Of course, many Canadian dignitaries were there, including Prime Minister Jean Chrétien and many members of his cabinet. One by one, dignitaries approached the podium to welcome the Ukrainian president and his wife. I also welcomed them. After I spoke, the president stood up, approached the podium, took my hand and kissed it. As a natural response, I kissed him on both cheeks. The second I did that, security personnel were on their feet and clearly alarmed that I had breached protocol. I returned to my seat, and soon thereafter, one of the president's security staff came up to me and whispered in my left ear, "You must never touch the president!" I was taken aback. I knew protocol but I didn't know that such a simple gesture could cause angst among the president's security. I didn't mean to do anything wrong and was embarrassed by the incident. At one point during the meal, I observed the president looking at me and I mouthed the words, "I'm sorry" to him. After the event, head table guests stood back again to let them leave the platform. As he walked by me, he made a point of stopping and once again, he took my hand and kissed it, a most kind gesture on his part.

Being an elected official myself, I fully expected that I would meet many politicians during my tenure, particularly at the civic and provincial levels. This included mayors and reeves from cities, towns, and rural municipalities in Manitoba, as well as many mayors and premiers from across Canada and some mayors and governors from cities in the United States. What I did not expect was to meet politicians at national and international levels, such as Canadian Prime Minister Jean Chrétien, or former President Jimmy Carter of the United States, or former President Kuchma of Ukraine. It was humbling to welcome these people to our city and I have some great memories of each encounter.

Many of the special moments I have just described were captured in photos, some of which I have included within these pages. The City of Winnipeg Archives has in its possession boxes of framed photos from my days in office. For me, however, the images are etched in my mind and in my heart, and I recall many of these moments as though they just happened yesterday.

Mayor Susan Thompson with the crew of HMCS Winnipeg "The BEST ship in the Canadian Navy."

Chapter 13
Unique Stories and Moments In Time

Being a mayor is a privilege. It is also an enormous responsibility. I was honoured to be given two clear majorities in 1992 and 1995 and to serve the citizens of Winnipeg for six years. During this time, it was critical for me to demonstrate accountability to the electorate and serve with integrity. Throughout my tenure, I assessed every aspect of the mayor's duties. I sought to find improvements wherever I could. I was driven to make a difference. As such, I have many stories to share about some rather unique experiences. In some cases, these are extraordinary moments in time that I will always treasure.

HMCS Winnipeg

Her Majesty's Canadian Ship (HMCS) Winnipeg is a patrol frigate in the Royal Canadian Navy. The vessel boasts one of the most advanced warship designs in the world. Over 130 meters long, she weighs more than 4,700 tonnes and features a helicopter deck and hangar. She houses a crew of 225. This ship has an exemplary record, protecting Canada's sovereignty in the Pacific and Arctic Oceans. Over the years, she has been deployed on numerous missions throughout the world. In 2009, she joined NATO in anti-terrorist operations in the Persion Gulf and the Arabian Sea, and a counter-piracy operation off the coast of Somalia. The HMCS Winnipeg has also escorted United Nations ships carrying relief supplies to East Africa.

In the early 1990s, the HMCS Winnipeg was one of twelve ships being built in Canada for the navy, a "made in Canada" defence industry initiative that hadn't occurred since the building of the Avro Arrow in the 1950s. Ours was the eighth ship being readied for delivery. The ships were state-of-the-art with highly sophisticated technology that was expected to be useful well into the next century.

All twelve ships were named after Canadian cities. All twelve ships are referred to as "she." Explanations abound about why this is so, from grammatical reasons in ancient languages, to being referred to in honour of the king or queen of the day. Whatever the reason, it is a historical tradition I heartily embraced.

As a matter of interest, the ship built in the early 1990s was not the first HMCS Winnipeg. The first Winnipeg was an Algerine Class Coast Escort built in 1942-43. The ship took up escort duties in the north Atlantic from the time it was built until the end of the Second World War in 1945.

In June 1995, the new Winnipeg ship was commissioned into Her Majesty's service and I was named her sponsor. It is a lifetime privilege and one I will treasure forever. The Canadian Navy has the tradition of naming a woman patron to each of its newly built ships. As such, I am the only Winnipeg mayor to hold this distinction.

Historically, the custom of having a woman christen a new ship dates back to the early 1800s in the United States. The ceremony (not necessarily by women) dates back even further. It is said that Romans, Greeks, and Egyptians held ceremonies to ask the gods to protect their sailors.

Modern-day honours are usually bestowed to women who have achieved distinction in their local communities. A Commissioning Committee, comprised of many prominent Winnipeggers, was struck to decide on who would receive this appointment. I was truly honoured to be chosen.

As the ship's patron, I was invited to two ceremonies. The first was held once the ship was built, and took place at the St. John

Shipbuilding shipyard in New Brunswick on June 25, 1994. St. John Shipyard was owned and operated by the Irving family, a very well-known family in the Maritimes. The event was organized to mark the naming of the ship. A number of dignitaries and guests from Winnipeg were invited. Over 500 people, mostly workers of the shipbuilding company, attended the shipyard ceremony. The pride of every person who helped build the ship shone that day and it was quite remarkable to witness. This had been a huge undertaking and it was evident that everyone was proud of their accomplishments.

Traditionally, the launching of a ship has always been a festive occasion and the ceremony for the launching of the Winnipeg was no different. I was asked to christen the ship with a modern-day, spring-loaded device that mechanically smashed a bottle of champagne onto the ship. All I had to do was pull a lever and it was done. Following the ceremony, guests were treated to a lovely lobster luncheon. I had the pleasure of being part of this celebration and had the opportunity to meet Mr. Arthur Irving, Sr., his sons, and other members of his family. I also met the dynamic Elsie Wayne, a New Brunswick politician who had been mayor of the city of St. John from 1983 to 1993. She too was the first woman mayor in her city, so we had a lot in common. She had recently been elected as a member of Parliament, the only Conservative MP other than Jean Charest in Québec. This was the federal election where the Conservatives were nearly wiped off the electoral map. Elsie was a dedicated and accomplished individual, and I was privileged to have met her.

Not long after the ceremony in St. John, in the fall of 1994, the Winnipeg set sail on contractor sea trials for a week. This is a custom for newly built ships to ensure that they are "sea-faring ready." The ship was officially accepted by the Canadian Navy and her crew was appointed in October 1994. She then sailed to her post in Esquimalt from Halifax, south around North America and via the Panama Canal. Once the ship arrived on the Pacific coast, another ceremony would be organized, this one to celebrate the commissioning of the ship to Her Majesty's Service.

On June 23, 1995, almost a year to the day of the naming of the ship, the HMCS Winnipeg was commissioned in Esquimalt. This is when the ship was actually given the designation "Her Majesty's Canadian Ship"and it was another festive occasion that I was privileged to attend. This was a day of sweltering heat...nearly 100 degrees farenheit...and most of the guests were challenged with heat exhaustion from standing in the midday sun. I was given the opportunity to say a few words and spoke to the crowd about the pride felt by Winnipeggers to have a ship named after their city. It was such a proud moment to be standing in front of this massive ship with HMCS Winnipeg emblazoned on its side. It really reinforced the fact that "she" was named in our honour.

The officers of the HMCS Winnipeg asked permission from the city of Winnipeg to adopt the same motto; "One with the strength of many." My reaction when they asked was "absolutely!" What a lovely tribute, I thought, to our great city and what a great motto for the HMCS Winnipeg crew to adopt. I also found out that that the ship has other "Winnipeg" touches. For example, one of the junctions inside the ship is aptly named "Portage and Main." Pieces of Winnipeg and Manitoba memorabilia adorn many walls in the frigate, including a buffalo head, our city crest, and artwork depicting Manitoba. The city of Winnipeg also provided some extras for the officer's dining room to enhance the look of the room for visitors.

As the ship's lifetime patron, I continue to be in touch with the commander and the HMCS Winnipeg crew. We have a unique bond. When members of the ship are in Winnipeg, I do my best to attend ceremonial events. The ship's officers and crew often take the opportunity to visit Winnipeg and are involved not only with Winnipeg but many Manitoba communities in raising money for local charitable organizations. Most recently, they were instrumental in raising funds for the Firefighters Burn Fund of Manitoba.

Winnipeg is fortunate to have a navy frigate named in its honour and has benefited greatly from this association. I am personally grateful to have been chosen as the ship's patron and will continue to be fully supportive of all of its endeavours.

International Winter Cities Conference

In 1996, Winnipeg hosted the International Winter Cities Conference and Showcase. Over 700 delegates from ten countries and forty northern communities attended. A combination of forums and panel discussions, exhibits, activities, entertainment, and an international tradeshow, this bi-annual conference is meant to examine all aspects of living in a winter city. We were to organize an array of seminars and presentations, including discussions relating to transportation, snow-clearing methods, and city planning in a cold climate city. The presentations would also expand on ways to promote tourism and resource development. Yet again, Winnipeggers demonstrated their incredible talents in putting this conference together. So many people involved in this initiative, including the chair and other leaders of the organizing committee, worked on a volunteer basis. The result — Winnipeg was seen on the international stage as a city with incredibly dedicated volunteers.

Winnipeg won the bid to host the International Winter Cities Conference in October 1992, just prior to me becoming mayor. Former mayor Bill Norrie and former councillor Shirley Timm-Rudolph were instrumental in winning this bid over Shenyang, China. They, and a bid committee made up of civic and provincial leaders, tourism and trade industries and other private and public agencies worked on the bid for nearly two years and successfully found ways to make Winnipeg the ideal city to host this conference. In early 1993, I appointed Harold Buchwald, a local lawyer and an active community volunteer, to head the host committee.

Penny McMillan, Harold Buchwald and I in Japan
(Photo courtesy of City of Winnipeg Archives)

In 1995, a year prior to our own conference, I was part of the meeting of the World Winter Cities Association of Mayors in Sapporo, Japan. This organization's roots began in 1982, also in Sapporo, when a number of mayors met at a Northern Intercity conference. The meetings began as a forum for cold climate cities to share best practices, but later became much more encompassing. At its first meeting, nine cities from six countries participated. By 1995, when I first attended this meeting, delegates came from over sixty cities. As host of the next Winter Cities Conference, the Winnipeg delegation was scheduled to give a progress report on our conference to be held in February 1996. Harold Buchwald, chair of the Winnipeg Winter Cities Committee and Penny McMillan, who at the time was the executive director of Tourism Winnipeg, were instrumental in this presentation.

At this meeting, I was introduced to the Japanese way of doing business. It would be a new learning experience for me. Our Japanese hosts were incredibly welcoming. Their attention to detail and thoughtfulness towards us was beyond excellent. They were polite and gracious. Once the business meeting started, I was introduced to yet another dimension of their culture. We found it very difficult to get specific answers to our questions. Unless they had a clear-cut answer, they would not say anything. Suffice it to say that our ways are different than theirs. The meeting went on for hours yet we had barely made any headway on what we were there to discuss. Try as we might, we could not get any answers to our questions regarding the expectations of the association. By the end of the meeting, it became quite tense as mayors from North American cities tried to comprehend what the Japanese mayors were seeking from us. At one point, I expressed to the mayor of Sapporo, Mr. Nobuo Katsura that I was most anxious to get an answer on a specific question. I apologized for my aggressiveness, but noted that it was important for me and my city to understand what they were expecting from us as the next host city. Mayor Katsura smiled ever so slightly as my words were translated for him. The answer that came back to us through the translator was "yes." All we could do was be patient, persevere, and be respectful.

The 1995 mayors' meeting was held in conjunction with Sapporo's annual snow festival. This festival is a huge affair that attracts millions of people. The snow sculptures stand three or four storeys high, run along an eight-block avenue and are absolutely spectacular. There were replicas of many major world landmarks — the Eiffel Tower and Buckingham Palace, just to name a few. Each sculpture was so intricately designed; the work of these artists was just incredible. I so enjoyed this part of the trip and was intrigued by how it all came about. We knew that snow was huge in northern Japan, but I was surprised to learn that snow was brought into the Sapporo festival site by the truckloads in massive Japanese army vehicles. This trip was a great learning experience.

Posing with Japanese citizens at the Sapporo Snow Festival (Photo courtesy of City of Winnipeg Archives)

The citizens of Sapporo were friendly and welcoming. The guests of the Winter Cities Association were given a lot of media attention and special treatment. We were served traditional delicacies everywhere we went. As delightful as this was, I do recall one time when Harold Buchwald craved for "something more familiar." After asking around for a place that would serve foods that were more traditional to us, we were recommended an excellent French restaurant that had recently opened. As soon as we walked through the door, the owner said "Mayor Thompson, welcome!" She had just seen a television news clip featuring the mayors around the world and recognized me from the broadcast. She also said she recognized my beautiful red coat. Prior to the trip, a friend of mine had volunteered to design and sew a coat for me that would be attractive and distinct, but more importantly, warm, as I knew that I would be spending much of my time outside at this festival. My friend Gayle and her sister Valerie painstakingly put together this beautiful coat, based on a photo from the cover of a Vogue magazine. It turned out to be absolutely stunning. They also were very ingenious at finding the materials for this coat and found a way to put it together at a minimal cost. The mandarin collar and cuffs were made of seal fur, which was taken from a used coat found at a Salvation Army Thrift Store. The beautiful red fabric and chamois lining came from a local fabric store. The coat turned out to be a real hit in both Japan and China. It is said that the Japanese and the Chinese like the colour red as it symbolizes good fortune and joy.

The trademark "red coat" made by friend Gayle and her sister Valerie (Photo courtesy of City of Winnipeg Archives)

While there, we also took the opportunity to travel to a few other cities in northern Japan. The protocol of hosting an International Winter Cities Conference was to personally visit the conference's founding city (Sapporo) and then visit as many other cities in northern Japan as possible, to invite them to come to our conference. As well, the tradition was to visit the next city to host the conference after Winnipeg, which in our case was Harbin, China. I was happy to have been given the opportunity to take this trip and personally invite the mayors of these cities to come to our conference. What transpired was great attention to our conference and our city.

We visited five cities throughout Japan. One of the cities we chose to go see was Setagaya. Though it is not located in northern Japan, we purposely chose to go there because it is one of Winnipeg's sister cities. Setagaya is the largest of Tokyo's twenty-three wards, with a population of roughly 800,000. Setagaya has the distinction of being Winnipeg's first "sister city." The suburb was bestowed this honour in a ceremony by Mayor Steve Juba in Japan in August 1970 and a simultaneous ceremony was held in Winnipeg in October that same year. Naming sister cities was meant to encourage cultural, student, and trade exchanges with cities around the world and became quite a popular thing to do in the late twentieth century.

When we first arrived at the Norita Airport in Tokyo, we were met by city representatives who immediately took us to the VIP line... quite a treat. We were driven to Setagaya in their mayor's private car, which was as well-equipped as any business office could be... quite impressive. We stayed at the famous Imperial Hotel in Toyko and I had to pinch myself when I saw the elegant exterior, the grand entrance, and the luxurious rooms. The people of Setagaya were charming and pleasant and made us feel so welcomed. I was made an honorary citizen of their city.

Penny McMillan, Harold Buchwald and I shortly after arriving in Harbin, China (Photo courtesy of City of Winnipeg Archives)

Next stop: Harbin, China. This again was a great place to visit and we were nicely welcomed and treated with kindness. I remember that we were there on February 14. As I met the vice-mayor of Harbin, Vice-Mayor Yue, I wished him a Happy Valentine's Day. The next day, he presented me with a heart-shaped charm made of jade. Mayor Yue and I developed a nice kinship on this trip and continued to get along well as we met a few other times during my tenure. To this day, I still wear my jade heart on Valentine's Day. Harbin is a huge city (2010 census population is 6.7 million) and widely known for its international Ice and Snow Festival. To say that these sculptures are fantastic would be an understatement. They are astounding. Most are illuminated with multi-coloured fluorescent tubes, creating glorious, stunning images. Most of the sculptures are made of clear ice taken from the frozen Songhua River. We took a tour of the sculptures, visited other attractions in Harbin, and met some wonderful people. If I had to find one word to describe my visit to China and Japan, it would be "breathtaking."

At the Harbin International Ice Festival
(Photo courtesy of City of Winnipeg Archives)

Upon our return to Winnipeg, we were invigorated by what we had seen, and were ready to host a most successful conference. Many mayors, city planners, business leaders and students from cities and northern communities around the globe were invited. The event would feature guest speakers covering relevant topics relating to living in a cold climate. There would be design competitions, sports events, entertainment, and a huge exhibit of winter products and services from all over the world.

The conference theme was, "Living, Working, and Playing in a Winter City." I found the event to be a great opportunity to showcase our city; to show the world how we take the challenges of our prairie winters and use them to our advantage recreationally, economically, and communally. It would also be another opportunity to show how very lucky Winnipeg was to have an overwhelmingly supportive volunteer base. From everyday volunteers who helped with transportation and guest services, to specialized communicators who created some wonderful marketing pieces, to architects who used their professional services to create ice and snow sculptures, the calibre of volunteers and their dedication was evident.

The event itself was held from February 9 to 13, 1996. This coincided with our largest annual winter celebration, the francophone Festival du Voyageur. This allowed us to take our guests to visit the festival ice sculpture competitions and participate in some good old-fashioned "joie de vivre." It also provided the opportunity for some to go skating on the Red and Assiniboine Rivers and enjoy toboggan runs and skidoo rides. The conference itself was well-represented with delegates from around the globe.

Many mayors from around the world attended our Winter Cities Conference. Representatives from over forty cities worldwide were in Winnipeg for the occasion. There was representation from other cities in Canada, China, Denmark, Finland, Iceland, Japan, Norway, Russia, Sweden, and the United States. My staff had arranged for me to meet with mayors individually in my office at city hall. On one particular morning, my scheduler came to my office and said the mayor from Bratsk, Russia was there to see me. This meeting had not been scheduled but the man had asked for the opportunity to meet with me. Once we began to talk to him, we realized that though he and a few of his delegates had been able to pay for their flights to Winnipeg, they could not afford a place to stay. We made special arrangements for suitable hotel accommodations for these guests, and ensured that the rest of their stay was pleasant. Quite often, when mayors visit each other's cities at international events such as this, the protocol is to bring a gift. I was not expecting that the mayor of this small Russian city of Bratsk (one-third of the size of Winnipeg) would follow this protocol. He did, however, present me with a gift wrapped in a blanket and tied with wool twine. He proudly helped me to unwrap a beautifully handcrafted piece of art. It was a nature landscape of trees, animals, earth, and sky, all made out of birch bark. It was simply stunning and the fact that this kind man, who could barely afford this trip, had brought such a unique gift to give to our city was a beautiful moment.

Over the course of four days, Winnipeg hosted a spectacular event. From an energizing opening ceremony (where the keynote speaker was Canadian Paralympian Rick Hansen) to the closing ceremony, guests were offered many interesting sessions, exhibitions, and events. Topics relating to transportation and accessibility, shelter and design, leisure and recreation, and remote and northern communities were discussed. Communication and environmental topics were also covered, which made for a well-rounded conference. We were thankful that our Winnipeg weather cooperated. Lucky for us, it was not too cold to be outside, but still under freezing so that the many sculptures created did not melt. We provided tremendous entertainment in two great shows at our Centennial Concert Hall. One was a family showcase that included a magic show and children's carnival. It was called the *Magic Glow of Winter.* The other was a gala evening spearheaded by Neil Harris, a multi-talented local producer and musical conductor, that showcased many of Manitoba's finest performers — Bramwell Tovey and the Winnipeg Symphony Orchestra, Evelyn Hart from the Royal Winnipeg Ballet, a mass choir that featured the Winnipeg Philharmonic Orchestra, other local choirs and soloists from Manitoba, and dancers such as l'Ensemble Folklorique de la

Rivière Rouge, the Rusalka Ukrainian Dance Ensemble, and the Chai Folk Ensemble. Everyone was enthralled by the array of talent. Our organizing committee received many compliments on this particular part of the event.

The Winter Cities Association was delighted with our efforts and complimented us for organizing such a great conference. Our many volunteers, who included many employees of the city of Winnipeg, worked extremely hard to make this a very successful event. I couldn't have been more thrilled with the way it all transpired and I was extremely proud of our city for taking on such a huge undertaking and showcasing Winnipeg's hospitality to the world.

Team Canada Trade Mission to Southeast Asia

In January 1997, I was invited by then Prime Minister Jean Chrétien to take part in a trade mission to Seoul, South Korea; Manila, Philippines; and Bangkok, Thailand. This was the third trade mission undertaken by this prime minister and the largest contingent to date — approximately 350 people. In addition to the prime minister and his entourage, there were several members of Parliament, all ten premiers, mayors from ten major cities, many of the top business people in Canada, and at least thirty members of the media. Locally, our business community was well represented, with the participation from the Canadian Wheat Board, Pioneer Grain, Manitoba Rolling Mills, and Palliser Furniture just to name a few. I saw this as an incredible opportunity to promote and market Winnipeg to the world, at the highest levels. It was also great timing, as we could convey personal invitations to all to join us in July 1999 as Winnipeg hosted the Pan American Games. Over the course of this trip, I could take the time to speak to the top politicians and major business leaders of this country. It also gave me the opportunity to get acquainted with the national media. This was helpful just a few months later, when the city of Winnipeg was faced with the flood of the century. I also got to know Jean Chretien somewhat, and when he was in Winnipeg for a press conference about the flood, he asked for me to be there.

Mayors of Team Canada visiting the Mayor of Seoul, South Korea (Photo courtesy of City of Winnipeg Archives)

When I first found out I was going to South Korea, I had hoped to plan a side trip to Jinju, which is one of Winnipeg's sister cities. Unfortunately, the city is much farther south than we first thought and we were unable to arrange this. Next, I thought we could perhaps visit Kapyong, just slightly north of Seoul. The city of Kapyong is where the Battle of Kapyong occurred in 1951. Many Canadian soldiers were involved in this battle, including members of the 2nd Battalion, Princess Patricia's Canadian Light Infantry (2PPCLI) based out of Winnipeg. Not long after the Korean War, the military base in Winnipeg was renamed Kapyong Barracks, so I thought it would be historically significant to visit there. Unfortunately, time did not enable us to leave the group, as we were all on one plane. We did visit Seoul and met with the mayor there. I was intrigued with Korea's beauty and history.

Fellow Winnipeggers and I visited with city officials from our sister city, Manila, Philippines. To my right is Mayor Lim. (Photo courtesy of City of Winnipeg Archives)

One of the absolute highlights of the trip was our visit to Manila, Philippines. Manila is a big city by Winnipeg standards and very densely populated (2010 census 1.65 million). I was quite pleased to be going there, as Manila is another one of Winnipeg's sister cities. Winnipeg has a significant Filipino population, due to a wave of immigrants that arrived in the early 1970s. At the time, we had a shortage of workers in both manufacturing and medical sectors. Many people from the Philippines had the experience we were looking for and saw Winnipeg as a great place to live. I was quite happy to be going to Manila and expressing our appreciation to its mayor.

I was able to set up a meeting with Mayor Lim. We had a lot in common. We were both elected in 1992. We both had the intention of raising our city's profile and improving its image. We both initiated reforms within our city government. As such, we had a lot to talk about and we had a wonderful visit.

It was in Manila that I was given the once-in-a-lifetime chance to meet Corazon Aquino, former president of the Philippines, and wife of assassinated Opposition leader Benigno Aquino. I had made a request to the Canadian Embassy in the Philippines to meet her. I admired her as a woman of great courage and thought she would be such an interesting person to meet. I was delighted to hear that she agreed to meet with me and Emoke Szathmary, former president of the University of Manitoba. She was adamant that if we met, there would be no media. I found that interesting, but I couldn't have been more pleased.

Dr. Emoke Szathmary, former President of the University of Manitoba and I had an extraordinary visit with Corazon Aquino. (Photo courtesy of City of Winnipeg Archives)

Our meeting ended up being much more special than I ever thought possible. She decided to come and meet with me in my hotel room. I was shocked to find out that she would come to meet me, not the other way around. Just imagine...I heard a knock on the door and there on the other side of the door was Corazon Aquino. It was surreal. I gladly welcomed her in. We immediately felt at ease with each other. We shared a private and stimulating conversation. We spoke about a number of issues and topics, from women in politics, to her husband's assassination (which tragically happened right in front of her), to faith and leadership. We were scheduled to meet for thirty minutes. The meeting wound up lasting well over an hour.

One of the most poignant moments was when she spoke about the days immediately following her husband's assassination at Manila airport in August 1983. Benigno Aquino had been in exile in the United States just prior to this. She said she was surprised when senior members of the government immediately asked her to step in as Opposition leader. Here was this petite woman with the weight of her country on her shoulders. It wasn't anything she had ever thought about doing, though her father did have a political background, so it was a life she understood. In order to make such a monumental decision, she took three days and went away to a convent to contemplate her future. A deeply religious person, she asked God to help and guide her. She spoke candidly about how her entire life had been guided by God and she told me that after three days of reflection and prayer, "God told me I must do this and I would become president." I was awestruck...not that this is how she had made her decision, but that she, too, had received a calling that was more powerful than her. I understood what she was saying because the same thing had happened to me. It touched my heart to hear another woman describe the same situation. I was moved to tears as she spoke with calmness and serenity and I was most honoured to have had the opportunity to meet and get to know her on such a personal level.

Corazon Aquino did become Opposition leader in the days following her husband's assassination, and three years later, she became president after the infamous Marcos regime. We spoke briefly about her term in office and the historic fact that she was the first woman president in the Philippines. We touched upon the years after her presidency, where she returned to a private life but remained vocal about politics in the Philippines. We also discussed her son's involvement in politics and her horror when she found out he had been shot during one of the three coups during her time in office. Her son was injured but not fatally, and today, he is the current president of the Philippines. I was moved by her entire life story, her sense of duty, and her conviction to do what was right. Meeting Corazon Aquino in Manila is a momentous time in my life that I will never forget.

Later that evening, I was invited to a dinner at the presidential palace. The Malacanang Palace is an exquisite mansion and the official residence (though not the living quarters) of the president of the Philippines, who at the time of our visit was Fidel Ramos. This historic building featured marble floors, mahogany walls, and finishing pieces made of various types of wood, wrought iron, and glass. We were led to a grand staircase made of mahogany, which took us to an impressive reception hall that featured historic paintings and intricately carved wood chandeliers. Even the outdoors was decorated for the occasion; white lights shone from the many sandalwood and mahogany trees on the grounds of the palace. Inside, each table was decorated with exquisite china, beautiful flower arrangements, and carved candles. It was magical...a beautiful setting for a state dinner.

The following day, I met the mayor of Manila, Alfredo Lim. Mayor Lim was a former decorated police officer and was extremely loyal to Corazon Aquino. He had helped defend her government in the 1980s. He was later appointed director of the National Bureau of Investigation and earned many commendations and awards. He was well-liked by his citizens and the Philippine community in Winnipeg knew who he was. A number of Winnipeg Filipinos had travelled to Manila for this visit and were invited to Manila City Hall to meet the mayor. The ceremony there was held in an outdoor courtyard and every detail was looked after. As we walked into the courtyard, our national anthem was playing. We then moved inside city hall, where many city employees were in attendance. The audience was receptive and kind. After the public function, we were able to meet privately for a short time and had a good rapport with each other.

My trip to Manila was truly a once-in-a-lifetime experience. Corazon Aquino was a true humanitarian and meeting her had a huge impact on me. I was very privileged to be a member of two Team Canada trips hosted by Prime Minister Chretien. These trade missions were, in my opinion, highly successful in promoting and marketing Canada, and provided a vehicle to establish relationships with many people in the world.

Thunderbird House

During my first election campaign, I met Mary Richard. At the time, she was president of the Urban Aboriginal Council of Winnipeg. I saw Mary as a true leader and a wonderful advisor when making decisions regarding aboriginal development. After I won the election,

I had expressed to Mary that I did not want to introduce my "white person" version of what needed to be done. I was convinced that any plans relating to aboriginals needed to come from the First Nations community. Before long, Mary became my aboriginal mentor.

Not long after I was elected, at Mary's recommendation, we held a "sharing circle" with elders at city hall. I can still recall one of the elders saying that this was the first time his people had been invited inside since 1874 (the year the city was founded). I don't know if this is true, but it was one of the sentiments expressed at that moment in time. As a result of this sharing circle, Mary came to me with the three goals for the city to undertake. As mayor, I felt that these goals were achievable and I embraced them as part of my mandate.

The first goal had to do with healing. The elders shared with us that a community building was needed for members of both the aboriginal and non-aboriginal community. They envisioned this as a gathering place — a healing centre and a celebration centre — to hold ceremonies, meetings, lectures, or private functions. This development had been first conceived in the late 1960s by the Winnipeg Indian and Metis Friendship Centre. Other aboriginal organizations supported the establishment of such a centre and a development corporation was established to see it come to fruition. The development body was named Neeginan, meaning "our place" in Cree.

At my suggestion, the aboriginal elders met with architect Douglas Cardinal, who created drawings for the building. Once this architect was involved, he told Mary that he felt that he had always been meant to design this building. His involvement was key. Under my tenure, the city provided the land at the corner of Main and Higgins for a nominal fee, and the plans to build Neeginan Place, what was later named "Thunderbird House" were underway.

The Neeginan launch was held in May 1995. Here I am standing beside my wonderful mentor Mary Richard. To the extreme right is architect Douglas Cardinal, who designed Thunderbird House. (Photo courtesy of City of Winnipeg Archives)

The next goal identified by Mary Richard and the elders was to appoint aboriginals to city of Winnipeg boards and committees. I immediately began to appoint aboriginals to various committees and encouraged businesses to do so as well. Within a few years, aboriginals were much more visible in the community. This was most evident on the various committees for the planning of the 1999 Pan American Games. Many aboriginals were involved with the Pan Am Games, and many were trained and took this experience to facilitate the North American Indigenous Games, which Winnipeg also hosted in 2002.

The third goal was to provide employment opportunities for aboriginals. Mary had expressed to me that it was important to establish positive connections to the aboriginal community, not only as participants on decision-making bodies but also as active in the local workforce. The city of Winnipeg had to lead in hiring First Nations people. Aboriginals had to serve in the police force, the fire department, and transit. My commitment to proactively hire First Nations people was not easy to implement. I was challenged with rhetoric about imposing a quota system (which I was not) and met with some resistance at first. Behind the scenes, City Hall bureaucrats definitely put barriers in place. During my tenure, I worked hard to encourage the City to be pro-active and recruit aboriginals, and eventually, the hiring of aboriginals in key sectors started to happen.

I must stress how important the construction of Thunderbird House was for the people of Winnipeg. This building was built, first and foremost, to be a healing centre for both aboriginal and non-aboriginal people. It is truly a gathering place for ALL people. Thanks to the vision and leadership of Mary Richard, who sadly passed away in 2010, Thunderbird House stands today, open for healing, educating, and providing opportunities to build a future for our community. The building is beautifully designed, thanks to architect Douglas Cardinal. It has a very spiritual quality. I was honoured to be a part of this initiative and consider it to be a critical centre as we build a future for Winnipeg.

The Chain of Office

Within society, and within various levels of government, there are traditional symbols of governance. In civic government, the custom is for the mayor to wear a Chain of Office, a collar or chain worn as an insignia of office during official or ceremonial duties. The tradition dates back to fourteenth century England. At the time, collars were bestowed upon kings, knights, and parliamentary figures. Soon thereafter, mayors and highest officials of educational institutions began to wear them as well. The tradition continued through the centuries, not only in Great Britain, but in other Commonwealth countries such as Australia, Canada, and New Zealand. It is particularly widespread amongst mayors across Canada. In the twentieth century, wearing a Chain of Office was seen as a way of honouring tradition and history.

I first wore the City of Winnipeg Chain of Office during my swearing-in ceremony in November 1992. This piece had originally been designed in 1972, when thirteen municipal governments amalgamated to form what was colloquially known as "Unicity." The chain consisted of thirteen maple leafs, each of them cast with a crest representing each of the amalgamated municipalities. Each leaf was cast in silver and linked by chain link to a centre disk, which carried the names of the mayors elected since unification. A second, smaller disk bore the city's new crest and motto. The entire collar was attached to a piece of burgundy suede.

When I began my first term, Councillor Jae Eadie encouraged me to wear the Chain of Office to every council meeting, citing it was proper protocol. I very much understood the importance of wearing the Chain of Office and when I did wear it, I wore it proudly. It wasn't until I went to a national meeting of mayors and was able to see the Chains of Office of most other mayors across the country that I realized how worn ours looked. Soon thereafter, I sought a way to replace it, at no cost to the city. I was determined to have a replacement by the time I left office, so that future mayors would have a chain that they could wear with pride.

In December 1997, I approached Roger Watson, a local jeweller and fellow Rotarian, to see if he could help me find a solution. We discussed what the ideal piece could look like and how it could be financed. Roger had some great ideas on both counts and accepted to take on this project. We kept the same look, which had originally been designed by Birks in Toronto, but we chose to reproduce it in gold and add a few intricate details. The end result was exquisite. Each of the thirteen maple leaves was cast with the crest of the amalgamated municipalities — similar to the first design — but in 14-carat gold. The links connecting each leaf were made up of much tinier maple leaves. We recognized the importance of the maple leaf as a symbol on this piece and thought this added touch would be fitting. Two links connected the leaves to each other and to the two round centre disks. The smaller disk bore the City of Winnipeg crest and the larger centre disk featured the more elaborate Coat of Arms of the City of Winnipeg. Both of these symbols include thirteen stars representing each of the amalgamated municipalities, the Fort Garry gate, a prairie crocus, and the Latin saying, "Unum cum virtute multorum" — "One with the strength of many." I had always loved our city's motto, embraced it, and referred to it often in my speeches.

This saying became ever so significant during the peak days of the 1997 flood.

After all was said and done, the cost of the new Chain of Office was $30,000. Roger Watson was instrumental in finding donors to contribute to the remaking of this lovely piece.[19] A number of individuals, mostly fellow Rotarians, and local companies contributed to cover most of the cost — $20,000. The remaining $10,000 price tag was donated by Roger Watson himself, donated in materials, in time to design the piece, and in work putting it together. The City of Winnipeg Chain of Office was completed in September 1998 at no cost to the city. I was most grateful for this initiative and had the opportunity to wear it proudly during my last year as mayor. (The new piece is shown below and on the front cover of this book.) It is a legacy for future elected officials of our municipal government, and the citizens of Winnipeg have every right to be proud of this historic city symbol.

19 The following companies and individuals contributed to the cost of the Chain of Office for the City of Winnipeg: Arthur Mauro, Can West Global Communications, Ernst P. Schell, Investors Group, N.M. Paterson and Sons, William A. Hutchison, Hugh Munro Construction, Ed and Margaret Danylchuk, Norman L. Coghlan, Taillieu Construction, George A. Keats, Roger Watson Jewellers

Photo courtesy of Albert Cheung

Part 3

THE NEXT CHAPTER

"Life is like a novel. You can guess what will happen on the next chapter, but you will not know until you're there."

Author Unknown

Official portrait of my appointment as Consul General of Canada to the United States of America (in Minneapolis)

Chapter 14
Consul General

Déja Vu

Remember those days in grade nine when you had to make a decision about whether you should be taking university entrance, general, or secretarial courses, and all of it hinged on what you chose as your future career? I remember feeling tremendous pressure during that time, as I had no idea what I wanted to do when I grew up. I did know that careers typically chosen by women, such as teaching and nursing did not appeal to me. My mother was very traditional and had ingrained in her daughters that our "role" in life was to be a wife and mother, and to support our husbands. There was a part of me that understood where she was coming from. She had been a "stay-at-home" mother, raising four children, and her duty was to her family first and foremost. However, I was the new baby boomer generation and women's roles were changing. To keep my options open, I made the wise decision of taking university entrance courses.

My guidance teacher insisted I needed to have a career goal in mind. I really did not know what that might be. She asked me to think seriously about what I wanted to do, and return to her the next day with my decision. I have no idea what happened during the night, but I awoke the next morning with a clear career path in mind. I returned to her office and announced that I was to be an ambassador. In a million years, I could not tell you where that idea came from, but I was convinced that this was now my calling. I could tell from the look on her face that she was less than impressed. She was as shocked as I was that I had landed on this path, but that was that, and I moved on to take university entrance courses. Ironically, over the years, ambassador roles, albeit not all traditional ones, became a part of my life.

One day, while I was studying at the University of Winnipeg, a notice was posted on a bulletin board outside the career office about dates and times for a foreign-service exam. *Ah,* I thought, *Writing this exam could lead me to becoming an ambassador.* I immediately began to look into the matter. It would have required me to go back and pick up some French courses. At the time, I had begun dating my future husband and my priorities shifted from ambassador to staying in Winnipeg, planning a wedding, and becoming a wife. Clearly, this idea of becoming an ambassador was no longer in the cards for me... or so I thought.

Fast-forward eight years and I was working for Eaton's in Calgary. I had been with the company for a few years now and was progressing nicely. I knew retail management and I loved my work. During a cosmetic fair, one of my suppliers approached me and said, "Wow Susan, you really are a great ambassador for Eaton's." I smiled and thanked him and thought to myself, *There it is again... ambassador*. I remember thinking that I may have previously been considering my destiny too specifically. Perhaps being an ambassador didn't necessarily mean foreign service. Perhaps I would be an ambassador in the more liberal sense of the word. An ambassador for Eaton's...it sounded nice and I took on the role proudly.

When I became mayor, it did not take long for people — media and citizens alike — to refer to me as a great ambassador for the city. Whether it was when I was participating in the Pan Am Games bid, working with other mayors and politicians on the Mid-Continent Trade Corridor or travelling on Team Canada missions with the federal government, I was often referred to as a great ambassador for the City of Winnipeg. Once again, this made me reflect on my discussion with my guidance counsellor back in grade nine and it finally occurred to me that I had indeed achieved my destiny. I had the honour of representing my city to the world on many occasions and this was just another way of interpreting my work. I felt lucky and blessed.

After my re-election in 1995, I emphatically stated to the public that this would be my last term, as per my election commitment. During an interview with our major local newspaper, I was asked what I would do next, after completing my term as mayor. I blurted out, "Oh, Ambassador to Chile or Consul General of Canada in Minneapolis." Honest to God...this is what came out of my mouth! Not long before this interview, a group of us had visited with Robert Dery, then Consul General in Minneapolis and we were invited to the Canadian Consulate. I remember having an eerie but comfortable feeling when I was there. It was like a déja vu. I knew I could do this job and I could envision myself being there again. I suppose that visit gave me the idea, subconsciously, that I could be the next Consul General in Minneapolis.

My quote on what I would do next must have sounded good, as it was reported in the newspaper that week and read by many. One of those people was Penny Collenette from Prime Minister Chrétien's Office. Penny was the director of appointments for the PMO's office and she was committed to recommending appointments for women and minorities. Soon after the article was written, she gave me a call. She asked me what this was about and my answer to her was, "A good idea?" She then went on to tell me that the idea wasn't as far-fetched as I thought. She explained to me that Chrétien wanted to see women in high-profile positions. And so the journey began...

Not long afterwards, still in 1995, Lloyd Axworthy, who was minister of Foreign Affairs at the time, called and asked if we could provide him with a meeting room at city hall for the Canadian Ambassador to the United States and the Canadian consuls in the United States for their annual meeting. I gave him the council chambers. During a break, Ambassador Raymond Chrétien, nephew to the prime minister, asked to meet with me in my office. It was a good meeting... just friendly chitchat about being mayor of a major city. Of course, he was "checking me out," but I was so naïve, I really did not get it. Subsequent to that, I was invited by the U.S. State Department to visit the United States for three weeks as their guest. The tour began in Washington, D.C. and during that visit, I was invited to lunch at our Canadian ambassador's official residence. What an honour! I swear I was pinching myself the whole way. I arrived at the Canadian embassy — the most incredible embassy in Washington D.C. in my opinion, and the only foreign embassy allowed on Pennsylvania Avenue. I met with Ambassador Chrétien and then we proceeded to the official residence. During our conversation, he asked me what I wanted to do next. I repeated the same answer that I had told our local reporter. He matter-of-factly said that I was "not a big enough fish" to be an ambassador. I remember thinking, *They've actually talked about this?* He then went on to say that I could possibly get a position as consul general. I was shocked. Even though I'd said these things publicly, I never in a million years thought the possibility might occur that I would be considered for such a prestigious position. Not being part of the Foreign Service, the only way that I could become consul general would be through a political appointment. Since I did not belong to any political party, I had always thought that my chances were slim to none that I would be in the running.

The process and momentum began to build. Other people and factors lent their influence. Senator Terry Stratton, who had been my 1992 campaign co-chair, lobbied for me to get an appointment. Jimmy Pattison, a Canadian business magnate and a friend, supported my appointment as well. Then Mother Nature had a hand in swinging the pendulum my way. The 1997 flood brought Prime Minister Chrétien to Winnipeg on two occasions, and I met with him on both visits. During these visits, we got to know each other a little better and he saw me in action during an actual crisis, which bode well for me.

Still, this political appointment was about as far-fetched as one can imagine for two very realistic reasons: (1) I was not a Liberal, and (2) the appointment could only be made on the recommendation of the minister of Foreign Affairs, who had already made his views known about whether or not I deserved the appointment. My odds of becoming mayor were 650,000 to 1; my odds of being consul general were 32 million to 1. For three years, the idea was off and on and then in late 1998, just when my term as mayor was about to end, I received a lunch invitation from Lloyd Axworthy. At that meeting, he advised me that he would recommend me for the appointment. Never underestimate what can happen when something is meant to be.

The one drawback was that the decision on the appointment was delayed to June 1999. My appointment as the next consul general in Minneapolis was likely to happen, but until the prime minister made the announcement it was not for certain and it had to be kept confidential. Since my term as mayor was ending in October 1998, and I had no pension, I needed a job as soon as possible. The rent had to be paid. This meant that I had to find something else to do for the next six months. Thank goodness for Terry Stratton, Murray Sigler, and Sandy Hopkins. Terry helped me greatly as I transitioned from mayor to private citizen. Murray and Sandy, then President and CEO and Board Chair (respectively) of the Winnipeg Airports Authority opened the airport's doors to me and gave me a new home...if only for a short while.

Soaring to New Heights

As mayor, I'd had many conversations with the Winnipeg Airports Authority's (WAA) board chair, Sandy Hopkins. He was an active member of the Winnipeg Chamber of Commerce and the instigator for the airport's change from federal government-regulated department to community-owned airport authority. Not long before the initial transfer, Murray Sigler was hired as the WAA's President and CEO. He was new to the city, but quickly became involved in a myriad of activities related to the city's economic development. I always thought both of these gentlemen were bright and energetic, and both played a pivotal role in revitalizing Winnipeg in the late 1990s. Somewhere in the back of my mind, I also thought they would be great to work with directly.

The feeling, I think, was mutual. Murray, in particular, would often tell me that with my connections, I would make a great PR person at the airport. "You know all the movers and shakers in this city," he would say. "I'm new here and you could introduce me to many key people."

What emerged was a new job at the Winnipeg Airport Authority. I was named the WAA's new executive consultant; Marketing and Public Affairs. Among my responsibilities, I would assist in developing a five-year strategic marketing plan, work on key initiatives such as the Mid-Continent Trade Corridor and the Winnipeg Airport Services Corporation and be part of a team working on the development of an airport industrial park. My responsibilities also included developing the vision and initial plans for a new terminal building. As well, the Pan Am Games were coming to Winnipeg in July 1999 and because of my involvement with the games as mayor, I was part of the welcoming committee on behalf of the airport authority. Again, I was to be an "ambassador."

Murray Sigler and Sandy Hopkins gave me my first "post-mayor" job at the Winnipeg Airports Authority in 1998.

Growing up in St. James and only a mile or two from the airport, I often watched the planes fly low over my home. For as long as I could remember, I had thought of the airport as an exciting place. Years later, as a business owner and as mayor, I met Lynn Bishop, then general manager of the Winnipeg International Airport. He ensured that I recognize the importance of this huge industry. I always saw its potential for growth. Now, taking on this new challenge, I would be a key member of the WAA team and be a part of the decision-making for this major economic pillar in our community. I was thrilled to be working with such a dynamic group.

For six months, I was very busy at the WAA. I loved the camaraderie among WAA staff and had a great time meeting and getting to know so many of them.

In March 1999, I received a call from Minister Axworthy's office asking if I was still interested in the consul general position. Of course, I emphatically said, "Yes." I was then told that everything was on track for an announcement in June but that this had to be kept strictly confidential. On another day — on April 30, 1999 to be exact — a woman from the Foreign Service Department called and exclaimed "Welcome to the Foreign Service of Canada" to which I responded, "I beg your pardon?" Nobody else had called me to say that the appointment was absolutely confirmed, but I took it as a very good sign.

Then, in late May, I received a telephone call from the prime minister's office. I was told that my appointment was confirmed and that the announcement was imminent. Everything still needed to be kept strictly confidential. I was also told that I had to go to Ottawa for a two-week orientation. While this was absolutely exciting news and I was ecstatic, I couldn't quite figure out how I would explain this to my new boss.

I walked over to Murray Sigler's office to explain the situation as best I could. "Murray, I need ten days off."

"When?"

"I need to leave tomorrow."

"Tomorrow? Where are you going?"

"I can't tell you. I can't tell you why I'm going, either."

"And you need ten days off." The entire conversation was bizarre. Luckily, I had a great boss; Murray granted me my leave, and off I went to Ottawa.

On June 10, 1999, the prime minister announced my appointment as consul general of Canada, representing our country in

Minneapolis, Minnesota, to an eight-state territory in the United States. I was now officially part of Canada's Foreign Service... a true and real ambassador for my country. **My grade nine vision had come true. It was absolutely uncanny.** My term was to start on July 1, 1999. The day of the announcement was one of the most exciting of my life. What a marvellous honour...an amazing moment in time.

I worked at the Winnipeg Airports Authority until just before the Pan American Games, which were held in July 1999. Though I was only at the WAA for a short time, I thoroughly enjoyed working there. I shall never forget the time I spent in one of our city's most vibrant places. I met some great people during that time of my life, some of whom I am still in touch with today, including my collaborator on this book.

Susan A. Thompson — A True Ambassador

Canada's Canadian Consulate in Minneapolis has been in operation since 1970. During my time as consul general, our consulate served an eight-state territory in the upper mid-west of the United States, which includes the states of Colorado, Iowa, Minnesota, Montana, Nebraska, North Dakota, South Dakota, and Wyoming. Billions of dollars in trade exist between Canada and this territory and our Canadian diplomats play an incredibly vital role in strengthening the ties that promote this type of activity. I was extremely excited about taking on my new role and couldn't wait to get started.

The position of consul general crystalized all of my work experiences into one. The lessons that I had learned as a retailer, entrepreneur, and politician served me well, as I began to build important relationships in my new role.

Being a political appointment allowed me to learn about Canada's Department of Foreign Affairs. It gave me a greater appreciation for our diplomats and the vital work that they do. Diplomats are the official representatives for Canadians in a foreign country. They are our voice in a foreign country...our eyes and ears. They are positioned to help Canadians take advantage of business and trade opportunities by promoting and marketing Canada. They can help to build relationships and influence decision makers. There are also times when these representatives can help to resolve disputes. During my time at the consulate in Minneapolis, I was involved in trying to resolve issues surrounding fishing regulations between Ontario and Minnesota, the Devil's Lake/Garrison Dam issue, the challenge by the United States regarding Canadian Wheat Board subsidies, endless trade disputes, and of course, the fallout of 9/11 and its impact on our borders.

Once I was inside the consulate, I was faced with some challenges. The first was acceptance. The career diplomats within the Department of Foreign Affairs in Ottawa do not look kindly on political appointments, so even though they were technically my employer, I was given the impression that I did not deserve this position. The dynamics of the organization are always present. As well, Canada had implemented a policy that only senior positions in consulates could be filled by Canadians. This meant that, out of a staff of eighteen in the consulate in Minneapolis, only three were Canadian. The rest were contracted Americans. Again, this made for very interesting dynamics. I was told by the operations manager that consul generals came and went.

As in all organizations, the Canadian consulate had some dedicated staff members. Then again, there were issues that needed to be solved. For example, one employee was on a fifteen-year performance "warning." There were factors of change that needed to be addressed.

Relationship-building is a key responsibility for consul generals, particularly with the governors, members of Congress and state legislators. I also met and maintained connections with the business community and the media in my territory. All influencers were important to develop.

One of the working relationships I enjoyed the most was with former pro wrestler Governor Jessie Ventura of Minnesota. Though he was "all business," he was also a joy to be around. He knew Canada. He had wrestled in many parts of Canada and actually finished his wrestling career in Winnipeg. He had been the mayor of Brooklyn Park, a bedroom community of Minneapolis, so we were able to share our civic experiences.

Former pro wrestler and Minnesota State Governor Jessie Ventura visited the offices of the Canadian Consulate in Minneapolis while I was Consul General. He was the first governor from the state of Minnesota to visit the consulate in over 30 years.

Part of my job was to increase trade between our two countries. Governor Ventura had done trade missions to Europe, China, and Mexico, and after I pointed out that Minnesota did more trade with Manitoba, Ontario, and Saskatchewan than Europe, China, and

Mexico combined, we embarked on trade visits to those provinces. During that time, he also formed good relationships with the premiers of Manitoba and Saskatchewan, Gary Doer and Roy Romanow.

Part of my job was also to promote and market Canada, and when you have a political figure like Governor Ventura, who has national media from both countries following him everywhere, you take advantage of that media coverage. Whenever the consulate did anything that involved Governor Ventura, the Canadian message got out.

I was quite pleased to have had the opportunity to meet this well-known politician. I thought he was a good governor. He had an excellent chief of staff and great people working for him and he was always a pleasure to work with. He did some good work for Minnesota, but took on the press with a vengeance. There were times it was like he was "back in the ring" but in the end, no one won.

Assisting Canadians in distress, a key role of the consulate, was never more apparent than on September 11, 2001. As soon as we were aware of the tragedies in New York City, Washington D.C., and Pennsylvania, our consulates went into high alert and we began responding to Canadians in our areas on a 24/7 basis. One of the situations we had to deal with was a plane that was scheduled to fly from Toronto to Calgary. The plane experienced some bad weather and dipped down near Minnesota. The flight crew was told to land in Minneapolis immediately. Not long after, all American airspace was shut down and this Canadian plane, bound from one Canadian city to another, was stuck in Minneapolis. The passengers were not prepared for this. Some did not have passports and none had American money. Some were in need of medication, particularly if they were going to be here for a few days, and all were distraught at the prospect of being "held" here for more than a few days. The consulate made arrangements to bring passengers to our office. We gave them the chance to contact relatives and for those who needed to, call their doctors for needed prescriptions. We generated proper identification where needed for each of them and worked with the airline to get them back to Canada as quickly as we possibly could.

Since 9/11, life has changed. Of course, all travellers now need a passport and are subject to much more stringent regulations to ensure safety. As a precaution, it is wise to know where your Canadian Consulates and/or Embassies are in foreign countries. Obtain telephone numbers and contact names before leaving for any foreign country, including the United States of America. Know the rules and regulations of the countries you are visiting.

As consul general, I was fortunate in attending various prestigious events. One such event — the National Prayer Breakfast — is held each February in Washington, D.C. It is hosted by the United States Congress, and every United States president since Dwight D. Eisenhower has made an appearance. The event, which is actually a series of meetings, luncheons, and dinners, is attended by approximately 3,500 guests from around the world. I first went as an invited guest. On my second visit, I was asked to speak. I was part of a forum that highlighted women in leadership roles in crisis situations. I was there to talk about the 1997 Red River flood of the century. Other women presenters included Benazir Bhutto, former prime minister of Pakistan and Lisa Beamer, author of *Let's Roll: Ordinary People, Extraordinary Courage,* a book that details the account of her husband and 9/11 hero Todd Beamer, as one of the passengers on United Airlines Flight 93, the plane that crashed in a field in Pennsylvania on the morning of September 11th. I was in awe to be part of such a prestigious group and felt extremely blessed to have met these two extraordinary women. At the breakfast itself, I was seated at the Texas delegation table. Needless to say, then President George W. Bush made a point of visiting this table and I got the opportunity to see him up close.

My sister Lenore and I at the official residence in Minneapolis

One of the most precious parts about my time as consul general was that my sister Lenore came to live with me in Minneapolis. Lenore had been recently widowed, and her children were all grown up and had moved out of the house. I saw this as an opportunity to give Lenore a change of scenery; to do something completely different with her life, if only for a short time. She agreed and moved from her home in Oregon to Minneapolis. The official residence did not have a permanent staff person. I really needed Lenore's help when it came to hosting, cooking, and entertaining American citizens at the residence. We were a good team. We are both good cooks and both have a creative flare. We simply rolled our sleeves and got the job done...together. Guests were treated to real home cooking...literally. Our years together in Minneapolis were very special, as we spent a lot of time just being together and reconnecting.

Spying

I must say that I had some peculiar moments when I lived in Minneapolis as well. It was no secret that our telephones at the consulate were tapped. I was surprised that I was also under surveillance at the official residence. On one occasion, as I was having a private conversation with a friend, I could hear somebody come on the line. This was followed by the sound of machinery in the background. Obviously, someone was listening in. I began to say, "Hello. Hello." to whoever was listening in, and continued by saying, "This is simply a personal call, but if you want to listen in, go right ahead." This did not deter the "listener" from hanging up. In fact, having my phones tapped happened with regular frequency. I understood that this was my reality as long as I was consul general, but I always thought it was rather peculiar that they would want to listen to my personal conversations, none of which were ever matters of national security.

I spent three years as consul general in Minneapolis and on a one-year assignment as a special advisor to the Government of Canada on U.S. / Canadian affairs. At this time, I was also in negotiations for a position that would end up being my new career for the next ten years of my life.

Life as a diplomat was a privilege. I had a great love for my country before my posting, but gained an even greater appreciation for Canada after representing it as consul general in Minneapolis. It had already been pretty special to be the mayor of Winnipeg, but to represent Canada was an even greater distinction. **For the most part, this time in my life was joyful and magical...and the "message" I had received in ninth grade that I would be an ambassador really did happen.**

The iconic Wesley Hall at the University of Winnipeg (Photo courtesy of University of Winnipeg Archives)

Chapter 15
University of Winnipeg Foundation

Coming Full Circle

Sometimes, the way life works is simply astounding. How I returned to Winnipeg after my consul general appointment was one of those surprising times in life. My appointment with the Government of Canada was good until the summer of 2003, but I knew that I had to get my next job before that. In early 2002, I began to actively explore what that might be...and where.

One day, in the spring of 2002, I was in my office at the Canadian Consulate when I received a telephone call from Sandy Riley. You may recall that Sandy was the person that I asked to be the volunteer chair of the 1999 Pan Am Games Committee when I was mayor.

Sandy is a prominent Winnipeg businessman, and in 2002, was chairman of Investors Group, Canada's largest distributor of mutual funds, diversified financial products, and financial planning services. On a volunteer basis, he had recently taken on the role of chancellor of the University of Winnipeg. When he called, he explained to me that the university was embarking on a ground-breaking endeavour. The university's Board of Regents had approved the establishment of an independent, arms-length foundation, a separate entity devoted solely to fundraising. He was calling to discuss the position of University of Winnipeg Foundation president and CEO.

As background to this historic move by the University of Winnipeg, the idea to establish a separate foundation was a suggestion brought forward to university administrators by Janet Walker. Janet was hired by the university in the spring of 2000 as their director of Advancement. She reported to then President Connie Rooke and worked alongside Joan Anderson, who was executive director of Advancement Services. The Board of Regents had established an external relations committee, who worked with the advancement group. Together, they first came up with a strategy to launch a major capital campaign for the University of Winnipeg.

Janet Walker spent much of 2000 and 2001 meeting with people who had a deep affiliation and connection to the institution. Former chancellors, presidents, and alumni were consulted and from these meetings, Janet understood the affinity many people had for this institution. She knew that the university was poised to embark on an unprecedented fundraising campaign, if the proper process was in place.

In January 2001, Janet and Sandy Riley went to St. Paul, Minnesota to meet with Dr. Doug Leatherdale, a United College alumnus (United College was the forerunner to the University of Winnipeg). Hailing from humble beginnings in south-western Manitoba, Doug was the first in his family to graduate from high school. He then became a university graduate and a politically active young adult. He went on to become a highly successful entrepreneur in Minnesota with the St. Paul Group of companies, and for many years, held the positions of both chairman and president and chief executive officer. As chair of the University of Minnesota Foundation, he was the perfect person to speak to about introducing a new funding model at the University of Winnipeg.

At this meeting, Doug introduced Janet to Mary Ellen Kuhi, director of development for the Minnesota Symphony Orchestra. Ms. Kuhi and Dr. Leatherdale had worked together on a highly successful fundraising campaign for the orchestra; in fact, Dr. Leatherdale was the campaign chair for that particular campaign. In a separate meeting with Janet alone, Ms. Kuhi shared her thoughts on how great campaigns worked and suggested the concept of a separate foundation, citing the University of Minnesota Foundation as an example. Janet liked the idea, and having previously worked at the Health Sciences Centre Foundation in Winnipeg, had some experience with it. On the flight home, Janet briefed Sandy Riley on her conversation with Mary Ellen Kuhi and he was keen on the idea. "Go ahead. Start the process," was his response.

In April 2001, Janet returned to Minneapolis to meet again with Mary Ellen Kuhi. This time around, she came to visit me at the consulate. Janet and I knew each other from previous affiliations and this was strictly a personal visit. The establishment of a foundation at the University of Winnipeg was still in preliminary stages and Janet kept this information confidential. We did talk about when my term as consul general would be up and that I was contemplating a return to Winnipeg. We agreed that someday we might work together again in some capacity, but did not have anything specific in mind.

In the meantime, the UW Development office hired a consultant to conduct a feasibility study on fundraising probabilities. The goal was to determine if the university could raise $27 million over five years for campus expansion and development, including renovations to Wesley Hall, a new science building, the development of a new building for the theatre department, and an expanded endowment fund for student scholarships and bursaries. Approximately forty-five community representatives, alumni, and donors participated in the study. While there was interest in the projects, the value of gifts suggested by respondents fell far short of the desired goal. Additionally, very few of the respondents were willing to sit on a campaign cabinet. The study also indicated that the professional capacity of the university's fundraising department fell short of expectations. A summary of the study's recommendations was reviewed by the university's external relations committee in late 2001. The study suggested that the university delay any fundraising efforts until the issues revealed in the study were addressed.

Despite the dismal revelations in this feasibility study, there was some recognition among the decision makers that establishing a separate entity could be the right way to go. Creating such a mechanism could boost donor confidence and attract large contributions from many of the city's philanthropists. The major stumbling block was that there would need to be a significant financial investment in the university's development office, and given the campus financial circumstances, this was unlikely to happen. Nevertheless, talks continued on how this could be accomplished.

Throughout this process, Janet worked tirelessly on the mechanics of establishing the foundation, incorporation of such an entity, and transition issues. Setting up a new entity required a lot of due diligence and Janet consulted lawyers and tax specialists as needed to get the ball rolling, if and when the university was ready to do so.

In 2002, the University of Winnipeg continued to weather some tough financial times. It was in a dispute with the provincial government over disproportionate post-secondary funding and a storm was brewing about shortfalls in the pension fund. Some of the university's buildings, both inside and out, were in dire need of repairs. Stone was literally falling off the historic Wesley Hall on Portage Avenue. The Province of Manitoba responded by announcing a $14-million grant for the restoration of the Wesley Hall building. A windfall such as this presented an opportunity. Could a new foundation be partially capitalized with the interest on this grant? Could the interest be used to pay the salaries of the new foundation staff?

As the possibility of a new entity became more achievable, Janet began to ponder who might be a suitable candidate to take the helm of this new organization. By then, the university had been developing financial rollouts for a foundation and steps had begun to obtain charitable status. Meetings were occurring on a regular basis to outline responsibilities, reporting scenarios, and proposed board appointments. Eventually, the topic of who could be president and CEO came up for discussion.

The manager of University Advancement at that time was Louise Humeniuk, and during discussions with Janet, Louise suggested me as a possible president and CEO of this new foundation. I'd had the opportunity to work with both of these remarkable women on past endeavours, and in particular, when they worked for the Winnipeg Core Area, a tri-government initiative to revitalize the economic, social, and physical core area of Winnipeg. They knew I had the experience to tackle something like this and we had always worked well together. Along with the university president, Connie Rooke, Janet took the suggestion to Sandy Riley. When Sandy first heard the suggestion, he responded positively and said, "Susan owes me!" referring of course to the fact that I had asked him to be volunteer chair of the Pan Am Games. And so, the phone call occurred.

Sandy made it quite clear during his telephone call that he wanted me for my vision and "can-do" attitude. He also explained that this was a significant new chapter in the university's existence, and that change was not always easy, so he wanted someone who could withstand any pushback and lead without fear.

I was delighted. The University of Winnipeg and its Collegiate had absolutely made my various careers possible. I had always credited the excellent teachers and professors at the UW for my successes. These professionals constantly encouraged me and "stuck with me" and my life would have been very different without their support. This was an opportunity to give back.

Moving back to Winnipeg and assuming this post was very appealing to me. I was at a point in my life where I wanted to return to my roots. In 1967, I had started my working life as a circulation clerk in the University of Winnipeg library, and now, thirty five years later, to be asked to become the founding president and CEO of its newly established foundation was truly a full circle moment for me. I was honoured to accept Sandy's offer. Arrangements were made with the federal government and I returned to Winnipeg.

The decision to move forward with the establishment of a foundation at the University of Winnipeg was made in the summer of 2002. In early August 2002, the University of Winnipeg Foundation was officially incorporated and by October 2002, the entity was granted charitable status. I met with Sandy Riley and Janet Walker at the end of October to discuss the terms of my employment, board structure, and critical dates.

The late fall of 2002, however, became even more tumultuous with financial instability and labour issues. Further revelations about the state of the university's pension plan had faculty and staff demoralized. By the end of the year, the university had lost its president, three vice presidents, two chief fundraisers, and several board members, including two table officers.[20] As such, delays in planning and development were put on hold.

In early 2003, Vice President Academic Patrick Deane was named acting president and he and the chair of the Board of Regents, Richard Graydon, proceeded to establish the foundation. On March 18, 2003, an announcement was made that the foundation would soon be up and running and that I would be president and CEO. I began to work for the University of Winnipeg Foundation that very day. The foundation "officially" became operational April 1, 2003.

On my first day of work, I remember walking up the front sidewalk leading to the entrance of Wesley Hall, the University of Winnipeg's iconic heritage building, fondly known as "the castle on Portage Avenue." The first thing that caught my eye was a gigantic green net draped across the front of the building. Its purpose was to catch the crumbling sandstone that was falling off the building's exterior. This was a bad omen, I thought. A crumbling building!

I first met with my staff — all three of them — and we had a quick conversation about the enormous task ahead of us. Clearly we were understaffed, yet we were about to embark on a major undertaking. It was apparent to me right from the start that the organizational structure would need to change and expand.

20 Taken from Dr. Neil Besner's remarks at the University of Winnipeg October 2013 Convocation Dinner, on the occasion of the 100th Convocation Awards.

Members of my team at UW Foundation in 2003: (from l to r) Louise Humeniuk, Terry Samborski, Nadine Kampen, Patti Tweed, Marlene Laycock, Janet Walker (Photo courtesy of University of Winnipeg Archives)

Once the foundation was established, Janet Walker became executive consultant to the new entity. She was my resource when it came to fundraising know-how and in most matters pertaining to the foundation. In our first meeting together, Janet and I reviewed the financial analysis and gift charts, which had been prepared for my arrival. It didn't take long for me to realize that with such an under-resourced organization, things were going to have to evolve in a very pragmatic manner. At this point in time, the overall goal was to raise $11 million. Janet's recommendation was that the lead gift be set at $500,000. I reflected on the gift chart and came to the conclusion that we should try to achieve ten lead gifts of $1 million. I then suggested the remaining million be apportioned accordingly. Janet was in disbelief as to what I was proposing. Her expertise in the science of fundraising simply did not compute that this would be possible. She thought it would be completely unrealistic to contemplate one one-million dollar gift, let alone ten one-million dollar gifts. I was positive that we could. To Janet's credit and extraordinary professionalism, she took one of those meaningful pauses before responding to my suggestion. She made a decision to trust my instincts and to develop a plan for this very ambitious goal.

Then I met with the vice president of Finance. He told me that the university had a $100 million infrastructure deficit and a pension crisis in the range of $10 million. He said that both faculty and staff members were restless and unhappy. He also advised that the university did not have a sufficient budget for the foundation and that this would be an ongoing problem. Finally, he told me that I was hired on a five-year contract to establish and build a foundation from scratch, change the culture within the UW, establish credibility and confidence within the community, launch a capital campaign, and raise $11 million.

So there it was. My first day and I was completely overwhelmed. I gathered my small team together, we had a chat and we decided what needed to be done. We built a plan, kept our heads down and got to work. With great hope and faith, we were prepared for the ride ahead.

"Hope sees the invisible, feels the intangible,
and achieves the impossible. Faith is the daring
of the soul to go farther than it can see."
Helen Keller

Building Another Dream Team

In my early discussions with Sandy Riley, I knew that he had to be the chair of the board of the foundation. It simply would not be successful without him. As chancellor, he possessed such insight and keen acumen to lead the university forward. He had the vision required to bring this colossal task to reality. For Sandy, this meant double duty in two highly demanding volunteer roles. Though reluctant at first, luckily for all of us, he agreed.

Realizing that this new chapter for the university required the help of many other great people, one of the first conversations Sandy and I had once I was hired, was about who could be on the board of directors. The first person Sandy asked me to approach was Doug Leatherdale. It was fortuitous that I had been in Minneapolis when I was asked to be president and CEO. Doug was the most successful Canadian in my territory while I was consul general, so I definitely knew who he was. In fact, in December 1999, I had been to his home for a Boxing Day celebration, a Canadian tradition. We had also met a few times in his offices at St. Paul Group of Companies.

I knew that Doug held the University of Winnipeg very near and dear to his heart. It was his alma mater and I suspected he was ready to move forward with some major donations, as long as there was a plan and a proper vision, and a proper structure. Doug and I went for lunch, I asked the question, and Doug's answer was, "I have been waiting to be asked. Of course I will be a board member." Doug Leatherdale was the first person we confirmed to be on the board. By the time the announcement was made, we had already locked in a few other key people.

One of Doug's very close university friends was Joe Martin, another United College alumnus who had graduated with a bachelor of arts (honours) in 1959. He was once executive assistant to former premier of Manitoba, Duff Roblin. A Harvard Business School graduate, Dr. Martin boasts a varied and successful business career, including consultant and later partner with Touche Ross and Partners. In 1995, Dr. Martin received an honorary doctorate of laws at the University of Winnipeg. Now living in Toronto and working as a faculty advisor at the University of Toronto's Rotman School of Management, Dr. Martin had the leadership skills and community affiliations to make him a prime candidate for our board. In addition, he too was frustrated about the state of the university. He had participated in many discussions and looked forward to seeking change. When we asked him to come on board, he gladly accepted.

We were very blessed with dedicated alumni. One such dedicated alumnus was Jim MacDonald. Jim was a former graduate of the University of Winnipeg Collegiate and he had always credited this unique high school for setting him on the right path. He graduated from the University of Winnipeg Collegiate in 1964, and in the early 1970s, he founded the UW Collegiate Alumni Association and became its first president. Continuing his interest in his alma mater, he joined the Board of Regents in 1980 and served for nine years. A successful vice president with RBC Dominion Securities, Jim, too, wanted to give back with a significant financial donation, but would not do so until a proper capital campaign was in place. There is no question that Jim Macdonald was a major impetus for the foundation and was most anxious to see it established. It was also Jim who absolutely "set the bar" for gifts to the campaign...more on that later.

In bringing Jim on to the board, we had a good chance of landing two additional UW Collegiate alumni who were now highly prominent and successful businessmen — Jim Richardson and Randy Moffat.

Jim Richardson, grandson of James A. Richardson, who was the founder of James Richardson & Sons Limited, graduated from the Collegiate at the University of Winnipeg. His close ties with both universities located in Winnipeg led him to being a regent on both the University of Winnipeg and University of Manitoba Boards. In 2002, Jim was vice president of the family business and involved in many community organizations. His illustrious background and experience in community organizations also made him a prime candidate for us.

Randy Moffat is best known as the former president and chairman of Moffat Communications Limited, a Canadian cable and broadcasting company. Randy had been with Moffat since 1963, as general manager of CKY Radio from 1964 to 1972, chairman of the board since 1972, and president of the company since 1979, until its sale in 2001. Active in the broadcast and cable industries in Canada, he also served as director on a number of corporate boards including Great-West Life Assurance Company. Randy was involved with many community organizations including the United Way of Winnipeg and the Business Council of Manitoba. He had just sold his company, so we were hoping that he would have the time and the inclination to join our board, and he did.

Over the course of his successful career, Bob Kozminski had been involved with many community boards, including the Winnipeg Jets, the Business Council of Manitoba, the Manitoba Institute of Management, and a number of organizations related to the car industry. He seemed a natural fit for us. Bob received his bachelor of arts degree from the University of Winnipeg in 1967. He later graduated from the University of Manitoba Law School and maintained a law practise for many years, before becoming involved with his family's business. Later, he became the president and CEO of Bob Kozminski's Keystone Ford Sales in partnership with Ford Motor Company. Thankfully for the University of Winnipeg and its foundation, Bob accepted the very important role of campaign chair for the University of Winnipeg Foundation Capital Campaign.

Leonard Asper, who also graduated from the Collegiate at the University of Winnipeg, was seen as another key person to have on our board. At the time, he was president and CEO of CanWest Global Communications Corp. His father, well-known entrepreneur and philanthropist Israel (Izzy) Asper had recently retired from CanWest Global and placed Leonard at the helm. Leonard was extremely busy. In 2000 and 2001, the company acquired the Hollinger chain of newspapers, including the *National Post*. Between that and his responsibilities at CanWest Global, he was forced to spend much of his time in Toronto. I was overjoyed when he agreed to come on board.

The university was required to name members to the founding board. They responded by naming Dr. Henry H. Duckworth, Dr. John Bulman, Sherman Kreiner, and Ida Albo. Also on the board by virtue of their positions were Richard Graydon, current chair of the Board of Regents, and Patrick Deane, acting president.

We were absolutely honoured to have the president emeritus of the University of Winnipeg, Dr. Henry Duckworth on the foundation board. His accomplishments, varied and many, include buildings named after him at both the University of Manitoba and the University of Winnipeg. He is an icon in the university world. A life-long educator, Dr. Duckworth started his career as a high school teacher, and went on to work at several universities, including United College. He contributed to governance and administration in a number of universities in both Canada and the United States, including Winnipeg where he served as vice-president, chancellor, and president emeritus of the University of Manitoba, and president, vice-chancellor, and president emeritus of the University of Winnipeg. A trained nuclear physicist, he brought recognition as a world leader in his field and authored five books, including his autobiography. We knew that Dr. Duckworth's wisdom and experience would be a tremendous asset to this board and were very pleased with the university's choice.

Dr. John Bulman, another pillar of the University of Winnipeg community, was committed to the institution in a variety of roles. Former chair of the Board of Regents, he served as chancellor from 1984 to 1996. The Bulman Centre, located on the UW campus, signifies the many contributions he has made towards the well-being of students, staff, and faculty. Amongst his many honours, he received an honorary doctor of laws by the university in 1983. He has been volunteer chairman and director of numerous organizations, including Wawanesa Mutual Insurance Company and the Manitoba Telephone System, and also served as vice chair and director of The Forks Renewal Corporation. His "senior statesman status" and experience was invaluable to us, and we knew he would be keen on taking on this new responsibility on our board.

Ida Albo is owner and managing partner of the historic Hotel Fort Garry in Winnipeg. She completed an honours degree in economics in 1981 at the University of Winnipeg, followed by a masters' degree in economics from Queen's University in 1982. As an economist, Ida lectured at both universities in Winnipeg and worked for the federal government. She then worked as a restaurateur and eventually, in the hotel business. She had been appointed to many prestigious boards over the years, including for the Tourism Association of Canada, the Asper School of Business, and Manitoba Children's Museum. I got to know Ida when she was involved with Centre Venture Development Corporation and the Mid Continent Trade Corridor Taskforce. She also served on the University of Winnipeg Board of Regents. I was delighted to have Ida join our board. At last, a woman!

Sherman Kreiner was an American who came to Winnipeg to run the Crocus Investment Fund. Prior to this position, Sherman worked extensively with business, labour unions, and state and provincial governments. He had written and lectured extensively on employee ownership. Appointed to the university Board of Regents by the provincial government, he was also named to the foundation board.

The chair of the Board of Regents at the time was Richard Graydon. Born and raised in Wellington, New Zealand, Mr. Graydon was a teacher by trade. He studied in New Zealand and in Winnipeg, earning a bachelor of arts and bachelor of education. He also spent a number of years as a principal in some Winnipeg schools. Richard brought two valuable traits to the table — dedication and integrity. This became vital during some tumultuous times at the beginning of the UW Foundation's existence.

The university's acting president and vice president academic, Dr. Patrick Deane had many responsibilities at the University of Winnipeg in 2002. By virtue of his position, he was automatically a member of the founding board of the foundation. Patrick's university credentials were impressive. He held bachelor's, master's, and PhD degrees in English. He received numerous awards and accolades for his studies. He was involved with a number of academic and professional societies and had been published widely in academic journals. We knew that this type of leadership would be essential for the foundation to succeed and gladly welcomed him on board. Dr. Deane is currently the president of McMaster University.

Each of these individuals accepted an invitation to sit on this board, knowing full well that this would be an enormous undertaking, but also one that would make history. In its entire existence, the University of Winnipeg had only ever had one campaign that went over the million-dollar mark. In 1988, it reported that it had raised $10 million. This board was poised to fundraise much more than that. In fact, the number that was eventually realized was unmatched and even surprised our own team.

The founding Board of the University of Winnipeg Foundation. Top row (l to r): John Bulman, Leonard Asper, Bob Kozminski, Joseph Martin, Doug Leatherdale, Richard Graydon, Randy Moffat; Bottom row (l to r): Jim McDonald, Patrick Deane, Sandy Riley (Chair), Ida Albo, Jim Richardson. Missing: Henry Duckworth, Sherman Kreiner (Photo courtesy of University of Winnipeg Archives)

If there was one thing that I learned in my career, it was that if you sat on a board, you had to give a major gift to that organization and I wholeheartedly adopted that goal. We recruited members that would give large, inspiring gifts. By the end of May, we had secured a number of outstanding leaders in the Winnipeg community and beyond and we were most proud that we had a stellar board...one of the most prestigious boards in the city.

"As in all things in life, it takes a team to make things work, and we indeed had a five-star team."

Reaching New Heights

However one wished to describe it, the University of Winnipeg Foundation was a start-up that was highly underfunded and under resourced. The expectations demanded of us were massive. Nevertheless, we started the foundation with a small staff of four and enough enthusiasm to fill an arena. Together with our newly-appointed and committed board of directors, we began to work on our goals, knowing full well that this endeavour was critical to the overall future of Winnipeg.

By early June 2003, the University of Winnipeg Foundation was beginning to get its feet wet. I had hired two additional staff, so we were now a group of six working strictly for the foundation. The university's Advancement Services Department provided us with support in the areas of data management, receipting, and record keeping. Together with the university, we had established some initial primary goals — to increase funding for scholarships and bursaries, to raise revenue for a capital development campaign, and to enhance programs, facilities, equipment, and technology. We had a huge task ahead of us and we knew it, but we were inspired by the people we had attracted to the board and we were excited to get started.

We created promotional materials to announce to the university family, former donors and the general public that we were in business, as we prepared for the first board meeting of the University of Winnipeg Foundation. We created operating agreements, by-laws and rules and responsibilities for our new board members and staff. We sorted through the responsibilities offered to us by the university, but soon realized that we would have to take care of our own financial administration and communications support. We shifted staff around, reorganized our priorities, and did what we could to make it work. In the end, we had financial statements ready for our first board meeting, which was held on June 17, 2003. We had invited quite a few additional people to this meeting — members of the Board of Regents, key faculty, and staff members from the university and the foundation, the president of the alumni association and other notable guests — and followed the meeting up with an exquisite dinner, courtesy of Ida Albo and the Hotel Fort Garry. It was important that all the people involved in this endeavour establish a bond and get to know each other. We needed buy-in. We couldn't survive without it. In the end, everyone who attended definitely did "buy in" and became part of the University of Winnipeg's most successful capital campaign ever.

There were two extraordinary start-up moments. The first occurred at a board planning session, organized in September 2003. The session was orchestrated to "get the board talking" about how much money the foundation should try to raise. More detail was needed to determine what to include in a Case for Support and we had to have a frank talk about expectations. The new board had been surveyed to determine what they deemed most important to least important and succeeded in engaging a fulsome discussion about the university's areas of greatest need. We talked about the future of student bursaries and the need for a larger endowment fund. Members began to recommend capital projects — lots of them — everything from renovating dilapidated classrooms, to the need for new buildings, to possible new facilities to accommodate expanding programs. This then led the group to recommend an aggressive target of $46 million, which sent me into heart palpitations. A defining moment occurred when Leonard Asper stood from his chair, removed his suit jacket, rolled up his sleeves, sat back down and exclaimed, "I'm not here for the ordinary. I'm here for the extraordinary." **A significant moment indeed.** Members continued to visualize the university's future and contemplated an even more aggressive, visionary goal of $125 million, perhaps linking this with a historic anniversary going forward. A business plan was approved at that meeting and the stage was set for a transformational fundraising campaign at the University of Winnipeg.

The second momentous meeting was held on March 16, 2004. This meeting was distinctive for two reasons. The first was that it was attended by Lloyd Axworthy, who had just been named president-elect of the University of Winnipeg. Though he wasn't going to be starting until May, he took advantage of his time away from UBC (where he was CEO of the Liu Centre for the Study of Global Issues) to attend the UW Foundation Board meeting. He told the board that he was looking forward to working with the foundation and indicated that one of the draws of taking on the position of president, was the establishment of this important and innovative entity. He shared with us that he was happy to be back in Winnipeg and looked forward to working with the people around the table to establish a vibrant, downtown campus.

This day was also special because during the meeting, one of the board members announced that he would be making a donation that set the bar for the rest of the campaign. Jim MacDonald announced that he was donating an unprecedented $1 million for student awards, benefitting students of The Collegiate. Jim explained, in a very touching oration, that his education at The Collegiate had turned his life around years ago. He credited the dean of the Collegiate in the 1960s — Lorne Tomlinson — for steering him in the right direction and starting him on a path towards a successful business career. This gift was a way of giving back to the institution that helped him succeed. Jim's wish was to reach students like him, who needed the Collegiate's special touch to help them succeed.

Jim also described his vision to raise $5 million for the Collegiate by throwing out a challenge whereby he would match gifts as part of his donation. The looks on the faces of everyone around the boardroom table foretold the future of an extraordinary campaign. As CEO, I was so thankful that we had board members like Jim. He really got the ball rolling. He was the first of the committed philanthropists around the table, who over the years provided wonderful opportunities for students.

And so it started. Our board stepped up to the plate, continued to raise the bar, and at the end of the campaign, achieved a 100% participation level, making up over thirty percent of the private funds raised. Five of the board donations surpassed the million-dollar mark and three more were in the realm of six-figures. From the get-go, we had the leadership and the lead gifts, and we were able to demonstrate to the community that the University of Winnipeg was in the fundraising business. The excitement was contagious. This played a key role in attracting revenue to the campus and contributed to the most successful capital campaign the university had ever known.

"I am proud of the role the University of Winnipeg plays in this city and I am moved by its attention to broader global issues. "A World of Opportunity" is a transformational campaign that will make a difference in the lives of our students for generations to come."

H. Sanford Riley

Surpassing the Goal and Being Part of History

Janet Walker, Sandy Riley and I "raising the curtain" on our fundraising goal at the launch (Photo courtesy of University of Winnipeg Archives)

The "World of Opportunity Capital Campaign" was officially launched on November 27, 2007. The kickoff event was spectacular... definitely an event to remember. Hundreds of guests packed the newly restored Convocation Hall, which is located in the historic Wesley Hall on Portage Avenue. There was a lot of fanfare; piano music playing in the background as guests arrived, Fubuki Daiko drummers just prior to the announcement, and silver curtain panels that were drawn to reveal the anticipated goal. A baby grand piano was loaned to the university from a local piano company and our very own board member, Leonard Asper, was one of the pianists. The campaign chair, Bob Kozminski, announced that the campaign goal was $70 million and that so far, over $55 million had been achieved.

Following the announcement, champagne and strawberries were served to help celebrate the occasion.

As the foundation's president and CEO, I was so proud to be part of this momentous occasion. For four years leading up to this event, the board and my staff had worked extremely hard to get to this day. This campaign announcement signalled the largest fundraising initiative in the history of the University of Winnipeg. The plans going forward were visionary and would change the downtown landscape. It was a day to celebrate what we had accomplished and what was still to come. It was one of the best days I had ever experienced at the University of Winnipeg.

I was particularly proud of the way the university internal family embraced the capital campaign. When all was said and done, the 700-plus members of the faculty and staff contributed over $4.9 million to student awards, from more than 1,650 individual gifts and pledges.[21] I met with many, many dedicated individuals who worked for the university and were completely committed to the institution. It warmed my heart to see such dedication.

The next four years brought euphoric highs and lows. While we continued to reap the benefits of generous donors, we were also faced with challenges because of the state of the economy. The world financial crisis in 2008 had an impact on every aspect of running our foundation.

The market crash in 2008 was a huge challenge. Month by month, day by day, our endowment reserves were being depleted. Moreover, once a year, the foundation was obligated to make a gift to the university from the interest earned on the endowment funds, funds that were also taking a kicking because of the global financial situation. It was a crisis that forced us to develop a new strategy. I am a great proponent of having a Plan B, and when the markets began to drop in June 2008, I anticipated that the worst was yet to come. I implemented a strategy and a mantra: New Reality, Uncharted Territory,

21 University of Winnipeg Foundation Final Report to Donors — September 2011, Page 16

Staying Ahead of the Curve. When something like this happens, weathering the storm depends on how quickly you can shift.

While we were at the stage of the campaign when we should have been ramping up staff and resources, I decided it would be best if we held back on all expenses. We didn't hire the staff we needed, putting a lot of pressure on the existing staff. We went without resources that would have made our jobs more manageable. Tough as this was, it turned out to be our saving grace, and by the end of 2008, we had weathered the crisis without too much damage to our reserves.

On September 16, 2011, the University of Winnipeg Foundation concluded the largest campaign in the university's history. Over $135 million was levered and raised, shattering the initial 2003 goal of $11 million, and nearly doubling the original campaign goal, set in 2007, of $70 million.

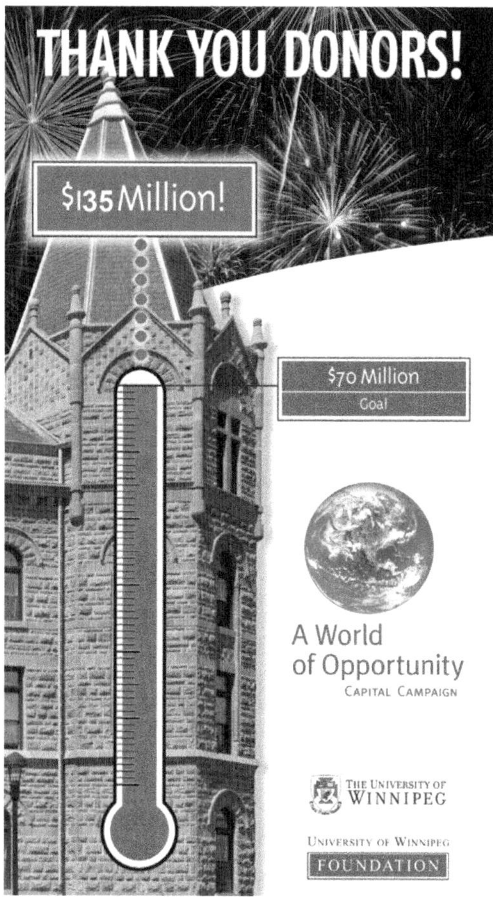

Courtesy of University of Winnipeg Foundation

So much was accomplished by the University of Winnipeg Foundation from 2003 to 2011. The university has some new and newly-renovated state-of-the-art facilities — the Richardson College for the Environment and Science Complex, McFeetors Hall Great-West Life Student Residence, UWSA Day Care Centre, the Buhler Centre Faculty of Business and Economics, the Asper Centre for Theatre and Film, and the restoration of Convocation Hall in Wesley Hall[22]. The endowment fund has grown from $18 million, when the foundation assumed responsibility for the management of

22 University of Winnipeg Foundation Final Report to Donors — Sept 2011

these funds, to more than $38 million[23]. This increase ensures that students at the University of Winnipeg will benefit from awards and academic enhancements for years to come.

Prior to the establishment of the University of Winnipeg Foundation, the university had never received a gift of a million dollars or more. By the end of the campaign, we had achieved sixteen gifts over $1M, twenty-two gifts over $500,000, seventy-two gifts over 100,000, nearly 300 gifts over 10,000, and an unprecedented 7,600 donors to the campaign. When I think back to the conversation I had with Janet Walker on my first day of work, when I suggested we aim for ten lead gifts of $1 million, I can't help but marvel at the feat we undertook and how the stars lined up to make it all happen. We always envisioned ourselves to be the little engine that could. In the end, we surpassed our goal and overwhelmingly responded to the needs of our university.

I began this chapter by saying that becoming president and CEO of the University of Winnipeg Foundation was a full circle moment for me...and indeed it was. By working and studying at this wonderful university and its collegiate, I was given the "life tools" necessary to achieve the many successes in my life. I have many good people to thank for this: Mr. Wright, the librarian in the mid-1960s, who hired me, even though I was a high school failure, and then gave me a work schedule that allowed me to return to high school and get my diploma; and Dr. Rais Khan, my political science professor, who taught me how to "think," weigh options, understand different viewpoints, and value history in every consideration. And in between, so many other teachers and professors, too numerous to mention, supported and encouraged me, with patience and understanding. This was, and still is, a university of excellence, hope, opportunity, and good people.

The University of Winnipeg's motto is "Let Light and Truth Flourish." To this day, this motto could not be more valid in how people need to conduct themselves in life. It speaks to a person's values and the importance of integrity in all aspects of life. The motto

23 University of Winnipeg Foundation 2010-2011 Endowed Fund Report

is indeed a guiding light to students to follow as they develop their own truth. I know it was for me.

Returning to my university in this pivotal role was such an honour. I am grateful that I was part of a team that transformed the University of Winnipeg. It provided me with a chance to give back to an institution that had been so important in so many chapters of my life.

My experience at the University of Winnipeg Foundation enabled me to see the depth of people's generosity. It allowed me to work with donors and to understand their passion. Whether a gift was small or large, donors displayed a commitment to try to make a difference in the lives of our students. I found this to be remarkable. The love and respect shown to our institution was heartfelt and heart-warming.

One of the things I learned during this time was how to build a personal endowment fund. I am not a person of wealth, but I was shown that small contributions over a number of years can result in an endowed fund. I therefore started the Susan A. Thompson Bursary, to encourage the study of history of women in politics. It is given to students who choose courses from the Women's Studies department.

Setting up the bursary also inspired me to dream about a Susan A. Thompson Foundation. Its purpose would be to raise money to be used for the betterment of women. Funds would be made available for young girls to achieve the education necessary to be successful in life. I haven't quite figured out how this is all going to happen, but it is a goal and dream in my life as I move forward.

This chapter of my life — the University of Winnipeg Foundation chapter — has taught me the importance of perseverance and integrity. It has reinforced in me that you can dream the big dream if you build the incredible team. I also learned, unfortunately, that politics — no matter where — can be as dirty as dirty gets. Despite all obstacles, I learned that not only can goals be achieved, they can be surpassed. Miracles do exist. Coming full circle was meant to be.

69 and joyful! (David Lipnowski/Winnipeg Free Press, January 18, 2014. Reprinted with permission.)

Chapter 16
What's Next?

The Next Chapter

So there it is...my story to date. I've been an entrepreneur, a politician, a diplomat, a founding president and CEO and a fundraiser. I am the proud patron of HMCS Winnipeg and have been named a White Feather Woman by my province's elders. I am a passionate Winnipegger, Manitoban, and Canadian. Every chapter of my life has been done with 100 percent commitment and devotion to the cause at hand. I have recently received two wonderful honours — an honorary doctorate from the University of Winnipeg and the Order of Manitoba.

I feel very blessed. I could die tomorrow and I would be all right with that. I have done what I was meant to do. I am not saying that there is not more for me to do, but at this stage of my life, I am joyful with the journeys I have undertaken.

Like many Canadians, even though I am officially of retirement age, I am not ready to retire. With no city or federal pensions, my finances are minimal. Yes, I have RRSPs, but certainly not enough to be able to manage the next decade and beyond in a suitable manner. My personal savings are enough to live by, but that's all. I need to continue working. To that end, I am preparing for the next chapter of my life. Lesson learned...when your parents tell you to save...LISTEN!

Just what does one do employment-wise after sixty-five? I continue to be available for public speaking and to sit on corporate boards. In 2011, I engaged in a fundraising contract for MacDonald

Youth Services–a capital campaign to raise money for an emergency youth shelter. I was delighted to be part of this initiative.

In 2014, Stephen Borys, director and CEO of the Winnipeg Art Gallery (WAG), offered me a contract as executive consultant to help raise $65 million for a world-class Inuit Art Centre. The WAG is the oldest civic art gallery in Canada and has the largest collection of Inuit art in the world. To celebrate the art and to honour the Inuit, the WAG is building an Inuit Art Centre, the first of its kind in the world. Through the Centre, the WAG will be a link, connecting people from the North and South to meet, learn, and create together. It will be a community hub for exhibitions and programs, research and learning, studio practice and art-making. A visit to the Centre will provide a unique opportunity to learn more about Inuit history, culture, and Canada as a whole. The building itself will be built right next to the Winnipeg Art Gallery and will be a four-storey 40,000 square foot facility. It will feature a visible vault — a cylindrical glass-walled art storage and conservation facility displaying thousands of artworks, — studios and classrooms, an interactive theatre and a gallery dedicated to Indigenous Art.[24] I have been passionate about this project since 1992, when I became mayor. I am so pleased to be part of this project and hopefully seeing it to fruition. It will be yet another incredible legacy for Winnipeg and for Canada.

And of course, I have spent a few years on this book and have another one in the works. Stay tuned!

I do still feel that I have the energy to pursue another calling. In that vein, I recently took a course to become a certified life coach. Over the years, I have had many people tell me I was their mentor, so I thought this would be a good fit. I would like to help those at executive levels in corporations, organizations, and the political arena. What many leaders do not realize when they first reach the executive level is that they are suddenly given extraordinary powers and can easily become entitled, arrogant, or corrupt. (Some become all three, unfortunately.) My goal is to assist new leaders through the abysses they will no doubt fall into and determine what corrective

---

24 Information obtained from the Winnipeg Art Gallery website.

action they can take. Having experienced the "minefields" firsthand, I understand the challenges of leadership and would like to assist new leaders down the path.

It took 118 years after the city of Winnipeg was founded for a woman to become mayor and now, over twenty years later, I am still the one and only woman to hold that distinction. The fact that today, in the twenty-first century, women are still struggling to get on corporate boards or to be at the executive level in companies is unacceptable. Even more worrisome is that there is such terrible violence against women globally. We also live in a world where women in movies and television are still portrayed as brainless, stupid beings or sex objects. Though women have made some progress, there is still a long way to go.

The first woman elected to the House of Commons of Canada was Agnes Macphail in 1921. Four other women stood as candidates in that same election, but were not successful. It took until 1935 for a second woman to be elected federally. It was not until 1979 for the number of women elected to the House of Commons to reach double digits, when ten women were elected. As of 2010, Canada ranks fiftieth in the world for women's participation in politics, with women holding just twenty-three percent seats in federal, provincial, and territorial legislatures.[25]

For a short time in Canada, in 2013, six women held the first ministerial position in their province or territory. In other words, six out of the thirteen provincial and territorial premiers were women. Less than two years later, this number had already slid down to two. Two of the women resigned before the next election was to take place. One was defeated in a subsequent election. One chose not to run as premier in the next election, but rather as an MLA. She lost. While many circumstances undoubtedly led to the subsequent resignations and defeats of these particular instances, the fact remains that the statistics do not bode well for women. After all these years, one has to ask the question. Why?

25 Statistical information obtained from Wikipedia.

At the mayoral level, Canadian women have definitely been more successful, though it did take a little longer. Canada's first woman mayor was elected in 1936 – Barbara Hanley in Webbwood, Ontario. In subsequent years, many more cities followed suit, however, and by the time I was mayor of Winnipeg in 1992, many major cities in Canada had women at the helm. Within our "Big Cities" organization (cities over 500,000 in population) in 1992, the following women were mayors of their respective cities: Jan Reimer, Edmonton; Jacquelin Holtzman, Ottawa; Barbara Hall, Toronto; Hazel MacCallion, Mississauga; and Suzanne "Shannie" McDuff, St. John's, Newfoundland. I was pleased to see that significant participation of women in municipal government existed and thoroughly enjoyed any meetings that involved the mayors across Canada for that reason.

I would like to emphasize at this point how important it is for women to continue to persevere and run for office at any level in government. It is vital to our country to have more balanced representation at all levels of government. Rosalie Abella, who sits on the Supreme Court of Canada, and in fact was the first Jewish woman to do so, once spoke at a National Women's retreat I attended. I will always remember her words. She told us that as women, we have to understand that we are governed by the laws of our country, and historically, the laws of Canada were made by men, for men. Women must participate in politics and become political leaders, for it is only at the government levels, through legislation, that the laws can be changed to better reflect a balance in our society.

I have consistently drawn on four fundamentals throughout my various careers. I believe that these basic principles have been critical to my ability to adapt and respond the challenges. They are a good work ethic, a positive attitude, a good education, and perseverance. As I have faced situations, whether it was a need to develop new skills or to rise above challenging circumstances, these attributes have seen me through. I take pride in having persevered through the many sudden or unexpected changes and shifts that came my way over the years.

So the next chapter of my life continues to unfold. Life is a journey...and my journey continues.

"Every great dream begins with a dreamer. Always remember, you have within you the strength, the patience and the passion to reach for the stars and change the world."

Harriet Tubman

Acknowledgements

This book would not have been possible without the assistance of a number of remarkable people who helped in so many ways. We gratefully acknowledge their support and list them here as an acknowledgement to their generous gift of time.

The staff at the City of Winnipeg Archives: Jody Balteson, Martin Comeau, Pam Hnatowich, and Sarah Ramsden were extraordinarily accommodating with their assistance in helping us go through boxes of binders, file folders, photos, and scrapbooks. Huge thanks to all of you.

My political campaign occurred over twenty years ago, so putting together the story all these years later proved to be interesting. I had diarized many things, which was helpful, and I sought the help of those who were directly involved. We spoke to Robert Gabor, Dennis McKnight, Eileen Stuebing, Jim and Gayle Carson, Guy Prefontaine, Paul Labossiere, Meryle Lewis, Tara Brousseau, Wally Hill, and Bill Watchorn. Each of them provided us with their recollections of what turned out to be a historic campaign. Bev DeGrave, my scheduler in the mayor's office, and former city councillors George Fraser and John Prystanski, helped us in many ways to describe my six years at city hall. Thanks to each of you for taking the time out of your busy schedules to meet or email us. Your contributions were wonderful.

Each chapter had its own set of challenges. In particular, I wanted the chapters regarding the 1997 Flood of the Century, the 1999 Pan American Games, and the loss of the Winnipeg Jets to be filled with many facts. As such, we interviewed many key players to help us describe the events as accurately as possible.

- For the chapter on the 1997 Flood of the Century, we contacted Doug McNeil, who worked for the city of Winnipeg in 1997 and was instrumental in fighting this incredible flood. We also obtained information from the book *A Red Sea Rising*, published by the Winnipeg Free Press. A number of public documents found at the City of Winnipeg Archives also helped to reconstruct the story.
- For the 1999 Pan American Games chapter, we spoke to Sandy Riley, chair of the games, along with Barbara Huck and Peter St. John, Don McKenzie, Mike Moore, Mike Sterdan and Colin Ferguson (who incidentally still had some old VHS tapes for us to view.) Each of them recounted their own version of events and their favourite memories. Many thanks to each and every one of you.
- For the chapter regarding the loss of the Winnipeg Jets, our research included articles written in the Winnipeg Free Press. George Fraser and John Prystanski, who were both city councillors during this time, also gave us their perspective of what happened.

From the beginning, I felt the inclusion of many photos would make this book more interesting. This created the daunting task of finding and/or creating high-resolution images of every photo we wanted to include. Many thanks to all who provided us with photographs. They include: Albert Cheung, Rob Mathieson (great neighbourhood friends shot!), Stan Milosevic, Alan McTavish, the City of Winnipeg Archives, the University of Winnipeg Archives, the University of Winnipeg Foundation, the *Winnipeg Free Press,* and my family. A special thank you to Doug Cook, who edited and re-sized a number of photos for us.

From time to time, we sought the advice and expertise of key people. The late Lindor Reynolds was instrumental in getting the cover "done right." She is the one who came up with the idea to have His Worship typed in and have the "His" crossed out with a red marker and replaced by "Her." Margo Goodhand took on the massive volunteer job of doing a content edit on the entire book...and she did a phenomenal job! Thank you so much Margo for your expertise, foresight, and friendship.

Many thanks as well to Gayle Carson, Arvel Gray, Janet Walker, Nadine Kampen, Patti Tweed, Teresa Murray, Barbara Huck, and Peter St. John. To each and every one of you...your guidance along this journey was invaluable.

My family was also instrumental in providing some great information to include in the book. My sister Lenore, the family historian, provided interesting information on our ancestors and family business. My sister Barbara and brother Norman answered questions when they could and offered their insights on our family history. Some of my closest friends also gave me some advice on what to include (and not include!) in the book...Gayle and Jim Carson, Eileen and Bob Stuebing, Doris Mae Oulton and Cam Mackie, Elba Haid, Carol Bellringer, Phillip and Judy Adam, Susan McMillan, Margie Isbister, and Brian Peel. Your suggestions and opinions throughout this process were invaluable.

I would like to extend a special thank you to my legal counsel and literary agent Rachel E.R. Margolis. Your assistance in getting this book to its final stages is extremely appreciated. I also take this time to thank FriesenPress for leading us through the final steps to get this book printed.

Last but certainly not least, I was extremely humbled by the show of support from friends who agreed to sponsor this endeavour. This book would not have been published had it not been for their kind generosity and unwavering support. Their names are noted in the front pages of this book, but bear repeating:

Tannis Richardson
Women of Winnipeg (WOW group)
Debbie and Sandy Riley
Carol Bellringer and Greg Doyle
Tom Dooley
John Prystanski
Margie Isbister
Sharon Boyd

Elba Haid and Edward Ransby
Gayle and Jim Carson
Eleanor and Tim Samson
Fiona Webster-Mourant

In 2011, towards the end of my term at University of Winnipeg Foundation, I asked my former executive assistant to help me archive files from the organization's founding and formative years. It was during this time that she overheard a conversation I was having with Janet Walker about what the next chapter of my life might be. I was mulling over my future, which would include turning sixty-five. Janet suggested this would be an opportune time to tell my life story.

For anybody who knows me, I am a storyteller. In fact, I had already started working on something. It did seem logical that I capture my history to date, but my priority was to write an inspirational book. I had no idea how I would focus on what would basically be a biography of my life and I wasn't sure where I would even begin. This is when my former assistant pointed out that many of my stories were already captured in speeches I had written, speeches that were filed in huge binders that she just happened to be holding in her hands. "All it would take would be to organize these into a book," she told me, to which I replied, "Well, maybe we should talk about this."

The next day, Terry Létienne marched back into my office with a message and a mission. She told me that she felt she was meant to help me write my life story. I told her I wasn't interested. Terry reminded me that I had always taught people to listen to what they were meant to do, and she reiterated again that she felt she could help me. She described to me what form this book could take and showed me a draft outline. At this point, I could see how eager Terry was about this and I had to acknowledge the fact that she had had a calling. It would have gone against the very essence of who I am not to embrace it. As reluctant as I was, from that point on, I knew that this was something that we had to do together.

And so our journey began. We met at least once a week for about a year, planning, researching, and revising the outline. We met with many people and did a lot of research. Then, over the course of two years, I began to recount my stories and Terry took notes. We then spent a whole lot of time writing and revising. When I moved to Vancouver, we continued to do so by email and telephone.

This book would not have ever happened had it not been for Terry Létienne's unshakeable faith in the project. God bless her for being unbelievably persistent, dedicated, and generous of time and talent.

The process of writing this book consumed over five years of our lives. Our journey has been remarkable. It speaks to a fundamental human trait, which is the importance of trust and respect. It resulted in a personal growth for each of us, a tremendous learning curve, and an everlasting friendship.

CPSIA information can be obtained
at www.ICGtesting.com
Printed in the USA
LVOW01s1253030916
502740LV00006B/6/P